War, Peace, and Power: Diplomatic History of Europe, 1500–2000
Part III

Professor Vejas Gabriel Liulevicius

THE TEACHING COMPANY ®

PUBLISHED BY:

THE TEACHING COMPANY
4151 Lafayette Center Drive, Suite 100
Chantilly, Virginia 20151-1232
1-800-TEACH-12
Fax—703-378-3819
www.teach12.com

ISBN 1-59803-385-9

Vejas Gabriel Liulevicius, Ph.D.

Associate Professor, University of Tennessee, Knoxville

Vejas Gabriel Liulevicius was born in Chicago, Illinois. He grew up on Chicago's South Side in a Lithuanian American neighborhood and also spent some years attending school in Aarhus, Denmark, and Bonn, Germany. He received his B.A. from the University of Chicago. In 1989, he spent the summer in Moscow and Leningrad (today St. Petersburg) in intensive language study in Russian. His dissertation research was funded by a German Academic Exchange Service fellowship and took him to Freiburg in Germany's Black Forest region and to Vilnius, Lithuania. He earned his Ph.D. from the University of Pennsylvania in European History in 1994, specializing in Modern German History.

After receiving his doctorate, Professor Liulevicius spent a year as a postdoctoral research fellow at the Hoover Institution on War, Revolution, and Peace at Stanford University in Palo Alto, California. Since 1995, he has been a history professor at the University of Tennessee, Knoxville. He teaches courses on modern German history, Western civilization, European diplomatic history, Nazi Germany, World War I, war and culture, 20th-century Europe, nationalism, and utopian thought. In 2003, he received the University of Tennessee's Excellence in Teaching Award. In 2005, he was awarded a prestigious National Endowment for the Humanities Fellowship for his research. He served twice as the Hendrickson Professor in the College of Arts and Sciences, for 2005–2007 and 2007–2009.

Professor Liulevicius's research focuses on German relations with eastern Europe in the modern period. His other interests include diplomatic history, the utopian tradition and its impact on modern politics, images of the United States abroad, and the history of the Baltic region. He has published numerous articles (which have also appeared in French, Italian, and German translation) and his first book, *War Land on the Eastern Front: Culture, National Identity and German Occupation in the World War I* (2000), published by Cambridge University Press, also appeared in German translation in 2002. His next book project is a larger study of German stereotypes of Eastern Europeans from 1800 to the present.

Professor Liulevicius has recorded two other courses with The Teaching Company, *Utopia and Terror in the 20ᵗʰ Century* and *World War I: "The Great War."*

Professor Liulevicius lives in Knoxville, Tennessee, with his wife, Kathleen, and their children, Paul and Helen.

Table of Contents

War, Peace, and Power:
Diplomatic History of Europe, 1500–2000
Part III

War, Peace, and Power:
Diplomatic History of Europe, 1500–2000

Scope:

Does an internal logic rule the seemingly unending and chaotic history of clashing European nations over the last five centuries? Why has European history seen such ferocious conflict within one civilization (including the Thirty Years' War, the Napoleonic Wars, and two World Wars)?

This course surveys these wars, intervals of peace, and the pursuit of power as a goal of statecraft over the last 500 years. We examine the roles of remarkable individuals, governments, overarching structures, and non-state organizations in European international history. This course critically assesses the concept of the balance of power (shifting coalitions of Great Powers in mutual competition, preventing any one power from gaining overwhelming might) and other ideas of order as potential keys to the dynamics of international politics, from modern diplomacy's birth in Renaissance Italy down to present-day summit meetings. Diplomatic history is not just the history of narrowly defined ambassadorial missions but in fact is a true international history. As such, it covers the shifting relations of both Great Power states as well as smaller powers—different levels of actors on the international scene—and explores distinct ideas about the state system and how it operates. Our topics include not only military outcomes, diplomatic settlements, and imperatives of grand strategy but also questions of peacemaking, international law, defense of human rights and minorities, abolition of slavery, pacific efforts of organizations like the Red Cross, challenges of foreign policy for smaller states, and ideal projects for achieving stable European order, culminating in today's European Union. Particular themes we pursue in this course include the crucial role of prior experience and precedent in shaping subsequent calculations; how persistent geopolitical problems across the centuries have created the world we live in today; the elusive pursuit of stability when the international scene is marked by constant change; and the significant observation that diplomatic methods and approaches can be as important as the substance of international questions. We also examine changing concepts of what the greater whole—Europe— meant for participants in the diplomatic drama of five centuries.

Our course is divided into three distinct periods. Part 1 covers from 1500 to 1815 and follows the European state system's development, involving many contending dynastic powers. In Lecture One we introduce key theoretical debates. Lectures Two and Three give an overview of Europe in 1500, marked by the growth of "new monarchies" and the birth of modern diplomacy in Renaissance Italy's city-states. Lectures Four and Five emphasize converging religious and dynastic bids for supremacy, cresting in the ferocious Thirty Years' War (1618–1648). Lecture Six introduces the Treaty of Westphalia of 1648, which launched a new political era. Lecture Seven reveals the rising new superpower, France. In Lectures Eight through Ten, we follow the intense competition to create centralized and efficient state structures. In the struggles of this epoch, key roles were played by talented monarchs like "the Sun King," Louis XIV of France, Frederick the Great of Prussia, and Maria Theresa of Austria. Lectures Eleven and Twelve focus on the culminating challenge represented by French revolutionary armies sweeping across the continent to overthrow monarchies and the self-made emperor Napoleon's meteoric rise and fall.

Part 2, spanning from 1815 to 1914, represents Europe's "classical balance of power," a period marked by the dynamic interaction of a smaller group of Great Powers, presided over by talented diplomats like Prince Clemens von Metternich of Austria, Benjamin Disraeli of Great Britain, and the "Iron Chancellor," Otto von Bismarck of Prussia (and later the German Empire). Lectures Thirteen and Fourteen examine how, after Napoleon's defeat, the 1815 Congress of Vienna sought to create a "Concert of Europe" to act together for stability, in spite of growing problems on the margins of the European arena, which are analyzed in Lecture Fifteen. Another challenge, covered in Lecture Sixteen, arose as a result of internal revolutions in 1848 and the ascent of an enigmatic French leader, Napoleon III, whose plans to restructure European politics cost him his throne. Lecture Seventeen outlines the British Empire—"on which the sun did not set"—and how its growth affected the political calculations of European diplomats. While a more general war was avoided, Lecture Eighteen reveals how and why the Crimean War (1853–1856) battered conservative solidarity and ushered in more dynamic change. Italian unification came about (Lecture Nineteen) and a unified German nation-state arose at the continent's center (Lecture Twenty), rocking European politics. Chancellor von

Bismarck had engineered German unification and now he in turn faced the daunting task of reconciling Europe to this key alteration. Lecture Twenty-One evaluates the Bismarckian system he constructed, as well as its eventual breakdown. Finally, in Lectures Twenty-Two and Twenty-Three, the paradoxes of this Victorian period are examined: While skillful diplomacy forestalled general European war, relentless European imperialist expansion carved up the globe. Regional crises increasingly flared up in areas of competition like the Balkan Peninsula, the focus of Lecture Twenty-Four. This age rich in paradox ended explosively with the outbreak of World War I in 1914.

Part 3 examines 1914 to 2000 to understand what followed the breakdown of the "classical balance of power": the repeated crises in the two World Wars, the decline of European global might, and the redefinition of the European state system in our own times. Lectures Twenty-Five and Twenty-Six reveal revolutionary changes produced by World War I as a global "total war," including the rise of the Soviet challenge to existing states. In Lectures Twenty-Seven and Twenty-Eight we evaluate peacemaking at the 1919 Paris Settlement, the Treaty of Versailles, and the League of Nations. Lecture Twenty-Nine shows the disappointment of peaceful hopes and the rise of Fascist Italy and Hitler's Nazi Germany, which overthrew the international order. World War II and postwar plans are the subject of Lectures Thirty and Thirty-One. The initial sense of promise after World War II gave way instead to a new bipolar confrontation of ideologies, the Cold War, as shown in Lectures Thirty-Two and Thirty-Three. We go on to explain in Lecture Thirty-Four how European countries—confronted by the loss of earlier overseas empires, diminished status in an age of superpowers, and Cold War division—sought to progressively redefine European political identity on a new basis. Lecture Thirty-Five recounts the amazing transformations of 1989–1991, with the Soviet collapse, the fall of Communism, and changed political realities. In our last lecture, we ask where Europe is headed today and what implications follow for the world at large. The aim of our course is a keener historical understanding of the dynamics of war, peace, and power—dynamics of undiminished relevance in our times.

Lecture Twenty-Five
The Outbreak of World War I

Scope:

This lecture examines the causes of the outbreak of World War I in the summer of 1914. This classic case of escalation is the object of one of the biggest debates in modern history, responsible for a voluminous amount of scholarship. We examine how it was that European diplomats and statesmen brought the continent to the brink of and then plunged it into an ever-widening war. We analyze in turn the main competing explanations for this route into catastrophe, weighing long-term and short-term causes, the role of intention versus accident, and the crucial question of contemporary expectations. Finally, we trace how scholarly debate has evolved and explore the current state of that debate.

Outline

I. Introduction.
  A. In 1914, a terrorist act in the Balkans triggered a diplomatic crisis that unfolded over six weeks, leading to World War I.
    1. After a long general peace since 1815, the war resulted from a failure in the European state system.
    2. World War I destroyed the earlier European state system and the operation of the balance of power, as the Dual Alliance (Germany and Austria-Hungary) faced the Triple Entente (Great Britain, France, and Russia).
    3. The rest of the 20th century was dominated by struggles to establish a new international order.
    4. World War I merits its description by historian and diplomat George Kennan as the "seminal catastrophe" of the age: The war left some 10 million dead; led to the collapse of four empires (Russia, the Ottoman Empire, Austria-Hungary, and Germany); ended European global predominance; ushered in the ideologies of Communism, Fascism, and Nazism; and was followed by an even more destructive world war.
    5. The stakes in understanding how this came about are high.

　　　　©2007 The Teaching Company.

B. The argument on the causes of (or guilt for) the war is one of the most voluminous historical debates, with an enormous literature dating back to 1914. The debate involves profound theoretical issues.

    1. Did long-term trends or immediate factors play the dominant role?

    2. Were individuals more important than structural factors?

    3. Did leaders understand or intend the results their actions produced?

    4. Can blame be assigned to particular actors or was it shared?

    5. Was the war inevitable or could it have been avoided?

C. Because the timing of events was crucial to the unfolding of the crisis, we need to review the sequence of actions and reactions.

II. Assassination at Sarajevo—June 28, 1914.

A. On June 28, 1914, the heir to the Habsburg throne, Archduke Franz Ferdinand, and his wife were assassinated in Sarajevo.

    1. Bosnia had been annexed by Austria-Hungary in 1908.

    2. Serbian nationalists and their Russian patrons were angered.

    3. Nationalism threatened the very existence of Austria-Hungary, a state of 50 million with many nationalities.

    4. The ill-timed visit of the noble couple came on the anniversary of the 1389 Battle of Kosovo, when Serbia had been defeated by the Ottoman Turks.

    5. The bumbling conspiracy almost failed, until a series of accidents allowed a young assassin to strike.

    6. The plotters belonged to a Serbian nationalist group aiming for union with the Kingdom of Serbia, a dynamic state of five million people.

    7. While the plotters had contacts with Serbian officials, they were not directed by the Serbian government as Austria-Hungary later claimed.

    8. Austro-Hungarian officials were convinced that decisive action needed to be taken, but at first nothing happened.

    9. Behind the scenes, diplomacy was expanding the crisis.

III. The July Crisis of 1914.

    A. Austria-Hungary consulted with its ally, Germany, and on July 5–6, 1914, received a "blank check" to act against Serbia with German support.

        1. Generals also contributed to deliberations, most wildly Austro-Hungarian commander Conrad von Hötzendorf, who constantly called for preventive wars.

        2. Germany's power was formidable, based on a modern army and a population of 65 million.

    B. Austria-Hungary sent an ultimatum to Serbia on July 23, 1914.

        1. The ultimatum (to expire in 48 hours) was designed to be unacceptable, with demands for Austrian investigations inside Serbia, and shocked European diplomats.

        2. Serbia turned to its ally, Russia—an empire of mighty potential and 165 million subjects.

        3. On July 25, Serbia accepted most of the ultimatum and mobilized its army; Russia also planned mobilization.

        4. Russia's 1894 alliance with France came into play, and Russia received encouragement from the French ambassador.

        5. On July 26, British foreign secretary Edward Grey pleaded for a conference to settle the crisis.

        6. Austria-Hungary declared war on Serbia by telegraph on July 28, 1914.

    C. The conflict now expanded beyond a regional crisis.

        1. Germany sought but failed to ensure British neutrality.

        2. On July 30, Tsar Nicholas ordered full Russian mobilization.

        3. On July 31, Germany sent Russia an ultimatum to stop mobilizing or face war, demanded French neutrality, and declared *Kriegsgefahrzustand* (a state of the danger of war).

IV. War is declared.

    A. When the German ultimatum expired on August 1, Germany declared war on Russia.

B. For a brief ambiguous interval, Germany thought it had secured British neutrality, but German war plans proceeded.

    1. The key German war plan was the 1905 Schlieffen Plan.

    2. It aimed to meet the threat of war on two fronts by attacking into France through neutral Belgium.

C. On August 2, Germany delivered an ultimatum to Belgium to allow entrance to its troops.

D. The British role was now clarified, with agreement in the cabinet; Britain had to enter the war.

    1. While the entente was not a full alliance, strategic questions now came into play, among them the crucial Belgian Question.

    2. British memories of Napoleon played an important role in the deliberations.

    3. The naval power of the British state of 45 million was reinforced by imperial resources.

E. On August 3, Belgium rejected the ultimatum, and Germany declared war on France while invading Belgium.

F. The same day, Sir Edward Grey sent an ultimatum to Germany.

    1. The deadline expired at midnight on August 4, and Britain entered the war.

    2. Grey declared, "The lamps are going out all over Europe. They will not be lit again in our lifetime."

G. Europe was now involved in a general war as it had not seen since 1815. Germany and Austria-Hungary faced off against France, Russia, and Great Britain, while Italy declared itself neutral.

V. The debate on causes.

    A. Debate on the war's causes began immediately and was colored by the political interests of the fighting powers.

    B. The debate itself has seen tremendous shifts of opinion.

    C. After the war, the Versailles Treaty's Article 231 in June 1919, proclaimed German guilt for the war.

        1. The claim undergirded demands for reparations.

        2. Rejected furiously by Germans, the claim led to a vast outpouring of diplomatic documents.

D. In the years before World War II, opinion shifted toward looking for collective responsibility and structural causes, denouncing traditional diplomacy.

E. After World War II, the debate was reopened explosively by Fritz Fischer's 1961 study, *Grab for World Power*.

    1. Fischer argued that Germany had caused the war in a bid for superpower status and had vast expansionist aims.

    2. His critics argued that German leaders had miscalculated the nature of the conflict.

    3. Fischer responded in a later book with the claim that the Kaiser had decided on war at the 1912 war council, but this claim met with less acceptance.

F. Other explanations have also been advanced but seem incomplete or inadequate.

    1. Some see diplomacy and alliances at fault, but these depended on policy choices. Historian Paul Schroeder argues that what needs to be explained is why peace ended more than why war began.

    2. Imperialism had raised European tensions since the 1870s, but these conflicts were not at issue in 1914.

    3. Arms races and military planning had escalated but were the tools of decision makers.

    4. A. J. P. Taylor argued provocatively that the war was an accident.

    5. Marxists argued that Capitalism was the cause, but economic interests suffered in the war.

    6. Some historians (following Fischer) argue the primacy of domestic politics in causing the war, but many elites understood that war often produces revolution.

    7. Some see Balkan politics at fault, but Great Power involvement expanded the crisis.

G. Most historians today see Germany as bearing primary responsibility for risking war but with other European statesmen also playing a role, even if by omission.

H. It is instructive to consider counterfactuals, as they help us see how events could have turned out differently, even if war in some form had become almost unavoidable.

    1. Elements of the equation could have been different (timing, localized conflict, British abstention), resulting in a different outcome.

2. The war had such huge effects on our later history and the present that the very prospect of a different outcome makes one stop and think.

Essential Reading:

Henry Kissinger, *Diplomacy*, pp. 200–17.

Supplementary Reading:

James Joll, *The Origins of the First World War*, 2nd ed.

Questions to Consider:

1. What would have been the best way to avoid the outbreak of World War I?

2. Is it useful to see World War I as a new Balkan War? Why or why not?

Lecture Twenty-Five—Transcript
The Outbreak of World War I

In this lecture, we will be examining the fascinating question of the causes of World War I. As we begin this exploration of World War I, we really leave behind in our course the period that we had been looking at previously, the classical balance of power in Europe—that long period of general peace between the Great Powers without a great general war involving all of the Great Powers that had extended such a remarkable record from 1815 all the way to 1914.

In this lecture, we will examine just how it was that by the summer of 1914 European diplomats and statesmen brought the continent to the brink and then plunged into an ever-widening war. We will analyze in turn the main competing explanations for this route into catastrophe. We will weigh long-term and short-term causes; we will consider the role of intention versus accident and the crucial question of contemporary expectation. In a sense, just what was it that people thought they were doing? Finally, we will also trace how scholarly debate on this crucial question in historiography in the writing of modern history has evolved, and we'll also consider the current state of that debate. Incidentally, I might also mention that for those interested in a much more detailed and comprehensive treatment of all of the aspects of World War I, not merely the diplomatic aspect, The Teaching Company in fact has a course titled, *World War I: The Great War*, by none other than yours truly that I would recommend to those who have further interest.

Let's set the stage for this cataclysm that brings to an end the classical balance of power. In 1914, a terrorist act in that troubled region, the Balkans in the southeast of Europe, triggered a diplomatic crisis, which unfolded over the following six weeks with remarkable and accelerating rapidity and led to World War I's outbreak.

After a long general peace that had held in Europe since 1815, this war resulted from a failure in the European state system, and our previous lectures have examined within that period of the classical balance of power how the balance of power had started to break down. Germany had feared encirclement, and out of its anxiety over encirclement had launched such an unpredictable and ill-considered foreign policy that others came to fear Germany. In sort of a triumph of self-fulfilling prophecy, German foreign policy in a sense produced the very encirclement it had worried about, as Europe divided in rigid alliance blocs with ever less flexibility inherent in the system.

World War I thus ended up destroying the earlier European state system and the operation of the balance of power. It would see a tremendous confrontation between on the one hand the Dual Alliance, Germany and Austria-Hungary, facing off against the powerful Triple Entente, the linkage of the Great Powers, Great Britain, France, and Russia. Indeed, after the catastrophe of World War I, the rest of the 20th century in some sense follows from that disaster because it's dominated by struggles to establish a new international order to somehow replace the one that was wrecked in the conflict of World War I. Thus, World War I truly merits, I think, the description by historian and practicing diplomat George Kennan as the "seminal catastrophe" of the 20th century.

The damage that it would inflict would be vast. The war would leave some 10 million dead. It led to the collapse of four empires: the Russian Empire, the Ottoman Empire, the Austro-Hungarian Empire, and the German Empire. It ended European global predominance, something that some Europeans were slow to recognize. It also ushered in the ideologies of Communism, Fascism, and Nazism in the wake of that conflict, and then was also followed by an even more destructive World War II.

Obviously, if its impact was this great, the stakes in understanding how this came to pass are tremendously high. Indeed, the onset of World War I is a classic case of the escalation to war. The argument on the causes of the war, or to put it another way who is guilty in terms of causing the war—if such a person or set of persons exists— is one of the most voluminous historical debates in all of historical writing, in all of historiography. It is probably on par with questions like: Why did the Roman Empire collapse? There's an enormous literature on this subject of why World War I broke out. That literature is really launched as sort of a tidal wave of historical writing from the very event itself. The first texts on this question start pouring out in 1914, itself immediately after the event.

One historian has gone to the trouble of actually counting up how many books there are on one part of the larger problem of the outbreak of World War I, and that historian has counted that there are thousands of books on the assassinations at Sarajevo in 1914 alone. This is an enormously huge historical literature on one topic;

one can see why this would be the case. The debate also involves not just these vast existential questions in terms of its effect on modern history, but it also for historians as craftsmen of historical narratives presents profound theoretical issues. These issues include the question of were long-term trends or more immediate, almost accidental details, or factors, the dominant ones? Another issue is: Were individuals more important than structural factors? Were particular statesmen more responsible in bringing this disaster to pass—or by contrast was it the unpredictable consequences of certain alliances or structures that brought this into being? Did leaders even understand or intend the results that their actions produced? One could write a history about unintended consequences. Is this a case of such an unintended consequence, or by contrast was malice aforethought in launching this war?

Similarly, can blame—the question of guilt, and this was very heatedly discussed in the immediate aftermath of the outbreak of the war—be assigned to particular actors, or was responsibility shared generally by all of the statesmen and all of the societies involved in the outbreak of the war? To put a further point to these questions, we might also ask: Should the war be seen as inevitable, simply fated to happen if not at that precise point in which it took place in 1914 maybe it could have broken out of necessity shortly thereafter for reasons that were structural, or was the war contingent? Here's a key question: Could the war have been avoided? Might Europe entirely have simply passed on this first "total war"?

Because the timing of events was crucial to the unfolding of the crisis that we will be talking about, we need to review the sequence of actions and reactions. What I would suggest would be the following: Rather than focusing on the details of the dates that I will inevitably have to mention or the hour-by-hour sequence, I think cumulatively one starts to feel the sense, and this is probably most important, of the gathering speed of this crisis as it moves forward. In particular, timing and the acceleration of events would be a crucial factor for participants in the crisis itself because they felt that the clock was ticking down on mobilization. I might define mobilization here usefully as the revving up of military plans to put armies into the field. Mobilization had become a fine art as a result of the massive arms races at the end of the 19th century so that all of the combatant countries had very closely scheduled time tables for when particular troops should be crossing which railroad bridges in which railroad cars, and the anxiety was that if you didn't put your troops into the field fast enough, you might lose the war in the first hours by simply falling behind. Time would be of the essence.

We now should turn to the event that sparked it all: the assassination at Sarajevo in Bosnia/Herzegovina on June 28, 1914, which really marks a historical watershed. On June 28, 1914, the heir to the Habsburg throne, the throne of the Austro-Hungarian Empire, Archduke Franz Ferdinand and his wife were both assassinated in the capital of Bosnia, Sarajevo. You will recall that Bosnia/Herzegovina had been annexed by Austria-Hungary in 1908. This had sparked an international crisis and had been denounced by Serbia and Russia who saw their own interests, they felt, being violated in this, and 1908 had been a moment when it seemed that general war might very well result. That had been smoothed over. The situation had cooled down, but nonetheless, Serbian nationalists as well as their great Russian patrons had been left infuriated by the humiliation.

Nationalism, in general we will recall, was a threatening force as far as the leaders of the Austro-Hungarian Empire were concerned because Austria-Hungary was a state of 50 million with many nationalities, some 11 or 12 major ones and many other smaller ones. The visit of the imperial couple was spectacularly ill timed one might say and you might almost think calculated to further inflame the nationalist passions of Serbian nationalists living in the region. The visit came on the precise day that marked the anniversary of a battle from the Middle Ages, the Battle of Kosovo in 1389. Think back all the way to the start of our course when we talked about the onslaught of the Ottoman Turks as they advanced into Europe. Serbia had been defeated by the Ottoman Turks at the Battle of Kosovo in 1389. So that date had enormous emotional significance for Serbian nationalists.

It seemed in a repetition of historical patterns that the enemy might have changed. The enemy might now be the Austro-Hungarians and the Habsburgs rather than the Ottomans, but the drama still had its emotional significance. The conspiracy of the terrorists who had converged on Sarajevo was a bumbling one. It was marked by tremendous miscalculation, failure of nerve and simply at a crucial juncture seemed to have failed. I mean, many of the terrorists felt it was time to call it a day and that nothing would result. Then a series of accidents, in particular the way in which the driver of the car of the imperial couple took a wrong turn, allowed one young assassin, who had given up just previously, to feel that this was the opportunity to strike. He leapt up close to the car as it drove by and at point-blank range emptied his revolver into that car and killed the imperial couple together. Indeed, one might mention that the car and the clothes of the murdered couple are still on display today in a Vienna military museum where almost in a shrine-like atmosphere these are held as relics of the martyred couple.

The plotters, as it turns out, belonged to a Serbian nationalist group whose aim was union of Bosnia/Herzegovina, which was currently under Habsburg rule, with the neighboring kingdom of Serbia, which was a dynamic state of 5 million people that saw itself imbued with a nationalist mission of achieving the union of the south Slavs. While the plotters did have contact with some Serbian officials, the terrorists were not directed by the Serbian government itself, which is what the Austro-Hungarian government claimed in reaction to this atrocity. Austro-Hungarian officials were convinced that a decisive crisis moment had arrived and they needed to take decisive action now. At first, however, apparently nothing happened. Many people felt that this was due to the sort of very relaxed and laissez-faire attitude of Austro-Hungarian officialdom in general. In fact, what was happening behind the scenes was diplomacy, which was expanding the crisis.

Let's turn to consider now the July crisis that follows immediately upon this assassination. Austria-Hungary reacted, first of all, by consulting its far stronger ally in the Dual Alliance, imperial Germany, and asked whether Germany would support energetic action against Serbia in reaction to this atrocity. On July 5–6, 1914, as a result of these communications, the Austro-Hungarian officials received what came to be called afterwards a "blank check" from the German officials to act against Serbia with German support. This represented the promise of Germany backing energetic action by the Austro-Hungarians. The man who was the servant of Kaiser Wilhelm II, the man who was in charge of the German government at this point, was a chancellor by the name of Theobald von Bethmann-Hollweg who had been chancellor from 1909 and was a fatalistic kind of conservative who later would look with dismay at events as they unfolded. It also needs to be mentioned that generals were making decisive contributions in arguing for energetic action, and the man who especially played this role was the wild Austro-

Hungarian commander, Conrad von Hötzendorf. One of his trademarks was to constantly call for preventative war against the neighbors of the Austro-Hungarian Empire. One historian has actually gone to the trouble of counting that in 1913, which was the previous year, Hötzendorf had 25 times called for war against Serbia. You get the impression that this is a man who if you asked him what he wanted for lunch might very well reply preventative war.

Germany's power as a backer of the Austro-Hungarian effort was formidable. Germany had a very modern army and a strong population of 65 million. Thus, the Austro-Hungarians now were emboldened to take decisive action. They drafted an ultimatum, a take it or leave it demand, which was leveled against the Serbian government and after strategic delay was sent to Serbia on July 23rd, 1914. The ultimatum, which was going to expire in 48 hours and the Serbs had to respond yes or no—that was the demand, was actually designed to be unacceptable. It's a really remarkable diplomatic document that you can read. It had demands for Austrian investigations within Serbia, which in essence would have abrogated the sovereignty of Serbia, and many European diplomats were shocked at the content of this ultimatum even though they had earlier had sympathies for what they saw as the justified complaints of Austria-Hungary.

Serbia now turned to its ally, its great Slavic patron, the Russian Empire. Russia was a mighty empire with vast potential, both economic and military, and 165 million subjects—truly a great power. On July 25, after consultations with the Russians, who had assured Serbia that they would back them as well, Serbia accepted most of the ultimatum. They tried to, in essence, accept all of the demands they felt they could but not all of it, and at the same time they mobilized their army. They prepared for war, and Russia also planned mobilization. At this point, Russia's alliance with France, which went back to 1894 and had been such a watershed in the change in the European balance of power, now came into play. The French ambassador in St. Petersburg encouraged the Russians in this regard.

On July 26, the British foreign secretary, Edward Grey, did something that was very characteristic of an earlier period, the age of the Concert of Europe. He pleaded for a conference to settle the crisis. In the tradition of the Concert of Europe, if there is a crisis, you call a congress or a conference. He was disregarded as events took their course. Austria-Hungary now declared war on Serbia after receiving what it felt was an unsatisfactory answer to its ultimatum by telegraph, and that suggests something of the speed that now was through technology inherent in the diplomatic process. They declared war on Serbia by telegraph on July 28, 1914, a month after the assassination. The conflict now expanded beyond merely a regional crisis. Germany at this point sought to ensure that in a future conflict that might now be unfolding that Britain would remain neutral, but it failed to do so. This was perhaps a somewhat naïve hope that it was still possible. They had received earlier warnings in this regard. On July 30, Tsar Nicholas of the Russian Empire ordered Russian full mobilization, and in a chain affect of these unfolding diplomatic consequences, on July 31st Germany sent Russia an ultimatum in turn to either stop mobilizing or to face war with Germany. It also demanded French neutrality and declared in a very long German word, *Kriegsgefahrzustand,* that there was now a state of the danger of war.

Let's move now to the advent of general war itself. When the German ultimatum against Russia expired on August 1 without satisfactory answer, Germany declared war on Russia. For a brief ambiguous interval, Germany thought that it might still have a chance of securing British neutrality, but German war plans proceeded all the same. The key German war plan was the secret Schlieffen Plan, which had been worked out long before as one of these very detailed mobilization plans. It had been worked out indeed by 1905, and it aimed to meet the threat of war on two fronts—the sort of thing that kept Bismarck awake at night, the nightmare of coalitions. It aimed to meet this challenge by attacking first with lightning speed against France in the west through neutral Belgium. This was obviously a violation of international law, but it was felt to be necessary by German generals—to strike France hard and fast, knock it out of the war and then turn against the far larger enemy of Russia in the east. As the plan unfolded, on August 2 Germany delivered an ultimatum to neutral Belgium demanding that its troops be allowed to pass through. That very ultimatum now clarified the British role emphatically.

In the cabinet, which had been debating on what the course of action should be given that an Entente did not obligate Britain to go to war, now there was increasingly consensus, and in the cabinet it was agreed that Britain had to enter the war. Strategic questions had come into play, and the crucial Belgian question was the threat of another Great Power occupying Belgium, which is directly across the English Channel and a natural jumping off point for invasion of the British Isles. This could not be tolerated, and indeed one of the themes of our course that we've come back to again and again has been the way in which prior experience conditions contemporary decisions.

British memories of Napoleon played an important role in the deliberations, and when you look at the statements of British policy makers in this period, they are often talking about a Napoleonic situation or even saying things like these Germans are worse than Napoleon. Clearly, the challenge of Napoleon and his bid for hegemony was present to mind. Britain, as a naval power with a population of 45 million in the British Isles, was also reinforced by vaster imperial resources—the colonies abroad.

On August 3, Belgium simply rejected the German ultimatum, and Germany declared war on France while invading through neutral Belgium. On the same day, Sir Edward Grey for Britain sent an ultimatum to Germany, and that deadline expired at midnight on August 4. Britain entered the war. Sir Edward Grey in a famous statement looking out upon this catastrophe as it unfolded declared, "The lamps are going out all over Europe. They will not be lit again in our lifetime."

He was right in this regard. Europe was now involved in a general war such as it had not seen since 1815. There had been the Crimean War where some Great Powers had fought against each other but no war involving all of the Great Powers. Now, Germany and Austria-Hungary faced off against France, Russia, and Great Britain. You will recall that when we had mentioned that Italy had become an ally of Germany and Austria-Hungary later in the 19th century that its adherence to that alliance had been questionable. Those anxieties on the part of German and Austro-Hungarian diplomats came true because Italy now declared itself neutral and not involved in this struggle.

Let's pass now to the historians' debate, the historians' clash, over what the causes of this onset of catastrophes really were. Debate began immediately, and it was colored by the political interests of the fighting powers. The debate itself over the decades has seen tremendous shifts of opinion. So, let me just broadly, sort of with a very broad brush, indicate some of the tremendous oscillation in terms of historical interpretation. After the war itself, the Versailles Treaty in Article 231—probably the most famous of all of the hundreds of articles of this treaty—when the treaty was signed in June of 1911 proclaimed a very simple explanation for the war. That was Germany was guilty of having started the war. This claim undergirded demands that were made in the treaty for reparations on the part of the victorious powers. Almost universally, Germans rejected that claim furiously even as they were forced to sign the Versailles Treaty that admitted it. This claim led to a vast outpouring of publication of diplomatic documents first by the German government and then all other involved governments as well, which really was sort of a windfall for historians who suddenly had a lot of documents that they could pour over. They realized eventually, however, that the ones that were released could often be quite selective to make the country that had published those documents appear in the very best light.

In the years before World War II, however, opinion shifted and began to look more towards collective responsibility emphasizing structural causes and denouncing traditional diplomacy and the balance of power as one of the reasons why Europe had gone to war rather than the primacy of German responsibility. Then the debate took another surprising turn after World War II when of all people a German historian re-emphasized Germany's particular role in unleashing the conflict. This historian was Fritz Fischer, who in his 1961 study that one might translate into English as the *Grab for World Power*—talk about putting your argument right into your title of your book—argued that Germany had caused the war in its bid for superpower status and had vast expansionist aims. Implicitly, there was a comparison here to Nazi Germany as well. His critics—and they were fierce critics—argued in fact that German leaders had merely miscalculated about the nature of the conflict even as the conflict set on. Fischer responded in a later book by ratcheting up his claims with the claim that the Kaiser indeed had decided on war as early as 1912 in that War Council that we had mentioned briefly in an earlier lecture, but this notion that there had been vast and early premeditation has not really been accepted by historians and has been quite skeptically met.

Other explanations have also been advanced, but they also seem as complete explanations rather inadequate. Let's consider a few of these in turn. Some historians have seen diplomacy and alliances as such at fault, but in fact these depended on policy choices that diplomats were making at the time. One might note that as in the case of Italy, which stayed out of the conflict, just because you had an alliance didn't mean that you inevitably got dragged in. Alliances could be broken as well. The eminent diplomatic historian Paul Schroeder also usefully complicates the issue by putting the debate on its head in this regard. He argues that what we really have to consider is not so much why the war began as why the long European peace ended. Why did habits of cooperation and consultation break down so fatefully?

Other historians have emphasized Imperialism, which played such an explosive role in the High Imperialism of the late 19th century. They claim that wave of European competition since the 1870s really raised the temperature of international politics. The only problem with this explanation is that many of the colonial conflicts were not the immediate issue in 1914, which centered on the Balkans and matters closer to home. Some historians have emphasized that arms races and the growth in armies and increasing intricacy of military planning had escalated, but in some sense to emphasize this too much might let the actual decision makers, who are the ones who start the military countdowns, off the hook. A famous British historian who has a tremendous love of paradox and I'm an admirer of his work even when I don't agree with the arguments that are being presented so vigorously, A. J. P. Taylor, had argued very provocatively that the entire war in some sense was an accident and that policy makers had become the prisoners of their own weapons as they didn't understand the full implications of courses of action.

Earlier in the 20th century, Marxists had argued that in some sense the war was caused by Capitalism itself and that increased capitalist competition had made a world capitalist war inevitable. The only problem with this explanation as one template for what happened is that economic interests suffered tremendously in the war and a lot of bankers and capitalists were dismayed at what they saw as war that would be bad for business when it came in 1914.

Some historians, returning to one of the very important themes of our course, following Fischer in essence, have argued that what you see here is a case where domestic politics matters a lot in diplomacy, and they argue that this is a case of the primacy of domestic politics in causing the war as a way of escaping as it were internal domestic crises. But in fact, many elite actually understood that war often produces revolution and were worried about it precisely for this reason. Some see Balkan politics as at fault drawing in the Great Powers against their will, but in fact Great Power involvement actually was instrumental in expanding the crisis.

Most historians today actually see Germany as bearing primary responsibility for having risked the war but with a role for other European statesmen as well, even if it was a role by omission. It's also instructive to consider "counterfactuals," that's to say alternative scenarios, because they help us to see how events could have turned out differently even if war in some form had become almost inevitable. Elements of this equation could have been different. There could have been differences in timing. The war could have come earlier or later with a very different international constellation. The conflict might very well have remained localized in the Balkans if one changes elements of the equation. One might also consider the way in which Britain staying out of the war, which was a possibility, might very well have produced a different outcome. An old undergraduate joke that I've heard in the past proposes an imaginary newspaper headline and this in and of itself is sort of a counter-factual. This imaginary headline reads, "Franz Ferdinand Found Alive—First World War a tragic mistake!" The very way in which this sort of sophomoric joke overstates the case suggests just how different history might have been if indeed but one or another element of this larger equation had turned out differently, and it's instructive to think about this.

The war had such huge effects on our later history and our present day indeed that the very prospect of a different outcome for it all makes one stop and think without World War I, no Communism, no Soviet Union, no rise of Fascism and Nazism, no World War II, no Cold War. Our own world might have been changed out of all recognition, but it was to be changed out of all recognition by a more all-encompassing general conflict, World War I, as "total war" that we will consider in its diplomatic aspects comprehensively in our next lecture.

Lecture Twenty-Six
World War I—Total War

Scope:

World War I (1914–1918) is often called a "total war" because of the all-encompassing mobilization of mass armies, entire economies, domestic societies, and allies demanded by the stakes of the conflict. The changes produced by the experience of war, in which at least nine million soldiers died, were correspondingly deep on the level of international politics. Long-standing diplomatic patterns were overturned under the pressure of war, war aims changed and grew more radical as the conflict dragged on, four empires collapsed (the Austro-Hungarian, German, Ottoman, and Russian empires), and two new ideological actors began their ascent to superpower status: Woodrow Wilson's United States and Lenin's Soviet Russia.

Outline

I. The war opens.

    A. The war involved a series of surprises, confounding contemporary expectations of what was to happen.

        1. Many were caught in the "short war illusion."

        2. The German Schlieffen Plan was to deliver victory in the west in six weeks; the plan was halted in northern France by October 1914 and static trench warfare set in.

    B. As the war continued, diplomacy had a role to play even during the fighting.

        1. In the past, one would have expected a conference to be called to reach a peace based on compromise; instead, war became more total in its scope and stakes.

        2. "Total war" refers to this all-encompassing conflict among entire societies (armies, economies, home fronts, mass psychologies) for ultimate defeat or victory.

        3. With the British blockade of Germany and German submarine warfare, the economic dimension was central.

        4. The intensity of sacrifice made compromise increasingly difficult.

II. War aims and allies.

    A. The prolongation of the war posed the question of what the war was being fought for, as the powers sought to outline their war aims.

        1. Germans saw this as a defensive war to break out of encirclement.

        2. Austria-Hungary fatalistically saw a war for survival.

        3. France fought a defensive war against German attack.

        4. Russia defended itself against German attack and in defense of Slavic goals.

        5. Britain intervened on the continent against German hegemony and for its own safety out of its concern for Belgium's neutrality (maintained since 1839).

    B. Beyond these first imperatives, the powers went on to elaborate more detailed programs and sought allies to tip the balance.

    C. In September 1914 the Triple Entente agreed in the Pact of London not to negotiate or make separate peace with the Central Powers (Germany and Austria-Hungary).

    D. At the same time, the secret September Program outlined Germany's expansive war aims.

    E. Both sides sought to add allies.

        1. Ottoman Turkey joined the Central Powers in November 1914 (declaring a jihad); Bulgaria joined in October 1915.

        2. Japan declared war on Germany in August 1914, seized German colonies, and expanded into China.

        3. Italy held a bidding war and joined the Triple Entente after the secret Treaty of London (April 1915) awarded it territories.

        4. Romania joined the Triple Entente in 1916; Greece joined in 1917.

    F. In the Straits Agreement of March–April 1915 (a startling shift in the Eastern Question), Great Britain and France dropped their century-old opposition to Russia seizing the Turkish Straits to keep Russia in the war.

        1. The importance of the Turkish Straits was demonstrated in the failed 1915 Gallipoli campaign (in present-day Turkey).

2. Some Russian leaders were relieved at its failure, which prevented British dominance.

G. The secret Sykes-Picot Agreement of February 1916, drafted by Sir Mark Sykes and Georges Picot, planned the division of the Ottoman Empire by Britain and France after the war.

    1. Britain was to control Mesopotamia, and France was to control Syria and Lebanon.

    2. In practice, these agreements clashed with other commitments in the region and affected problems in the area that continue to this day.

H. Russia and Germany bid for Polish sympathies with declarations of a future Polish state; these bids were met with indecisive results.

I. The British Balfour Declaration of November 2, 1917, by Foreign Secretary Arthur J. Balfour declared that the British government viewed:

> with favor the establishment in Palestine of a national home for the Jewish people … it being clearly understood that nothing shall be done which may prejudice the civil and religious rights of existing non-Jewish communities in Palestine.

J. Both sides also attempted to sway neutrals; a crucial arena was public opinion in the United States, which remained neutral at the urging of President Woodrow Wilson (1856–1924).

    1. As the neutral United States traded by sea, both British blockades and German submarine warfare created conflicts.

    2. The sinking of ships with American citizens at first led Germany to restrain its tactic, but on February 1, 1917, it again risked unrestricted submarine war.

III. Peace initiatives.

A. Socialists tried to gather international conferences to end the war on the basis of their political program for the future.

B. The Vatican, under Pope Benedict XV (1854–1922), launched peace initiatives without result and antagonized all sides with its neutrality.

C. In December 1916, President Wilson asked all sides to state their war aims as a prelude to conciliation, and in January 1917 he proposed the formula of "peace without victory."

D. Austria-Hungary's last emperor, Charles, tried to secretly negotiate with the entente in 1917 and was humiliated.

IV. The Russian Revolution.

    A. The discredited Tsarist regime fell with astonishing speed in February and March 1917.

        1. The Tsar abdicated, ending three centuries of Romanov rule.

        2. In spite of general war weariness, the liberal provisional government promised to continue the war.

    B. To destabilize the new Russia, the German high command sent exiled revolutionary Vladimir Lenin back in a sealed train.

        1. He praised war as a "giant accelerator."

        2. On his return in April 1917, he preached "revolutionary defeatism."

V. United States entry into the war.

    A. In spite of neutrality, economically the United States had become linked to the Triple Entente.

    B. Public outrage broke out at the revelation of the Zimmermann Telegram, which Germany had sent on January 1917 to the Mexican government to lure it into the war.

        1. British officials intercepted the message and passed it to Washington.

        2. On April 6, 1917, the United States declared war on Germany.

    C. American involvement offered economic reserves, boosted Triple Entente morale, and began shipping American troops to Europe.

    D. Even as it entered the war, the United States did so as an "associated power" rather than as an ally, underlining distinctive aims and motives.

    E. Wilson outlined these aims and motives in his January 1918 Fourteen Points speech to Congress.

1. These aims and motives included open diplomacy, freedom of the seas, free trade, disarmament, resolution of colonial questions, autonomy for the peoples of Austria-Hungary and the Ottoman Empire, a free Poland, and an international League of Nations.
    2. Later speeches elaborated on nations' right of self-determination.
    F. Wilson was hailed by many Europeans.
VI. Lenin and the Brest-Litovsk Treaty.
    A. A different radical departure from traditional politics took place in Russia, where radical Socialist Bolsheviks under Lenin seized power.
    B. The Bolsheviks declared a Soviet government—led by people's commissars—and took Russia out of the war.
    C. They immediately mounted an international campaign to speak "over the heads" of elites and overthrow the international system.
        1. On November 15, 1917, they declared a right to self-determination in the former empire.
        2. Leon Trotsky became people's commissar for foreign affairs.
        3. He famously announced that his role would be to publish secret treaties found in the safes of the Foreign Ministry and then close up shop as international revolution broke out around the world.
        4. Reflecting their ideology, the Bolshevik ceasefire negotiation team included working class representatives and a woman revolutionary.
        5. Diplomatic ranks were abolished.
    D. As negotiations with the Germans began in December 1917 at the fortress of Brest-Litovsk, they offered a moment of truth: a vision of the peace the Central Powers intended.
        1. Both sides argued in spectacularly bad faith about self-determination.
        2. Trotsky's verbal brilliance did not work, as the Germans advanced when he quit the negotiations in February.
        3. On March 3, 1918, the Bolsheviks signed the Treaty of Brest-Litovsk, losing huge territories and a large amount of the population to save the revolution.

4. Triple Entente opinion hardened toward the Central Powers at the news of this iron peace and the treaties with Ukraine and Romania that also were signed.

VII. Collapse of the Central Powers and the armistice.

A. A last German offensive on the Western Front scored frightening successes in spring 1918 and then ground to a halt.

B. Germany's allies dropped out.

C. Austria-Hungary, once the indispensable support of the European state system, began to dissolve.

    1. In recognition of its earlier traditional role, the Triple Entente had been reluctant to call for its dissolution.

    2. The nationalism of "submerged peoples" and the imperatives of territorial promises eroded that reluctance.

    3. Czechs, Slovaks, South Slavs, and other peoples of the monarchy declared independence, shattering the Habsburg realm, which signed an armistice on October 4, 1918.

D. Exhausted, Germany signed the armistice on November 11, 1918, on the basis of Wilson's Fourteen Points.

E. The peoples of Europe now awaited a new kind of peace settlement after this "war to end all wars."

Essential Reading:

Henry Kissinger, *Diplomacy*, pp. 218–227.

Supplementary Reading:

Aviel Roshwald, *Ethnic Nationalism and the Fall of Empires: Central Europe, Russia, and the Middle East, 1914–1923.*

Hew Strachan, *The First World War.*

Questions to Consider:

1. Without the intervention of the United States, what other outcomes might the war have produced?

2. If the Bolshevik coup had failed and Russia had remained in the war, what effect would that have had?

Lecture Twenty-Six—Transcript
World War I—Total War

In this lecture, we will be considering the diplomatic dimensions of World War I from 1914–1918. In our previous lecture, we looked very closely at the tremendous debates that surround the outbreak of the war itself, its diplomatic chain of affects, reactions, and counteractions. In this lecture, by contrast, we will look at World War I itself from a diplomatic point of view vindicating an insight that we had announced in an earlier lecture that simply because a war breaks out doesn't mean that diplomacy ceases entirely. Even if the enemies are not speaking with one another or willing to compromise, diplomacy still goes on even between one's own allies and one's self. World War I, from 1914–1918, is often called a "total war." What is meant by that is an all-encompassing mobilization of mass armies, entire economies, domestic societies as well as allies, all of this demanded by the enormous, indeed total, stakes of the conflict. The changes produced by the experience of this war in which at least nine million soldiers died and additional civilian fatalities were experienced were correspondingly deep as well on the level of international politics.

We will observe how long-standing diplomatic patterns were overturned under the pressure of war. We will experience some real surprises in this regard. We will see how war aims changed and grew more radical as this total conflict dragged on, and we'll observe also the collapse of four empires that we've talked a lot about in our earlier lectures: the Austro-Hungarian, German, Ottoman, and Russian Empires. We'll also finally see the rise of two new ideological actors as they begin their assent to superpower status: the United States under Woodrow Wilson and Soviet Russia under Vladimir Ilyich Lenin.

Let's begin with the opening of the war itself because the war, once it had begun, involved a series of surprises that often confounded entirely contemporary expectations of what was to happen. Many were caught in what historians have since called the "short war illusion," the conviction as the saying went that war would be over by Christmas. The boys would come home after experiencing glorious adventures, and there would be triumph that one was sure one's own nation would experience.

The German Schlieffen Plan was to deliver victory in the West in the course of six weeks of tremendously quick and decisive battle against France. This was intended to be really a replay of the triumph of the Franco-Prussian War of 1870–1871, but contrary to the expectations of military planners, the Schlieffen Plan offensive was halted in northern France by October 1914 due to the tremendous efforts of French soldiers and British soldiers who were thrown into the breach. By the fall of 1914, a more static trench warfare had set in with a line of trenches extending for hundreds of miles from the Alps to the English Channel rather than decisive battles fought gloriously on those battlefields.

As the war continued, diplomacy had a role to play even during this embittered fighting. One surprise that immediately presented itself was this: In the past, in the tradition of the Concert of Europe, one would have expected that once war had not delivered decisive results, let's say by 1915, a conference would have been called. The Great Powers would have gathered, maybe even while the fighting still went on in the battlefield, to somehow reach a peace based on compromise recognizing that no decisive result had been brought about. That's not what happens; this is a clear indication of the breakdown in the Concert of Europe tradition that earlier had been so important. Instead, by now war had become more total in its scope and its perceived stakes, precisely what the war was being fought about. Here we return to that crucial definition, which is so useful in this regard—the notion of "total war." "Total war" refers precisely to this more all-encompassing nature of the conflict of entire societies including their armies, their economies, and their home fronts, which is a very evocative phrase that suggests this total commitment to "total war," as well as mass psychologies of the people involved, mobilized comprehensively for ultimate defeat or ultimate victory.

Another aspect that was very important in this regard was the economic dimension, and certainly the economic dimension had been present before in the Napoleonic Wars that we talked about with blockades. Here, this weapon was used to an even more decisive effect. The British blockaded Germany, which as a modern economy was tremendously dependent both upon imports and exports. The Germans responded by using modern technology to launch a counter blockade, as it were—German submarine warfare that aimed to put the squeeze on the British economy in turn. It was precisely the intensity of sacrifice, the way in which legions of young men went to their death in the trenches that made compromise increasingly difficult. If one were to call a conference and if one were to negotiate for a compromised peace short of total victory, well, the question would then loom up—what had those initial sacrifices of such great magnitude been for? What had it all actually brought in the final analysis?

We need to turn then to the fascinating question of how war aims and alliances developed out of this question of how one would win this war as the stakes seemed to continually grow. The prolongation of the war itself led to the crucial question of what the war was being fought for. It led the powers to seek to outline their war aims. We might review this in sequence.

The Germans saw the war as a defensive war to break out of encirclement and what they sometimes styled a world of enemies surrounding Germany. Few Germans were self-critical enough at this juncture to note that it was in fact Germany's erratic foreign policy that had brought that sense of encirclement to pass, but this was a dominant emotion nonetheless.

For their part, the leaders of Austria-Hungary fatalistically saw a war for survival. If they were not able to stave off what they saw as the threat of smaller Serbia, what hope might there be for the further existence of the venerable Astro-Hungarian Habsburg realm?

France, for its part, fought what it understood to be a defensive war—I hope you see, by the way, a pattern growing here. Everyone is convinced that they're fighting a defensive war. France had good reason for feeling it was fighting a defensive war. After all, it had been attacked by Germany, and northern France was bearing the brunt of the German invasion. Russia, for its part, also felt it was fighting a defensive war against German attack as German forces also would move into the realm of the Tsarist regime and also in defense of fellow Slavs who it felt were imperiled in the Balkans. Now, there were some more remote ideas of eventually reaching some comprehensive solution to the Eastern Question—that long-standing problem of what would happen with a failing Ottoman Empire, and perhaps the notion that one might some day win those long-coveted geopolitical strategic points: the Turkish Straits between the Black Sea and the Mediterranean linking Europe and Asia and the glorious capital of Constantinople as well. That was more remote. The defensive imperative was truly crucial.

Britain was different in this regard. Britain intervened on the continent in a defensive way to starve off what it felt was German hegemony, the anxiety that Belgium in the hands of the Germans might threaten Britain's own safety. Indeed, Belgium's neutrality had been guaranteed since 1839 by the Great Powers and was an existential concern for Britain even in its earlier splendid isolation for precisely this reason. In the British case the motives were also seen as defensive but maybe in a way that as less immediate and had more to do with the balance of power than in the case of continental nations.

Beyond these first imperatives though, the powers went on to elaborate more detailed programs and also sought allies, to bring allies to their side to tip the balance decisively in this conflict. It was tremendously irksome to a lot of the leaders of the Great Powers that at least in these first stages the Great Powers and their blocs, the Central Powers against the Triple Entente seemed to be so evenly matched.

The first thing to accomplish, in this regard was to make sure that one's own alliance bloc actually held, and in the case of Germany and Austria-Hungary, the latter was so weak that the Germans felt that they were bound together indivisibly in a community of fate. In the case of the Triple Entente—that is to say Great Britain, France, and Russia—they actually signed a pact, the Pact of London, in September of 1914, which guaranteed that they would not negotiate unilaterally or make a separate peace any one of them with the Central Powers of Germany or Austria-Hungary. They would stick through to the very end.

At this point, Germany was crafting a more extensive outline of what this war was all about. This was the so-called September Program of 1914, which outlined increasingly expansive war aims for Germany. That involved somehow throwing off encirclement through the gains of territories in the east and west, and the shopping list tended to get longer as time went by in order to make sure that in some future conflict Germany wouldn't face quite so perilous a situation again. Both sides also sought to add allies to their side. A tremendous stroke for the Central Powers of Germany and Austria-Hungary, since they had lost Italy as an ally at the start of the war, was to gain Ottoman Turkey for their side in November of 1914. They were also very hopeful when Ottoman Turkey declared a jihad or a holy war against, in particular, British colonial rule as a religious dimension to this conflict. Bulgaria joined the Central Powers in October of 1915.

For its part, half a world away, Japan declared war against Germany in August of 1914. It had a long-standing relationship with Great Britain. However, it didn't as much participate in the European struggle but instead concentrated on seizing German colonies in the Far East and also expanding at the expense of China.

Italy, for its part, had held out of the war at the start in a gesture that was sometimes styled to be an act of sacred egoism on the part of Italian realist politicians. Italy, in essence, held a bidding war for its services. Which side would offer it most to join its alliance bloc? The winners in the last analysis were the Entente because they managed through the secret Treaty of London in April of 1915 to promise territories and colonial gains for Italy. Many of the territories that it promised actually belonged to Austria-Hungary at the time, which was an easy thing to promise given that it was enemy territory. Romania, for its part, also joined the Entente in 1916 and Greece in 1917.

In the process of alliance diplomacy, a fascinating thing happened. Great Britain and France promised Russia that it would be allowed to gain the Turkish Straits and Constantinople. Now, this is an appropriate moment for a sharp intake of breath and surprise on your part. Did the lecturer just misspeak? Could this be right? Indeed, in a startling shift in the longer history of the Eastern Question, Great Britain and France, which had long objected to Russia moving in to this territory, at long last changed this old tradition. In the Turkish Straits Agreement of March and April of 1915, Great Britain and France finally dropped their century-old opposition to Russia seizing the Turkish Straits precisely because they felt it was so important to make sure that Russia didn't drop out of the war as it was experiencing very serious setbacks that we will talk about shortly. To make sure that Russia did not make a separate peace, it was necessary to offer Russia the ultimate prize. We see here a fascinating and startling reversal of long-standing traditions.

The importance of the Straits and its geopolitical significance was further demonstrated in a failed campaign, the so-called Gallipoli Campaign, when Great Britain and France had attempted to force passage through this geopolitical strong point from April of 1915 and failed. The reaction of their Russian allies was quite surprising actually. Some Russian leaders were actually relieved at their failure because they worried that otherwise the British might control the Turkish Straits and rob Russia of this prize that it had been promised at the end. That was not a very generous thing to feel towards allies, but it speaks volumes about the aims of the Russian long-term planning.

Also, further planning was taking place that would be fateful in its results. The secret Sykes-Picot Agreement of February 1916 was signed. This was not a treaty; it was an agreement. But it would shape later policy toward the Middle East. It was drafted by the British diplomat Sir Mark Sykes and the French diplomat Georges Picot; it in essence planned a further revolution in the Eastern Question. It agreed to the division of territories of the Ottoman Empire by Britain and France after the war. Britain was to control Mesopotamia, what is today's Iraq, and France would gain Syria and Lebanon under its control.

In practice, these agreements clashed with many other commitments that were being made in the region in part including promises of Arab independence to encourage an Arab revolt against the Ottomans concurrently. Indeed, problems in the area in this day, and some of the turmoil one sees there, have a lot to do with these earlier clashing commitments.

Russia and Germany at the same time back in Europe were bidding for Polish sympathies with declarations of a future Polish state, but the Poles were more inclined to wait to see how things would turn out and then revive the national independence they had longed for for so long a period. The British Balfour Declaration of November of 1917 was also crucial in setting the terms of the future. This was a declaration by British Foreign Secretary Arthur J. Balfour in which he declared that the British government viewed:

> with favor the establishment in Palestine of a national home for the Jewish people … it being clearly understood that nothing shall be done which may prejudice the civil and religious rights of existing non-Jewish communities in Palestine.

This was a great encouragement to Zionists who hoped to establish a Jewish state as a homeland in that region. Both sides in the World War also attempted to sway neutrals, and a crucial arena thus was public opinion worldwide, especially in the United States, which remained neutral in this period at the urging of the American president, Woodrow Wilson.

As the neutral United States traded by sea with both sides, both British blockade and German sub warfare, created conflicts. Increasingly the sinking of ships with American citizens led to conflict with Germany. The British blockade, precisely because it didn't involve the actual sinking of ships but simply interdicted German ports, was seemingly more subtle in this regard and seemed less offensive. The sinking of ships with American citizens at first led Germany to restrain its submarine warfare, but then on February 1, 1917, Germany gambled in the awareness that this might bring America into the war. It again risked unrestricted submarine warfare.

Let's consider briefly peace initiatives because certainly such initiatives were taking place. In particular, socialists championing, as they saw it, the claims of the working classes tried to gather international conferences to emphasize socialist community and brotherhood across national lines to end the war on the basis of their political program for the future—an end to capitalism. But these efforts didn't yield results. Workers in France, Germany, and Russia continued to rally to their national cause.

The Vatican, under Pope Benedict XV, launched peace initiatives as well, but these were without result in part because the Vatican by insisting on neutrality in a war in which Catholics were fighting on both sides, managed to antagonize all of the combatant powers as a result. In December of 1916, President Wilson of the United States tried to play the role of outside broker. He asked all sides to state their war aims as a prelude to conciliation. In January of 1917, he proposed a formula that had a lot of appeal to a lot of Europeans at the time, the notion of "peace without victory," some compromise at long last.

An attempt at a more traditional, old-style kind of diplomacy was launched by the last emperor of the Austro-Hungarian realm, Emperor Charles, who succeeded Franz Joseph who died after a long, long reign during World War I. He tried through his wife's aristocratic relatives who had ties with the Entente to secretly negotiate in 1917, but when the French revealed these peace feelers, he was humiliated. One might say that with him a whole tradition of secret aristocratic diplomacy also was being phased out.

A key break was the arrival of the Russian Revolution. The discredited Tsarist regime fell with startling rapidity ending centuries of Romanov rule, three centuries indeed, with the abdication of the tsar as the revolution took hold in February and March of 1917. In spite of a general war weariness, however, the liberal government that succeeded tsarist rule, known as the Provisional Government, promised to stay in the war in order to secure gains as well as out of loyalty to its Entente allies.

In order to destabilize this new Russia, the German High Command, its generals, conceived a plan. They sent an exiled Russian revolutionary by the name of Vladimir Ilyich Lenin who had been in exile in neutral Switzerland back into Russia—in a sealed train through the German lands so that he wouldn't be able to actually spread revolution in Germany—in order to infect the new Russia with revolution. Lenin was happy to use the Germans just as they were using him. He praised war as a "giant accelerator" of social progress. When he returned to Russia in April of 1917, he preached what was called "revolutionary defeatism," the necessity of losing the war so that the revolution might win—his radical Russian Revolution to replace the democratic style one that had just been enacted.

Another milestone was the entry of the United States into the conflict. We see here the theme of the advent of American power as a European factor as well. In spite of American neutrality economically, in terms of loans as well as trade, the United States had become linked to the Entente side. Public outrage broke out at the revelation of the so-called Zimmermann Telegram, which was a secret communication that had been authorized by Germany's foreign secretary, Arthur Zimmermann. It had been sent in January to the Mexican government promising the Mexican government the prospect of winning back lost provinces, New Mexico, Texas, and Arizona, in exchange for entering World War I on the side of the Central Powers.

British officials in the battle for public opinion had intercepted this message and passed it on to Washington. As a result of both this outrage as well as the submarine warfare, on April 6, 1917, the United States declared war on Germany. American involvement offered economic reserves, boosted Entente morale at a crucial juncture, and began shipping American troops in massive numbers to Europe.

Even as the Americans entered the war, however, the United States was not termed an ally. Instead, Woodrow Wilson insisted upon the term "associated power." What he meant to do by this was to underline the fact that from his perspective the United States was pursuing very different aims and motives than the Europeans with their balance of power tradition. Woodrow Wilson outlined what he saw as America's distinctive and exceptional motives in his January 1918 Fourteen Points speech to Congress. The Fourteen Points was essentially a shopping list of American war aims, which were intended to have universal appeal. They included a new kind of open diplomacy, openly arrived at and democratic in its nature; also freedom of the seas, free trade, the beginnings of general disarmament, resolution of colonial questions, autonomy for the subject peoples of Austria-Hungary and the Ottoman Empire, a free Poland—this had long been a liberal intention in Europe as well, and a new institution for international cooperation—an international League of Nations. Later speeches of Wilson's elaborated in particular on what came to be a tremendously powerful slogan of this new kind of diplomacy he was advancing. That involved the "right of self-determination" of nations—democratic self-determination for sovereignty. Woodrow Wilson's message was hailed by many Europeans. He was sometimes known as "Wilson the Just" and was greeted with tremendous fanfare when he would arrive in Europe as the war ended.

We need to turn now to what Lenin had been doing in the meantime. A different radical departure from traditional politics was taking place in Russia where radical socialist Bolsheviks, as they were called, under Lenin seized power on November 7, 1917. These Bolsheviks later would come to call themselves Communist as a badge of just how radical their commitment to Socialism was. The Bolsheviks declared a new revolutionary Soviet government led by people's commissars, and they immediately took Russia out of the capitalist war. They immediately also mounted an international campaign whose aim was to speak "over the heads" of Europe, "over the heads" of crowned monarchs and traditional diplomats, and their aim was to completely overthrow the international system, to abolish the balance of power, to overthrow old diplomacy by ushering in a world revolution of the working classes.

On November 15, 1917, the Bolsheviks declared a right to self-determination in all of the former Russian Empire. Leon Trotsky, one of the famous Bolshevik leaders, became the people's commissar for foreign affairs, and he very famously announced that his role would be a simple one in his capacity as people's commissar for foreign affairs. He would simply bust open the safes of the Foreign Ministry and after they had blown open the safes publish the secret treaties that he found in there and then close up shop because the outrage at the old style of diplomacy would be so strong among the downtrodden of the world that revolution would erupt. As international revolution broke out, one would not even need foreign policy any more, as Lenin suggested. He asked: Do we even need foreign policy?

Reflecting their ideology, the Bolsheviks now launched a team to enter into ceasefire negotiations with the Germans. To reflect their radicalism, they included in their number representatives from the working class as well as, and this was something new in diplomacy, a woman revolutionary to represent the egalitarian message of Bolshevism—or alleged egalitarian message of Bolshevism. One might note that the working-class representative who was a peasant became a real social hit in the negotiations and the parties that followed afterwards once he had gotten over his initial discomfort at being someone quite humble in origins amongst such elites.

The Russians also abolished diplomatic ranks. This was an innovation among their own teams that they quickly reversed because it led to tremendous confusion. It was unclear who was in charge at all. Now, negotiations with the Germans began in December of 1917 for a ceasefire and for a permanent settlement at the fortress of Brest-Litovsk, and they offered a moment of truth because here one could see what kind of a peace the Central Powers Germany and Austria-Hungary, intended to enact for everybody. Both sides—the Germans leading the Central Powers as well as the Bolsheviks—argued in spectacularly bad faith about self-determination and what it would entail because it was a value that neither side really cared about.

Trotsky was verbally brilliant. He was able to drag out the negotiations interminably, and his goal in fact was to play for time because he was sure that the international workers revolution was about to break out everywhere. Finally, when a crisis was reached,

Trotsky tried one last stroke of rhetorical sophistication. He declared to the puzzled Germans that he was now announcing a state of neither peace nor war, and he left the negotiations. The Germans, once they got over their surprise, did something quite old-fashioned in the face of this new revolutionary diplomacy: They simply sent their troops forward and they advanced further into Russian territory in February of 1918.

The result was that the Bolsheviks found themselves forced back to the negotiating table. Lenin argued that it was necessary to sign some kind of peace just to save the revolution. On March 3, 1918, the Bolsheviks at long last were forced to sign the Treaty of Brest-Litovsk, which has been called the "forgotten peace," because Versailles—that we will talk about later in a coming lecture—would loom over the forgotten peace, the Treaty of Brest-Litovsk. Russia lost huge territories and population in order to just save the revolution. Entente opinion in the West hardened against Germany and the other Central Powers at the news of what was really an iron peace, and it embittered later negotiations between those allies in the West and Germany. Treaties with the Ukraine and Romania that were equally harsh were also signed.

Let's conclude with the collapse of the Central Powers and the Armistice that follows. A last German offensive on the western front, after Germany seeming to have won the war on the eastern front, scored initial frightening successes in the spring of 1918 because the American troops had not yet arrived in sufficiently large numbers to tip the balance. Then after these initial successes ground to a halt revealing that though Germany still was a formidable power, it had exhausted its reserves. That was doubly true of Germany's allies. They were exhausted and now after Germany seemed to have lost its momentum, dropped out of the war one by one.

Austria-Hungary—and this is another watershed moment that we should pause and appreciate the surprise of—which once had been an indispensable supporter of the European state system, so invested in the balance of power, seemingly so necessary in spite of its many weaknesses, now just began before the eyes of contemporaries to dissolve out of existence. It was melting away. Earlier in recognition of its traditional role as part of the balance of power, Entente countries had been reluctant to call for the dissolution of the Austro-Hungarian multi-national state, but the Nationalism of "submerged peoples," as they were called, the subject peoples and the imperatives of territorial promises that were made to all and sundry eroded that reluctance. Czechs, Slovaks, South Slavs, and other peoples of the monarchy declared independence.

In part, it's fascinating to know that the Czechs and the Slovaks had done some of their prior negotiating on a common project of union in Pittsburgh in the United States where there were exile communities. You can walk by a parking lot today in downtown Pittsburgh where dramatic statehood was being negotiated in precisely these terms. As these demands for independence grew, the Habsburg realm was shattered, and it signed an Armistice in October of 1918 at a time when it was essentially losing its own existence. Exhausted Germany finally signed an Armistice on November 11, 1918, acknowledging that it was defeated on the basis it hoped of Woodrow Wilson's generous Fourteen Points.

The peoples of Europe now awaited a new kind of peace settlement after this "war to end all wars" had ended. What kind of peace settlement they actually got we will consider when we discuss the Paris Settlement, the comprehensive peace, in our next lecture.

Lecture Twenty-Seven
The Paris Settlement

Scope:

After four years of devastating war, the victors of World War I gathered in Paris in 1919 for a grand diplomatic conference to draft a comprehensive settlement and create a new international order replacing that of the Congress of Vienna in 1815. Many factors were involved: the strong personalities of the negotiators (Clemenceau of France, Lloyd George of Great Britain, and Wilson of the United States), their pursuit of national interest and common stability, as well as chaotic realities on the ground in remote parts of Europe. These all combined to shape a controversial peace settlement, including the Treaty of Versailles imposed on a defeated Germany and the plan for an international League of Nations to replace the balance of power with collective security.

Outline

I. Significance of the Paris Settlement.

    A. The task before the leaders gathered in Paris in 1919 was to draft treaties with five defeated powers (Germany, Austria, Hungary, Bulgaria, and Turkey) and to create a new international order.

    B. The Paris Settlement was the fourth of the great international meetings (after the Treaty of Westphalia, the Treaty of Utrecht, and the Congress of Vienna).

    C. For a brief time, the negotiators at Paris disposed of tremendous power in shaping the world.

        1. Wilson announced: "We are the State."

        2. However, as at the Congress of Vienna, at the same time the clock ticked down on the victors' cohesion.

        3. Changes beyond their control also unfolded on the ground.

        4. A string of new nations appeared, not artificially created by the Paris Settlement (as revisionists claimed) but created out of the will of local nationalists.

D. A new factor in this congress was the American role.

    1. As opposed to the European powers, the United States asked for no territory.

    2. Wilson practiced strikingly personal diplomacy as the first U.S. president to go to Europe in office.

    3. He pressed his vision of a new international politics, rejecting the balance of power as "forever discredited" and to be replaced with "the moral force of the public opinion of the world."

E. Many participants were determined to produce something new—one delegate recalled the common aspiration to "create great, permanent, noble things."

F. Inevitably, the result was an uneasy mixture of the new and the traditional.

II. The atmosphere of the Congress.

    A. The peace congress was held in Paris, not a neutral venue.

        1. It was chaired by French Prime Minister Clemenceau as president.

        2. Representatives of 27 victor states came, but defeated powers were excluded, as was Bolshevik Russia (committed to the overthrow of the state system).

    B. The official opening was on January 18, 1919.

        1. English and French were the official languages.

        2. More than 100 meetings took place in the French Foreign Ministry.

        3. The essential work was done in six months (January–June 1919).

        4. In a troubling dynamic, what was meant to be a set of maximal demands as a basis for discussion became permanent.

    C. More than 1,000 delegates participated.

        1. While the British delegation at Vienna had 14 delegates, now 400 delegates were sent.

        2. Experts played new roles.

    D. At the same time, the counsels grew narrower.

        1. Lloyd George observed that "diplomats were invented simply to waste time."

2. To speed up deliberations, meetings were set up for the Council of Ten, made up of state leaders and their Foreign Ministers.

3. Informally, special influence was wielded by the Big Five (France, Great Britain, the United States, Italy, and Japan), then reduced to the Big Three (France, Great Britain, and the United States).

4. Wilson's open diplomacy was undermined.

E. There were fascinating contrasts with the 1815 Congress of Vienna.

1. Some were conscious, as British diplomats studied the Congress of Vienna for lessons.

2. The Paris Congress was larger and emotions were more heated.

3. Films of events showed increased public attention.

4. The exclusion of defeated powers changed the dynamic.

III. Principles of the settlement.

A. Clemenceau stressed the need to win the peace.

B. Wilson's Fourteen Points were the guidelines of the peace but increasingly were sidelined.

C. In practice, national self-determination and security came into conflict.

IV. The Big Three and others.

A. Woodrow Wilson had been a professor shaped by academic habits, and he employed a rhetoric of inflexible Idealism.

1. Wilson brought a board of experts—The Inquiry—charged with finding a just solution to any problem that might arise.

2. His personal diplomacy could be both an asset and a liability.

3. Another problem was that his health began to fail at this time.

4. Wilson was not inclined to compromise and even after a Republican victory in November 1918, he did not bring along prominent representatives.

B. Prime Minister Clemenceau, although already 78 years old, was a formidable figure nicknamed "the Tiger."

    1. His fierce priority was French security and anxiety about the German threat.

    2. He frequently mocked Wilson's Idealism.

C. Prime Minister David Lloyd George, "the Welsh Wizard," saw himself mediating between his colleagues.

    1. After a bellicose election, he increasingly reverted to Britain's traditional balancing role on the continent.

    2. British priorities were imperial: establishing a balance of power against any continental hegemony.

D. Other participants also played significant roles.

    1. Italian Prime Minister Vittorio Orlando, upset at Italian demands on the Adriatic not being met, stormed out on April 14, 1919.

    2. Many supplicants arrived in Paris to plead their cause and distribute propaganda.

V. The terms of the treaties.

A. The Treaty of Versailles with Germany imposed terms to contain a renewed German threat.

    1. Germany lost its colonies, 13 percent of its population, and 10 percent of its territory (to Belgium, France, Denmark, and Poland).

    2. The so-called "Polish Corridor" split off Germany's eastern part, and Danzig was made a free city.

    3. The Saar, a crucial coal region, was temporarily occupied.

    4. Germany was disarmed (as an alleged prelude to general disarmament) and left without a draft, and with only a small army and no air force or submarines.

    5. France sought to split off the Rhineland as a buffer, but in April 1919, the United States and Britain offered instead a guarantee of support against German aggression, along with a demilitarized Rhineland.

    6. Reparations were exacted, but sums were so large that the final bill ($32 billion) was only decided by May 1921.

    7. Article 231, the "War Guilt Clause," undergirded reparations.

     8. On May 7, 1919, a German delegation led by Foreign Minister Ulrich Graf von Brockdorff-Rantzau was given the terms, and outrage ensued.

B. Other treaties were also imposed.
     1. The Treaty of St. Germain with Austria (September 10, 1919) took away territory and banned a union with Germany.
     2. The Treaty of Neuilly with Bulgaria (November 27, 1919) gave territory to Greece.
     3. The Treaty of Trianon with Hungary (June 4, 1920) gave territories to Czechoslovakia, Yugoslavia, and Romania.
     4. The Treaty of Sèvres with the Ottoman Empire (August 10, 1920) dismembered the realm but was not ratified.

C. In a significant departure from earlier traditions of sovereignty, new eastern European states signed minority rights treaties.

D. Suspense centered on whether Germany would sign.
     1. German public opinion denounced this as a "diktat" (although milder than the Treaty of Brest-Litovsk) violating self-determination for Germans.
     2. Since war was threatened and blockade continued, Germany signed.
     3. The signing in the Hall of Mirrors on June 28, 1919, was heavy with symbolism.

VI. The League of Nations.

A. Wilson saw this new international organization as a priority—a crucial "clearinghouse" for problems—and hence was willing to overlook many flaws.

B. The idea was not Wilson's own invention, but it had antecedents in liberal British and pacifist thinking.

C. The League of Nations Covenant was written into the peace treaties.

D. In a radical departure from the earlier balance of power, the league enshrined the concept of collective security.

E. Institutionally, it was not a world government but a union of states to consist of a General Assembly and a smaller council.

F. The new structure did not do away with European Imperialism.
   1. Instead, the mandate system was established, promising to prepare for independence.
   2. The Middle East was divided up between France and Great Britain as mandates (the United States turned down a suggested mandate for Armenia or Constantinople).
   3. A Japanese proposal on racial equality was not passed.

VII. Outcome and verdicts.
   A. Criticisms were soon heard.
   B. John Maynard Keynes published *The Economic Consequences of the Peace*, warning of the league's effects and reflecting significant British opinion that the settlement was too harsh.
   C. The United States did not approve of the Paris Settlement.
   1. Wilson won the Nobel Prize in 1919 for his peacemaking but lost the ratification battle on March 19, 1920.
   2. Anxieties over sovereignty and Wilson's unwillingness to compromise played a role.
   3. As a result, the United States abstained from the league and guarantees to France were not put into effect.
   D. Individual states demanded revision and changes. Germany and even victorious Italy denounced the treaty.

Essential Reading:

Henry Kissinger, *Diplomacy*, pp. 227–45.

Supplementary Reading:

Margaret MacMillan, *Paris 1919: Six Months That Changed the World*.

Questions to Consider:

1. Do you see Wilson's overall role as positive or negative?
2. Was the Paris Settlement a failure or the best that could be done at the time?

Lecture Twenty-Seven—Transcript
The Paris Settlement

In this lecture, we will be considering the Paris Settlement of 1919. The Paris Settlement was that group or series of treaties that were signed with the defeated powers by the victors of World War I. The Versailles Treaty, probably the more familiar of these in terms of general historical knowledge, was but one of a series of treaties making up together the Paris Settlement. In our earlier lecture, we had examined the tremendous ordeal and suffering associated with World War I and the inability to arrive at a compromise settlement. What we will examine in this lecture is the peace that resulted. After four years of devastating war, the victors of World War I gathered in Paris in 1919 for a grand diplomatic conference in which they set out to draft a comprehensive settlement and to create a new international order to replace the one that had been drafted at the Congress of Vienna in 1815 and that had obviously broken down. Many factors were involved in the Paris Settlement and its results. They included the strong personalities of the negotiators, Clemenceau of France, Lloyd George of Great Britain, and President Wilson of the United States.

We also will examine the way in which these statesmen pursued national interests as well as the value of common stability, and we will evaluate the chaotic realities on the ground as well in remote parts of Europe. All of these elements combined to shape a controversial peace settlement, including the Peace of Versailles imposed on defeated Germany and the plan also for an International League of Nations to replace entirely the balance of power with a new concept that we will discuss—collective security.

First of all, we might pause for a moment to think about the tremendous challenge that lay before the peacemakers in 1919. The task before the leaders who gathered in Paris was to draft treaties with five defeated powers—the Central Powers of Germany; Austria; Hungary, now treated separately from Austria; Bulgaria, and Turkey—and in a larger sense beyond settling with the defeated powers to create a new international order with some coherence that would bring stability. The Paris Settlement of 1919 was the fourth in a series of great international meetings, the last in fact in the series so far at least, that we have already examined in earlier lectures. We will recall the Treaty of Westphalia. We will recall also Utrecht and the Congress of Vienna. This was the fourth in the series. For a brief time, thus, the negotiators at Paris disposed of tremendous power in shaping the world, and indeed in what was certainly a conscious echo of the glorious days of King Louis XIV who had said that he was the state, Woodrow Wilson announced to the gathered negotiators, "We are the State."

A new dynamic was at work, but we need to keep in mind throughout and let this run in the back of our minds as a theme even as we discuss the negotiations themselves—that just as was the case of the Congress of Vienna back in 1815, at the same time as the negotiations were going on the clock was ticking down. The clock was ticking down both on that enormous gathering of power that had been achieved by the victors, and the clock was ticking down on the victors' cohesion among themselves as well because inevitably demobilization would begin. The fever pitch of preparedness that war had implied would start to wind down and so too the cohesion of the victors would start to erode as their own interests would reassert themselves. Changes would also unfold on the ground beyond the control of these negotiators. I think it's very important to avoid falling into the trap of seeing these negotiators in an all-powerful role. Clearly, there were limits to what they could achieve under the circumstances, and the clock was ticking down on their power.

A key example of how change was taking place on the ground was the appearance suddenly of a string of new nations in Central Europe running from Finland in the north all the way to a new South Slavic or Yugoslav State in the south of Europe. We will talk more about these new nations appearing as a result of the determination of local nationalists who aimed to finally achieve national independence or in the case of the Poles to recreate the national independence they had lost in the 18th century. These new nations, as they appeared, were not artificial creations of the negotiators of the Paris Settlement. They, in fact, had been created out of the will of local nationalists, and revisionists would later see them as things that were abominations, creations, of the Paris Settlement. That was not an accurate assessment. A factor in this congress that separated it from the Congress of Vienna was the important new American role.

America's role, as Woodrow Wilson jealously insisted upon, was an exceptional one. As opposed to the European Great Powers, the United States was not asking for any territory, no growth in its own borders in Europe. Woodrow Wilson also was practicing a strikingly personal diplomacy, trying to use the tremendous hopes that had been vested in him and one might say projected onto him by war-weary Europeans. He was indeed the first American president to go to Europe while in office, and while this brought some advantage in terms of being able to use his personal role, it also cut him off from developments at home. We will see that could have a fateful result as well. Wilson pressed his vision of new international politics, and one needs to appreciate for a moment how innovative his message might be in a more traditional context. He rejected the balance of power, and he ringingly declared it "forever discredited" by the war that had just ended. What was to replace the balance of power? A new system whereby "the moral force of the public opinion of the world" would be the decisive force, and it's easy to see Wilson as playing a somewhat ridiculous role as a prophet of other worldly moral foreign policy. But in fact, Wilson's message had tremendous resonance at the time and indeed for many eastern Europeans still has to this very day. There are streets and train stations named after him in Eastern Europe in the present. Many participants who gathered at Paris shared Wilson's determination to produce something new. One British delegate, for instance, recalled the common aspiration to "create great, permanent [and] noble things," to re-write human politics. Inevitably, given such high expectations and hopes, the result would be something less. The result would be an uneasy mixture of the new and traditional in diplomacy, and we will analyze precisely this.

It might be worthwhile to take a moment to just conjure up in our minds what the atmosphere was of this Paris Settlement. The peace congress that was held was held in Paris, and that was significant. That was not a neutral venue. It was not held in Switzerland or somewhere in Scandinavia. It was held precisely in the capital city of one of the victor powers, and that had been insisted upon by the French. The chairman of this peace negotiation would be none other than the French Prime Minister, Clemenceau, who would function as president and preside over the negotiations.

The representatives of 27 victor states were invited to the conference, but there was a decisive difference from how negotiations had been conducted back at the Congress of Vienna in 1815. The defeated powers were excluded from the negotiations. They would learn later of the results that had been agreed upon. Another country also was excluded, and that was Bolshevik Russia. In a way, it's not surprising that it was not included. After all, the Bolsheviks had left the war to the dismay of the Entente who hoped that they would stay in the war against the Germans, and the very fact that the Bolsheviks announced to everybody that they were totally committed to the total overthrow of the state system and the abolition of diplomacy as well as capitalism makes it less surprising that they were not included given these commitments and this revolutionary zeal.

The official opening of the Paris Settlement came in January of 1919, and English and French would be the official languages that would be used over the course of over 100 meetings that would take place in the French Foreign Ministry, the Quai d'Orsay. The essential work was done over the course of six months of hard bargaining, consultation with experts and countless hours of pouring over complicated maps.

In a troubling dynamic, what was meant to be a set of maximal demands that might be a basis for later discussion increasingly because of the press of time—remember, we have talked about the ticking down of the clock on power and cohesion on the part of the victors, those maximal demands tended to become the permanent demands that would be the final take it or leave it basis of the settlement. It's also instructive to think about it in terms of conjuring up the atmosphere—what large numbers of people participated. Over 1,000 delegates had been sent to the peace negotiations, and this was a real contrast from the Congress of Vienna back in 1815. That had been a large social occasion. This was an even larger one. Let me just indicate the order of magnitude involved here. The British delegation that had gone to the Congress of Vienna in 1815 led by Castlereagh had—are you ready for this—14 members. Now, the British sent 400 members, and included in that number were not just the highest diplomats and functionaries from the foreign office. Experts, including historians of all people, were sent as well, and they played new roles in diplomacy because their expert opinions would be called upon to settle questions of ethnicity and where self-determination should or should not be applied. Historians now were playing a key role in a way that they had not in the past.

At the same time, however, there was an interesting dynamic, and it was one that was a little bit troubling. It had to do with this—the way in which the councils, the meetings of who was involved in negotiation, tended to get smaller. David Lloyd George, the British leader, had observed I think with some justice that "diplomats were invented simply to waste time." Now, this was an expression of personal frustration on his part, but I think he had hit on something quite serious and in fact valid except one should give it a different valuation than Lloyd George did. Diplomats, indeed, sometimes are able to use protracted negotiations as a way of perhaps allowing facts to change on the ground, tempers to cool, for compromise to perhaps be creatively arrived at. So, this role of diplomats as time-wasters is probably not sufficiently appreciated, as it should be. To speed deliberations, the meetings that were really crucial to the settlement were set up for the Council of Ten, not all of the victorious powers but the ten main ones. These meetings were made up of state leaders, the heads of state if they were attending, with their Foreign Ministers. But real influence was wielded by the Big Five more informally, and the Big Five among the victors were France, Great Britain, the United States, Italy and Japan.

When Italy and Japan tended to be shut out for really crucial, more intimate discussions, this number was reduced to the Big Three, France, Great Britain and the United States. This might have been effective in terms of arriving at conclusions among the more narrow council, but a problem was that Woodrow Wilson's promise of a new open diplomacy, transparency in deliberations was being undermined. Wilson was, of necessity he felt, going along with it. There were finally fascinating contrasts between this set of negotiations and the earlier 1815 Congress of Vienna. Some of those contrasts or continuities were, in fact, conscious because the British diplomats had sent historians back into the archives to study the Congress of Vienna for lessons as to what had worked and what had not worked.

The Paris Congress was much larger, as we've mentioned, than the Congress of Vienna, and emotions were more heated. The reasons for the more heated nature of those emotions and passions had everything to do with the fact that this more "total war" had created such an upwelling of nationalist passions on the part of the entire peoples and societies involved. This increased public attention was also reflected in the fact that many negotiations were actually caught on film, and this was presented to a much larger audience in the form of newsreels.

The exclusion of defeated powers, which was another difference with the Congress of Vienna when defeated France had been a very important negotiating partner, very much changed the dynamic. What were the principles that were announced for this set of negotiations in contrast to the legitimacy and the solidarity that had been announced at the Congress of Vienna? Well, the French leader, Clemenceau, stressed the need to win the peace, and he argued with a lot of justice that winning the peace or making peace might be much more challenging than simply fighting a war. Woodrow Wilson, however, was concerned not with such mundane things as winning the peace and gaining security, but rather, we will recall, Woodrow Wilson's revolutionary Fourteen Points were meant to be the guidelines for an entirely new kind of politics and peace. Increasingly, they were sidelined or relegated to the margins. In practice, as we will see, demands for national self-determination that Wilson had fatefully raised and demands for security that would be paramount especially in the minds of the French came into conflict.

Who participated in really dominant roles? We need to examine this key question. Well, we need to know two things to begin with. The first thing to note is obvious but crucial. The Big Three, the representatives of France, Great Britain and the United States, were not kings or primarily servants of kings as had been the case at the Congress of Vienna but rather representatives of peoples wielding a new kind of democratic politics. A second thing to emphasize, and this will become obvious shortly, is the Big Three also apparently spent much time driving each other crazy. This inevitably had a result in terms of negotiations as well.

So, let's turn to examine the Big Three as well as some other actors in the negotiations. Woodrow Wilson, the president of the United States, had been a professor before he launched his political career. He had been shaped by some academic habits. He was prone to pontificating and professing, as some professors are, and also employed a rhetoric of inflexible idealism that some felt gave him an aura of self-righteousness. One person who definitely felt so was the French leader, Clemenceau, who said that talking to Wilson was a lot like talking to Jesus Christ himself. But Clemenceau was not in the majority on this necessarily. European crowds had cheered deliriously when the man they called sometimes "Wilson the Just" had arrived in Europe and had been greeted by some of the largest European crowds in history.

Wilson didn't come alone. He brought a board of experts with him, academics and historians. This was known as The Inquiry, and this board of experts was charged with finding a just solution to any problem that might arise. Wilson promised them he would fight for that just solution. Wilson's personal diplomacy, the fact that he had not delegated the task of negotiating to someone else, could be both an asset as well as a liability. In terms of assets, the charisma that he enjoyed was something he could wield in terms of influence. It was a liability in the sense that if Wilson made a mistake in negotiation, it wouldn't be possible to deny it or to backtrack as might have been the case if he had delegated those responsibilities to a subordinate. Another problem was that Wilson's health began to fail during these negotiations in part because of the exertions and the tension of negotiation itself.

Wilson, in terms of his inflexibility of character, was also very disinclined to compromise, and even after the Republicans scored victory at home in congressional elections in November of 1918, Wilson did not bring along prominent representatives or invite Republican representatives to co-opt them for the solutions that he was trying to carve out in Europe. On the French side, the French Prime Minister, Clemenceau, although he was already 78 years old, was a formidable negotiator. He very much deserved his nickname, "the Tiger." His fierce priority was to secure French security, and he was anxious about the German threat. He felt, as he said at one point, that there were several million too many Germans, and that was the real German problem. Legend has it that he asked when he died to be buried standing up facing Germany so he could give warning of the German threat if it ever gathered again, and he frequently mocked Woodrow Wilson's idealism as that quip about talking to Jesus Christ himself indicated. He also, just to add another instance, had declared that God himself had given us ten commandments and we had broken all of those, and that Woodrow Wilson, doing God one better, had given fourteen commandments. Well, as for Wilson's commandments, we will see.

On the British side, Prime Minister David Lloyd George was known as "the Welsh Wizard." He was a man who was born for politics, something that he loved, and he saw himself in a mediating role between his colleagues. This was maybe a reassertion of Britain's old role of being a balancer on affairs in the continent. After a very bellicose, war-like election in Great Britain when he had promised to really make Germany pay as a result of its defeat, after that passionate election was passed, he turned in a more gentle and soothing direction by increasingly reverting to a more dispassionate British role, again absenting Britain's traditional balancing role on the continent. Britain's priorities that Lloyd George would follow in these negotiations were imperial—that is to say putting British imperial interests that were global in scale first and concerned with establishing a balance of power against any continental hegemony. Now, that last part needs to be fleshed out.

If Britain's priority was not to allow any power continental hegemony that meant not just making sure that Germany was not in a position to become a hegemon but also making sure that Germany itself wasn't so weakened that French continental hegemony might result. One can see here already growing differences between even these chief negotiators. Other participants also played significant roles. The Italian Prime Minister, Vittorio Orlando, who was upset at the fact that Italian demands on the Adriatic were not being met, in part because so many of them offended rather deeply against the notion of self-determination for nationalities that Wilson had championed, finally stormed out in April of 1919. Also, many supplicants arrived in Paris to plead their causes and to distribute propaganda championing their cause to anyone who would listen at all, and a remarkable archival collection—that of the Hoover archive in Stanford, California, in some sense was started by just the collecting of some of these pamphlets that would get shoved under the hotel room doors of the prime negotiators during the negotiations themselves.

So, what were the terms of the treaties that were arrived at after these tortuous negotiations? The Versailles Treaty with Germany, in particular—one of several of these treaties, imposed terms that were meant to contain a renewed German threat in the future. Germany lost its colonies overseas, 13% of its population at home, and 10% of its territory on the margins of Germany. It lost territories to Belgium, France, Denmark and Poland and in particular Alsace and Lorraine, those coveted lost provinces of France, were returned. In the east, the so-called "Polish Corridor" for a revived Poland split off Germany's eastern port, East Prussia, and the port of Danzig was made a free city. German nationalists would later denounce this mutilation, as they saw it, of Germany where one part was cut off from contiguity with the rest of Germany. The Saar was temporarily occupied in western Germany, and this is a crucial coal region where France, Luxemburg and Germany meet that came under French occupation.

Germany was to be disarmed. This allegedly was presented as a prelude to general disarmament in the coming more blessed age of collective security. They would have no draft, no ability to bring young men in for military service, and a small army, little better than a police force, of about 100,000 men, no air force, and no submarines. France sought more than this for its own security, however. France sought to split off the Rhineland as a buffer zone to create in some sense an independent Rhineland, but in April of 1919 the United States and Britain, worried that this would go too far, instead offered France a guarantee on the part of America and Great Britain against future German aggression along with a merely demilitarized Rhineland. The Rhineland would remain exposed without military defenses so that if Germany ever again became aggressive, the French might have a head start in meeting that threat.

Economic measures also were meant to weaken German economic revival, and they included a ban on naming German sparkling wine "champagne." Champagne was to be reserved, along with the name cognac, exclusively for the French productions of these diplomatic staples that otherwise are so often seen at diplomatic receptions. Germans would have to give some other name to their sparkling wines. On top of all of this reparations—payments, fines in essence—were exacted for the damage of the war, but the sums were so large that the final bill was not even settled at that time. Germany just had to agree to pay it. Finally, a bill was only decided upon in May of 1921 involving $32 billion. One final article was especially a thorn in the side of nationalist Germans, and that was Article 231, the so-called "War Guilt Clause," which was meant to undergird reparations and advance the notion that Germany alone had been responsible for launching the war.

On May 7, 1919, a German delegation led by Foreign Minister of Germany Ulrich von Brockdorff-Rantzau—his name very much drips with aristocratic associations—was given the terms that had been arrived at. The German negotiators had arrived with crates full of documents to debate, but no debate was to be allowed. German public opinion was outraged when they saw the terms.

Other treaties were also imposed. Let's look at them only very briefly. The Treaty of St. Germain with Austria on September 10,

1919, and by the way the treaties were named after the palaces or locations where they were negotiated, took away territory from Austria and banned future union with Germany, which seemed to many Austrian-Germans to be a violation of self-determination. The Treaty of Neuilly with Bulgaria in November of 1919 gave territory to Greece. The Treaty of Trianon with Hungary in June of 1920 gave large territories of the former Hungary to Czechoslovakia, Yugoslavia, and Romania, and this was violently rejected by the Hungarians. On a recent visit to Budapest, I saw a map being sold on the street that showed the older territories and the irredenta of Hungary even just a few years ago. The Treaty of Sevres with the Ottoman Empire in August of 1920 dismembered the realm but was not ratified, and we will talk in a later lecture about why that was the case.

In a significant departure from earlier traditions of sovereignty moreover, the new Eastern European states were also imposed upon to sign minority rights treaties guaranteeing ethnic minorities treatment that was seen as commensurate with their rights in Eastern Europe. Many Eastern European countries, even as they signed the treaties on minority rights were accused, the Western Powers, of hypocrisy in this regard because they were not treaties that the Western Powers themselves were willing to impose as conditions for their own minorities.

The real suspenseful question was whether Germany would agree to sign. German society from one end to the other of the political spectrum was caught in an almost universal consensus for revision. They didn't like the terms of the treaty. Many Germans were, in fact, not convinced that they had even lost the war. They saw this treaty as a "diktat," a dictated peace, one that was unfair and unjust and meant to cripple Germany. Few of them paused to reflect on the fact that it was actually a lot milder than the Treaty of Brest-Litovsk that Germany had imposed upon defeated Russia. German public opinion also again and again claimed that self-determination for Germans had been violated repeatedly.

Since war was threatened and blockade was continued, Germany had no choice but to sign, and the signing in the Hall of Mirrors in the Palace of Versailles of Louis XIV on June 28, 1919 was heavy with symbolism. The German delegates who came to sign looked like zombies. They actually brought their own fountain pens to sign the treaty so as not to have to sign with enemy fountain pens—this by way of trivia is the first treaty that was signed by fountain pen rather than quill. In the jubilation afterwards, Woodrow Wilson was almost pushed into a fountain by crowds that had come to celebrate, and that, I think, is a very vivid example of public involvement in diplomacy that had not been the case before.

I want to close by just saying a few words about the League of Nations that was seen by Woodrow Wilson as really a new international organization that would be a crucial "clearinghouse" for problems and led him in fact to overlook many flaws that he saw already in the settlement. This idea of a League of Nations was not Woodrow Wilson's own invention because it had antecedents in liberal British and pacifist thinking for a European Federation that we talked about in earlier lectures. The league itself was written into the peace treaties; in a radical departure from earlier balance of power, the league was meant to enshrine the concept of collective security. Collective security meant that rather than balancing, everyone should cooperate in order to ensure that no aggressor ever arose. Everyone would be responsible for everyone else's security. This was not to be a world government but rather a "union of states," which would have a General Assembly and then a smaller Steering Council, as it were. The structure didn't abolish European Imperialism. Instead, the so-called "mandate system" was established, which promised to prepare other countries for independence.

The Middle East was divided up into these mandates between Britain and France. The United States turned down a suggested mandate for Armenia or Constantinople, and a Japanese proposal, which was put forward to endorse racial equality was not passed either. So, it shows the break with Imperialism didn't take place.

I want to conclude with some verdicts. Criticisms were soon heard. The British economist, John Maynard Keynes, published immediately a book called *The Economic Consequences of the Peace* that denounced this peace as unfair, and soon a lot of British people were feeling that the settlement was too harsh. For its part, the United States did not approve the Paris Settlement. Even though Woodrow Wilson won the Nobel Prize in 1919, he lost the battle for ratification of the treaty in Congress in March of 1920. Anxieties over sovereignty and Wilson's unwillingness to compromise at all had played a role in this result. As a consequence, the United States abstained from the league, and the guarantees that had been given to France were not put into effect. Individual states would now demand change. Germany had denounced the treaty, and even victorious Italy felt that it had gotten a raw deal.

After so much longing for peace, many Europeans now would ask themselves what sort of final result would be the reality in practice and just what the interwar period would look like. What the results would be of this structure we will observe closely in our next lecture.

Lecture Twenty-Eight
Interwar Europe

Scope:

This lecture, which covers the turbulent years from 1919 to 1929, first outlines the new diverse map of Europe and traces the great hopes vested in the League of Nations, its internal dynamics, efforts to protect minorities in the new Europe, and urgings for disarmament. Relations between France and Germany, however, remained tense; eastern Europe was in a state of turmoil as the new states of the region contended over borders, and the United States withdrew from European politics. The 1925 Treaties of Locarno seemed to offer a new beginning, pacifying wartime hatreds in Europe. A key figure of the period was the controversial German Foreign Minister Gustav Stresemann, who sought a new international role for Germany before his untimely death.

Outline

I. The new map of Europe.

   A. With the collapse of the Russian and Austro-Hungarian Empires, a series of new democratic states appeared in central and eastern Europe.

   1. These states included Finland, the Baltic states (Estonia, Latvia, Lithuania), Czechoslovakia, Yugoslavia, and Poland.

   2. This was in a sense an internal expansion of the European state system, as these countries joined the diplomatic exchange.

   3. Defeated and reduced states (Germany, Austria, Hungary, Bulgaria, Russia) were revisionist, promising instability.

   B. Russian and German weakness was a feature of the political map for now.

   C. France and Britain bore the burden of trying to uphold the Paris Settlement without American help.

   D. Through the interwar period, Germany's democratic Weimar Republic sought a revision of the Treaty of Versailles.

E. While battling internal crisis, Soviet Russia pursued a dual track: an ideological policy of spreading its control and international revolution while also participating in the diplomatic system.

    1. In the Russian Civil War (1918–1920) the Bolsheviks defeated the Whites and foreign intervention (British, French, American, and Japanese forces) and murdered the Romanovs.

    2. In March 1919, the Comintern (Third or Communist International) was established to promote revolution worldwide, with parties abroad looking to Moscow.

    3. Soviet foreign policy was a mysterious blend of ideology and pragmatism.

    4. A former Tsarist official, Georgy Chicherin (1872–1936) became commissar for foreign affairs from 1918 to 1930.

    5. To split the capitalists, the Soviets made peace with the Baltic states in 1920, and the Comintern supported revisionist Germany starting in 1922.

    6. Incorporating reconquered former imperial areas (Ukraine, Belarus, Caucasus), the Soviet Union or Union of Soviet Socialist Republics (U.S.S.R.) was established in December 1922.

    7. Britain and France recognized the Soviets in 1924.

    8. In spite of their revolutionary spirit, Soviet diplomats were sticklers for form and procedure.

F. A reflection of the new political spirit of the times was the proliferation of initiatives for regional cooperation, including movements in the Scandinavian, Baltic, and Black Sea regions.

G. The British Empire was also reorganized, with the Dominions (Canada, Australia, New Zealand, and South Africa) gaining independence in foreign policy from 1926, while Ireland was partitioned and the Irish Free State established in 1921.

II. Operation of the League of Nations.

    A. The league's headquarters were located in Geneva, Switzerland; the Palace of Nations was built starting from 1929.

1. The first meeting of the General Assembly took place in November 1920 with representatives of 41 nations (the United States was not a member).
   2. The council had a set of permanent members and rotating members.
   3. Its aims were to establish peace and avoid conflict by institutionalizing collective security in which all members would oppose aggression together.

B. The league's collective security never fully replaced older balance of power politics, but it was a useful arena. Critics labeled it a "victors' league," as Germany was excluded until 1926.

C. Smaller powers could play a special role.

D. An international civil service grew up around its institutions.

E. League arbitration scored some successes, including the peaceful settlement of the Swedish-Finnish problem in the Aaland Islands, which gained autonomy in 1922.

F. Enthusiasts spoke of a "league spirit" in Geneva that overcame national differences, but others criticized that very sentiment.

III. Alliances.

A. Implicitly contradicting collective security, France sought alliances to contain German revival.
   1. France signed a treaty with Belgium in 1920.
   2. It especially sought alliances with eastern European countries.

B. This cordon sanitaire hemmed in Soviet expansionism and deterred Germany.
   1. In respect to Germany, this was an attempt to revive the dynamic of the Russo-French alliance of 1894.
   2. France signed treaties with Poland (1921), Czechoslovakia (1924), Romania (1926), and Yugoslavia (1927).
   3. Czechoslovakia, Romania, and Yugoslavia also formed the Little Entente by 1921.
   4. These alliances were problematic because they involved weaker powers and faced a multitude of revisionist states.

> **5.** Mutual conflicts between eastern European countries prevented effective cooperation.
>
> **6.** A strong Poland clashed with its neighbors, poisoning relations with Lithuania (over Vilnius, taken by Polish forces in October 1920), Czechoslovakia (over the coal region of Teschen), and Germany (over Upper Silesia in 1921).

IV. Troubles.

> **A.** Wars also raged as aftershocks of World War I.
>
> **B.** In the Soviet-Polish War (1920–1921), Polish marshal Pilsudski advanced into Ukraine and was thrown back to Warsaw, where the Red Army was halted in the "Miracle on the Vistula."
>
> **C.** The Greek-Turkish War redrew the map of the East.
>
> > **1.** Turkish nationalists rejected the 1920 Treaty of Sèvres. Led by Mustafa Kemal (1881–1938), later known as Atatürk, they declared independence.
> >
> > **2.** Greek armies that had invaded Anatolia in 1919 were thrown back in 1921.
> >
> > **3.** The Treaty of Lausanne of July 1923 replaced the earlier settlement, demilitarized the Turkish Straits, and dropped promises of Kurdish autonomy.
> >
> > **4.** The Eastern Question was now ended.
> >
> > **5.** In a dreadful precedent of ethnic cleansing, population transfers were enacted, with 1.5 million people sent to Greece and 0.3 million people sent to Turkey.
>
> **D.** This tragedy illustrated the wider problem of stateless refugees.
>
> > **1.** Millions of people fled unrest in Russia or were dispossessed.
> >
> > **2.** The League of Nations established "Nansen passports" to validate the identities of those who were stateless, homeless, and dispossessed (named after High Commissioner for Refugees Fridtjof Nansen, who won the 1922 Nobel Peace Prize for his work).

V. The Treaty of Rapallo.

> **A.** An economic conference was held in Genoa, Italy, in April and May 1922, with Soviet participation.

B. The Soviets and Germans slipped away to sign the Treaty of Rapallo on April 16, 1922.

    1. The treaty renounced mutual claims, encouraged trade, and paved the way for German-Soviet cooperation in illegal weapons.

    2. Symbolically, it showed that pariah revisionist states could make common cause.

VI. The Ruhr Crisis.

    A. French president Poincaré was determined to hold Germany to its obligations.

    B. When Germany fell behind in reparations payments, France and Belgium invaded on January 11, 1923, seizing the Ruhr, a heavily industrialized zone of western Germany.

    C. Their aim was to extract reparations by force, but this backfired and international opinion turned against French policy.

        1. Economic shock in Germany created hyperinflation and instability, and France gained little.

        2. France evacuated the Ruhr by 1925.

        3. This failure demonstrated that France alone could not enforce the Treaty of Versailles.

        4. Afterward, French policy took on a more defensive stance, withdrawing to build the Maginot Line on the frontier.

VII. Gustav Stresemann.

    A. A conservative representative of business and an ardent imperialist during World War I, Stresemann went on to be German Foreign Minister (and briefly chancellor) from 1923 to 1929 and has been called "Weimar's Greatest Statesman" and "First of the Europeans."

        1. Pragmatically, he ended passive resistance in the Ruhr and pursued a "fulfillment" policy.

        2. The 1924 Dawes Plan afforded a loan to Germany and regularized reparations.

    B. Stresemann's foreign policy sought repaired relations with the West and peaceful revision. He sought to promote reconciliation with France, lessen tensions, strengthen economic cooperation, and restore Germany to the ranks of the great powers.

C. Stresemann was and is a controversial figure.
  1. His own statements produced doubts about his sincerity.
  2. He was always clearly a German nationalist, but his views on how to pursue German interests changed.

VIII. The Locarno Treaties.

    A. Together with French Foreign Minister Aristide Briand, Stresemann worked out the Locarno Treaties, signed on October 16, 1925.

    B. In the Rhineland Pact, Germany, France, and Belgium recognized mutual frontiers as permanent and undertook not to change them by force.
  1. Britain and Italy guaranteed the settlement.
  2. Germany regained its status as an equal in international negotiations.

    C. Ominously, borders to Germany's east were not guaranteed, creating two kinds of frontiers.

    D. Nonetheless, this created a sense of relief called the "Spirit of Locarno."
  1. Germany joined the league in 1926.
  2. Stresemann and Briand shared the Nobel Peace Prize in 1926.

    E. Stresemann died at the age of 51 in 1929. Some say World War II might not have taken place had he lived.

IX. Peace efforts.

    A. The Czechoslovakians, led by Edvard Beneš, pressed for disarmament and collective security.

    B. Naval agreements were negotiated at the 1921–1922 Washington Conference and the 1930 London Conference.

    C. The peace diplomacy climaxed with the Kellogg-Briand Pact in Paris in August 1928.
  1. It was negotiated by U.S. Secretary of State Frank B. Kellogg and French Foreign Minister Aristide Briand.
  2. Signatories renounced war as a tool of national policy.
  3. Eventually, 62 states signed, but effects were negligible.

    D. The Geneva Convention of 1929 established rules for the humane treatment of POWs.

E. The league made little progress in promised disarmament.

   1. National interests dominated complex negotiations.

   2. The World Disarmament Conference opened in February 1932 in Geneva with 59 countries and collapsed in June 1934.

Essential Reading:

Henry Kissinger, *Diplomacy*, pp. 246–87.

Supplementary Reading:

Carole Fink, *Defending the Rights of Others: The Great Powers, the Jews, and International Minority Protection, 1878–1938.*

Jonathan Wright, *Gustav Stresemann: Weimar's Greatest Statesman.*

League of Nations Photo Archive at Indiana University: www.indiana.edu/~league/

Questions to Consider:

1. Does it really matter if Stresemann's professed peaceful intentions were sincere or not? Why or why not?

2. If earlier disarmament efforts had made more progress, how would that have changed the descent into crisis in the 1930s?

Interwar Europe

In this lecture, we will be examining interwar Europe. In our previous lecture, we looked closely at the Paris Settlement of 1919 that had tried to both end World War I as well as establish durable structures for stability in the years to come. Even as we consider this interwar period and its eventual descent into crisis, I think it's important to keep in mind that contemporaries certainly didn't think of it, unless in their nightmares, in terms of an "interwar" period. To them, it was the time after the Great War, as World War I was known, and we need to keep in mind the intensity of hope that so many people had that peace might somehow still be preserved rather than a repetition of worldwide conflict.

In this lecture, we will cover the turbulent years of 1919–1929 when the descent to crisis begins in earnest. We will outline the new diverse map of Europe. We will examine in operation some of those great hopes that were vested in the League of Nations as well as its internal dynamics—the way in which it tried to protect minorities in the new Europe and its urgings for disarmament. Yet, relations throughout this period between France and Germany were unstable remaining tense at first until remarkable new steps were taken. Eastern Europe remained in a state of turmoil as new states in the region contended with one another over borders, and the United States withdrew from European politics.

We will examine the fascinating 1925 Treaties of Locarno, which seemed for so many a shining example of hope offering a new beginning and pacifying wartime hatreds in Europe. A key figure in this period was the controversial German Foreign Minister, Gustav Stresemann, who sought a new role for Germany internationally before his untimely death, and we will examine closely his pivotal role.

First of all, we want to look closely at the new map of Europe. With the collapse of the Russian and Austro-Hungarian empires in particular in Central Europe, a series of new democratic states appeared in Central and Eastern Europe. These included in a belt between Germany and Russia the states of Finland; the Baltic states, that's to say Estonia, Latvia, and Lithuania; Czechoslovakia; Yugoslavia, the formal name for the South Slav state from 1929; and a resurrected Poland.

64   ©2007 The Teaching Company.

In a sense, we might even think of this as in line with one of the themes of our course as an expansion of the European state system but not an external one, instead an internal expansion of the European state system for these countries, many of them smaller, now join the diplomatic exchange as sovereign nations and gave it added intensity and diversity as well. Defeated and reduced states, and these included Germany, Austria, Hungary, Bulgaria, and Russia, were emphatically revisionist. They aimed to overthrow the Paris Settlement that they felt had been unfairly imposed, and all of this remained always in the background as a promise of instability.

Taking a long view of European history, we might say that in this period important features of the political reality were the weakness of the once great power, Russia, and the weakness of the once great power, Germany. These were features of the political map that mattered a lot, but they were features for now. What would happen when Russian and German strength revived? For their part, as a harsh reality, France and Britain found themselves bearing the burden of trying to uphold and keep up the Paris Settlement without American help that initially had been expected. We will recall that Woodrow Wilson's inflexibility had in part contributed to American legislators not agreeing to ratify the Versailles Treaty, and thus the United States had been kept out of the sort of role that had been envisioned earlier within the Paris Settlement. This has led to tremendously varied estimates of Woodrow Wilson's role and legacy as a politician—not least among American historians.

Another very important implication was this: Through the interwar period Germany's democratic Weimar Republic—so named because a very democratic constitution had been written in the City of Weimar in Germany—labored under burdens that it might otherwise not have had to bear. The Weimar democracy was burdened by association with the Versailles Treaty, which was viewed by many Germans who had an almost consensus of revisionism in the day as a cruel, corrupt, and unfair settlement. As a result, the Weimar Republic, as well as many Germans, would enthusiastically subscribe to the slogan of revision. What form that revision would take, whether it would be peaceful or something even more vigorous, remained open, but a consensus extended across the German political landscape in terms of demanding revision and change to the status quo.

For its part, the Soviet Union battled serious internal problems, civil war as well as internal crisis, and the Soviet state, Soviet Russia, at this time began to pursue a dual track. It's fascinating to observe how on the one hand the Soviets advanced revolutionary diplomacy and the aim of overthrowing the status quo in diplomatic terms—indeed abolishing diplomacy as such, the Great Power system and the balance of power, while on the other hand even as they pursued this ideological policy of spreading control and international revolution, also seeking at the same time to find ways of participating in the diplomatic system and using or exploiting some traditional diplomacy for their ends. We will trace this fascinating duality even in the case of this revolutionary Soviet Russia.

In the Russian Civil War from 1918–1920, which was one of the aftershocks of World War I, the Bolsheviks, against the odds, defeated the White forces, as counter-revolutionary and democratic Russian forces were known, and foreign intervention in the shape of forces that were sent by Britain, France, Japan, and the United States in order to secure ports and bases where supplies had been landed or that were strategic locations. The Bolsheviks defeated these forces and murdered the Romanov imperial family emphatically showing that there was no going back to the earlier way of things.

Another sign of the novelty and the revolutionary nature of Bolshevik policies came in March of 1919 when the Bolsheviks established the so-called Comintern, or Communist International, sometimes known as the Third International, to replace earlier socialist international organizations that had aimed to promote worldwide revolution. Now, the Comintern would spearhead the cause of international revolution with parties, Communist parties, around the world looking to Moscow, the homeland of the revolution, the socialist motherland in a sense, as the natural leader in that effort.

Throughout this period, Soviet foreign policy would be a mysterious and often shifting blend of on the one hand ideology making total claims for total revolution to come, and on the other hand pragmatism, a willingness to engage in negotiation with those who were willing to talk to this revolutionary outlaw state whenever possible. It's worth mentioning here in this context a famous saying of Winston Churchill that he uttered a good deal later, but in which he called Russia always, "a riddle wrapped in a mystery inside an enigma." I think that's a very apt summation of a longer historical record as well.

A fascinating blend of revolution as well as continuity was offered in the very figure of a former Tsarist official by the name of Georgy Chicherin, who became the commissar for foreign affairs after Trotsky in 1918, and he lasted in this post until 1930. His earlier training in Tsarist diplomacy carried over now into Bolshevik affairs but now was put to more revolutionary uses. The Soviets as an outlaw revolutionary state that was preaching worldwide revolution did find occasion to sometimes engage in negotiations that they hoped might split the capitalist world because we should never forget that from the perspective of the Bolsheviks they were inevitably going to face a united front of capitalists unless diplomacy could split them who were determined to throttle the young revolution in its cradle.

To split the capitalists, the Soviets tried to talk to those who would be willing to talk with them. The Soviets made peace with the Baltic states in 1920, and the Communist International, the Comintern, also supported in a strange sort of gesture German demands for revision of the Paris Settlement from 1922 seeing this as a way of breaking down capitalist unity by provoking fights and conflicts in what otherwise would be a unified capitalist camp. At the same time, the Bolsheviks were also in another gesture to continuities with the earlier Tsarist regime working to incorporate or reabsorb former imperial areas that had claimed self-determination and had moved away from the imperial heartland centered on Russia. These were the former imperial areas of Ukraine, Belarus, and the Caucasus, which together with Soviet Russia were fused into the Soviet Union, also known by its initials as the U.S.S.R. standing for the Union of Soviet Socialist Republics, a state that was established in December of 1922.

For a long time, the state did not receive recognition. Britain and France finally recognized the Soviets with many hesitations in 1924 and the United States only much, much later. In spite of its revolutionary spirit, Soviet diplomats representing the Soviet state were often sticklers for form and procedure; this is a fascinating turn of events because one would suppose that revolutionary diplomats would shed the striped pants and the other formal wear of traditional diplomacy and instead be right in your face to traditional diplomats with their novelty, and their newness, and their challenge. That was not the case here. To the contrary, the Bolshevik diplomats insisted even more than others on proper protocol, proper procedure, and this was in part I think a way to disarm the suspicions of more traditional diplomats. There was also a fascinating continuity. At the start of our course, when the principality of Muscovy had been a far off and very exotic location, Muscovy had been famous for the intricacy of its diplomatic procedure and protocol. One might say that in some sense here the Bolsheviks were taking on earlier Russian traditions as well.

A reflection in Europe as a whole of the new political spirit of the times, when we shift our focus now away from the Soviet Union and towards the rest of Europe to the west, Europe saw a proliferation of initiatives for regional cooperation. I think this was born out of that longing for peace at long last and stability that should follow after the horrors of World War I. These initiatives included Scandinavian regional cooperation. There were initiatives for Baltic federation and common cause, which unfortunately didn't get very far, and also fascinating movements for regional cooperation in the Black Sea region as well that were given in the case of the Black Sea initiative the really wonderfully poetic name of the "Promethean" movement. What this meant was that it harkened back to Classical times when the figure Prometheus who in myth had brought fire and was chained in punishment to the mountains that were in fact the Caucasus; it harkened back to earlier cultural unities in trying to carve out something new.

For its part, the British Empire was also reorganized in this period with the Dominions—that's to say Canada, Australia, New Zealand, and South Africa—gaining independence in foreign policy from 1926, much more freedom in that regard even as they retained their tie to Britain while Ireland for its part after a civil war was partitioned and the Irish Free State established in 1921.

Let's examine for a moment the operation of the League of Nations, which had seen such hopes vested in it. The league's headquarters were located in neutral Switzerland, in Geneva, where the imposing structure of the Palace of Nations was built from 1929. The first meeting of the General Assembly took place in November of 1920 with representatives of 41 nations. Let's recall that the United States was not a member, was not participating. The Council, which was the sort of steering committee of the General Assembly, had a set of permanent members and rotating members. The permanent members represented the victors of World War I so one could say that this was not perfectly democratic or representative in that sense.

The aim of the League of Nations was to establish peace and to avoid conflict by institutionalizing this new concept of collective security in which all members would oppose aggression together. Any country that took up arms against others was to be viewed as an aggressor who had to be stopped by all members acting together. This was to replace the earlier conventions of balance of power and balancing. The league's collective security, however, as a concept in action, never fully replaced older balance of power politics, as we will see in a moment, but the league remained a very useful arena for discussions and negotiation.

It was not without its critics. Many critics labeled it a "victors' league," in particular Germans as Germany was excluded until 1926 until it had proved itself worthy of such participation. Smaller European powers could in fact play a very special role in the League of Nations trying to advance agendas of disarmament or of arbitration; their record is a very interesting one. An international civil service grew up around the league and its offices, organs, and institutions, and indeed league arbitration actually scored some remarkable successes including conflicts that might very well have led to war in earlier periods. There was, for instance, the peaceful settlement of a Swedish-Finish conflict over the Aaland Islands in the Baltic Sea, which gained autonomy but retained their identity as part of Finland in 1922—a conflict, as it were, solved through mediation. This led enthusiasts to speak of a "league spirit," a spirit of belonging to the league that was said to hover over Geneva and the League of Nations, overcoming national differences and almost representing an emerging world citizenship. Some, who distrusted the league because of what they saw as its erosion of national sovereignty, criticized precisely that sentiment as being illegitimate.

I want to turn next to the question of how balance of power politics still continued to act alongside the proclamation of collective security through the League of Nations, and this was in the form of alliances. Alliances didn't disappear, and in fact implicitly contradicting the promise of collective security, France for its part sought alliances to contain a future German revival. France was not convinced that collective security would be the answer to its dilemma in this regard. So, France signed a series of treaties, a treaty with Belgium in 1920, and it especially sought alliances with Eastern European countries on the principle of being able to threaten Germany some day with war on two fronts by posing enemy alliances on both the east and west against a future Germany on the principle of my enemy's enemy is my friend.

These alliances represented what came to be called a cordon sanitaire, a safety belt as it were, that hemmed in a future aggressive Germany and also hemmed in Soviet expansion, a dual purpose in a sense. In respect to Germany, the cordon sanitaire and the alliance system was an attempt to revive the dynamic that had worked before World War I so formidably, the dynamic of the Russo-French alliance that had been signed in 1894. France signed a series of treaties with Poland in 1921, Czechoslovakia in 1924, Romania in 1926, and Yugoslavia in 1927. Meanwhile, it also was able to link its hopes in this regard to the forming of a so-called Little Entente in Eastern Europe of Czechoslovakia, Romania, and Yugoslavia in 1921 who together banded their forces in order to stop any resurgence in particular of Hungarian revisionism.

These alliances in Eastern Europe cultivated by France were problematic, and I think one may have noticed the problem already just by hearing the list of the nations involved. They involved weaker powers, smaller by orders of magnitude than the Great Power of Russia had been from 1894 on, and in Eastern Europe they faced a multitude of other revisionist states that wanted to change the status quo. If this weren't bad enough, there was the reality that needs to be mentioned that mutual conflicts between Eastern European countries, even ones linked in alliance with France in these structures, often prevented effective cooperation. In particular, that long-standing fulfillment of the dream of Polish patriots, a resurrected Poland, in its drive for strength managed to clash with very many of its neighbors and poisoned relations with many of them—for example, to the north poisoned relations with Lithuania over the City of Vilnius, which had been taken by Polish forces in October of 1920 but was claimed by Lithuania as a capital. Relations with Czechoslovakia were embittered in clashes over the coal region of Teschen, and relations with Germany fraught as a result of conflict over Upper Silesia in 1921.

There were also further troubles on the European scene as a result of wars that really were aftershocks of World War I. Let's mention a few of the main ones of this nature. In the Russian-Polish War of 1920–1921, Poland and Soviet Russia had clashed. Polish Marshal Pilsudski had advanced into Ukraine and sought to expand the new resurrected Poland in that direction, but Polish forces were soon thrown back almost to Warsaw by the Red Army as it counter-attacked, a counter-attack indeed that was only halted by another counter attack at Warsaw by Polish forces—the so-called "Miracle on the Vistula [River]." Polish patriots see this as another example of Poland saving Europe echoing the lifting of the Ottoman siege of Vienna in 1683.

Another war spoke to some of the issues of the Eastern Question that we have mentioned in earlier lectures. That was the Greek-Turkish War. Turkish nationalists rising up out of the ruins of the Ottoman Empire and now seeing for themselves not an imperial identity but a Turkish nationalist one rejected the 1920 Treaty of Sèvres that had been part of the Paris Settlement, and led by Mustafa Kemal, who later would be known as Atatürk, the father of the Turks, declared Turkish independence and challenged the Great Powers in this regard.

Greek armies invaded Anatolia in 1919 in pursuit of a larger Greek territory, a "greater Greece," and these were thrown back in 1921 by resurgent Turkish forces. The result of this conflict was the signing of the Treaty of Lausanne of July 1923 that replaced the earlier Treaty of Sèvres, which demilitarized the Turkish Straits and dropped promises of Kurdish autonomy. To this very day, the Kurds remain as one of the main groups of ethnicities that don't have a state of their own. The Eastern Question in a real sense now had finally been brought to a conclusion. The question of what would follow after the Ottoman Empire was now answered in the carving up of its once imperial domain.

There was also a dreadful sidelight to this Treaty of Lausanne. It established a terrible precedent: a precedent indeed of ethnic cleansing or as contemporaries called it in a polite and somewhat veiled term, population transfers, as both Greece and Turkey exchanged populations of people who were seen as ethnically foreign. One and a half million people were sent to Greece from

Turkey, and a third of a million were sent to Turkey—uprooted from places where they had lived and identified with for centuries.

This terrible innovation of population transfers to solve problems of ethnicity or borders also illustrated a wider problem of stateless refugees. Millions had fled Russia or were dispossessed in the dislocations of fighting in Eastern Europe; their fate remained uncertain. Here the League of Nations stepped in in a very useful role to establish its own passports, so-called "Nansen passports," that validated the identities of people who otherwise were stateless, homeless, and dispossessed. "Nansen passports" took their name from the High Commissioner for Refugees Fridtjof Nansen, a man of Norwegian background, who won the 1922 Nobel Peace Prize for his work.

A surprising event took place with the Treaty of Rapallo, which grew out of an economic conference that was being held in Genoa, Italy in April and May of 1922 with Soviet participation as a sign of how the Soviets were trying to participate in Western diplomacy. The Soviet and German representatives did something unexpected. They slipped away from the Genoa negotiations and together signed the Treaty of Rapallo after the town where they had met in April of 1922. That treaty seemed mild on the surface. It renounced mutual claims, encouraged trade, and this wasn't openly said but also paved the way for German-Soviet cooperation in illegal weaponry as well. Symbolically, this was worrisome for many European diplomats because it showed that pariah or revisionist states, otherwise outlaws in the international system, could come together to make common cause. Some diplomats see this as an early anticipation of a later German-Russian agreement, the Nazi-Soviet Pact of 1939 that we will discuss in a later lecture.

For now, however, a main crisis that needed to be dealt with was the Ruhr Crisis. French President Poincare was determined to hold Germany to its treaty obligations for reparations, and when Germany fell behind in them, France and Belgium invaded Germany in January of 1923. Their aim was to extract by force reparations, but this backfired and international opinion quickly turned against French policy that was seen as heavy-handed and unreasonable. In Germany, economic shock, hyperinflation, and instability were the results while France itself gained little for the expense of occupation. France was forced eventually to evacuate the Ruhr that it had taken, which is a territory in north Rhineland, Westphalia in western Germany, a densely populated zone of heavy industry very valuable to the German economy. The French were forced to evacuate by 1925, and their failure demonstrated a deeper truth: France alone could not hope to single-handedly enforce the Versailles Treaty.

After this aggressive move that had failed, French policy took on a more defensive stance and withdrew to build the Maginot Line on its frontier as what some have called a "defensive crouch" against a future threat. For now, there was a hopeful sign, a hopeful portent, in the figure of one man whom we want to consider in conclusion. That was the German statesman Gustav Stresemann, a conservative representative of business and oddly enough a very ardent imperialist during World War I. Stresemann had gone on to be the German Foreign Minister and very briefly chancellor from 1923–1929, and he has been hailed as "Weimar's Greatest Statesman," and sometimes even the "First of the Europeans," because of the way in which he it seems helped Europeans to turn the corner towards a more peaceful beginning. Pragmatically, as a German nationalist, which he remained throughout, he nonetheless saw the need to end passive resistance in the Ruhr, compromise the question with the French and pursue the so-called "fulfillment" policy of trying to meet reparations in good faith while in the process showing that it was necessary to revise these demands precisely because of their severity. He scored some successes as a result of this new compromise policy.

The 1924 Dawes Plan, negotiated with American help, afforded a loan to Germany and regularized reparations. Stresemann's foreign policy, in general, sought to repair relations with the West and to achieve a peaceful rewriting of the terms of the Versailles Treaty in especially those areas that were most objectionable to German opinion. He sought on the way to peaceful revision to promote reconciliation with the French, which we saw is key to lesson tensions generally internationally, to strengthen European cooperation throughout Europe, and as a result of these new departures, to restore Germany to the ranks of the Great Powers.

Stresemann was at the time, and remains, a controversial figure. Some of his own contradictory statements when he addressed different kinds of audiences have produced doubts about his sincerity. When he spoke to German nationalists, he sometimes spoke about the need to make the most of the situation or to finesse it, and that leads some people to worry that perhaps Stresemann was in some sense rhetorically pursuing one route and in practice another. I think that the problem resolves itself for all of the complexity of his character in this sense—Stresemann always remained clearly a German nationalist, but his views on how best to pursue German national interest changed over time. One might think of it in these terms—in time, his emphasis in the phrase "peaceful revision" shifted from the "revision" part to the "peaceful" part. That in and of itself would have been quite a contribution to the cause of giving Europe a new beginning, and one might mention also that Stresemann, as he went about his busy diplomatic work, actually invented a new form of formal wear, which allowed him to change only his jacket when he went from the informal office to the formal meeting halls and negotiations. To this very day in Germany there is still a Stresemann suit that's named after him. This is another kind of immortality.

The triumph of Stresemann's departure came with the Treaties of Locarno. Together with French Foreign Minister Aristide Briand, Stresemann worked out a new departure known as the Locarno Treaties, signed on October 16, 1925. In one part of these treaties, the so-called Rhineland Pact, Germany, France, and Belgium together recognize their mutual frontiers as permanent and promised not to change them by force. Britain and Italy guaranteed this settlement. As a result, there was a wave of good feeling. Germany regained its status as an equal in international negotiations and soon would join the League of Nations. A little more ominously, not many people were noticing that borders to Germany's east in Eastern Europe, were not similarly guaranteed. Stresemann wanted to leave them open for future revision, and this tended to create two kinds of frontiers, stable and unstable, in Europe. This could be an ominous development, but nonetheless, there was a great sense of relief in Europe at the time that was called the "Spirit of Locarno," as Germany joined the league in 1926. In that same year, Stresemann and Briand shared the Nobel Peace prize for their efforts. Stresemann died, unfortunately, at the age of 51 in 1929, and some people muse that if he could have continued these efforts, World War II might very well not have taken place.

I want to conclude by just noting a few very important peace efforts in this period as well. The Czechoslovaks, led by Edvard Benes, pressed for disarmament and collective security showing the role that smaller nations could take. Naval agreements were also negotiated in the 1921–1922 Washington Conference. You see that the United States is still somewhat involved in international politics, not totally isolationist, and there were more naval agreements in the 1930 London Conference.

Peace diplomacy climaxed with the Kellogg-Briand Pact signed in Paris in August of 1928 negotiated by the U.S. Secretary of State Frank B. Kellogg and French Foreign Minister Aristide Briand. The signatories all formally renounced war forever as a tool of national policy. Even though 62 states signed, the effects were negligible. The Geneva Convention of 1929 did more perhaps establishing rules for humane treatment of POWs. The League of Nations made little progress in the promised disarmament that it wanted. National interests tended to dominate the complex negotiations, and for instance even a five-day meeting negotiating failed to define what "war material" meant. This was not promising in terms of further progress.

The ceremonial and hailed World Disarmament Conference opened in 1932 and then collapsed in 1934 unfortunately just at a point when Europe was descending into crisis, a process that we will follow in our next lecture.

Lecture Twenty-Nine
Europe into Crisis

Scope:

The promise of the interwar period rapidly ebbed, however, as the Great Depression of 1929 and the shift toward Authoritarianism and Fascism in European politics moved the continent toward another plunge into disaster. This lecture covers the darker period from 1929 to 1939 and tracks the rise to power of Mussolini in Fascist Italy, Hitler in Nazi Germany, and the calculations of Stalin in the Soviet Union. We observe Hitler's aggressive racist ideology of domination and his diplomatic revolution, overthrowing the Treaty of Versailles and exploiting the appeasement policies of the Western democracies before launching World War II in 1939 after signing the Nazi-Soviet Pact—an unexpected and strange alliance.

Outline

I. The slide into authoritarianism and disorder.

  A. The Great Depression of 1929 compounded instabilities that had appeared earlier, as a wave of authoritarianism spread in Europe.

    1. In Italy, a country deeply disappointed at its "mutilated victory" of World War I, Benito Mussolini led the Fascist movement, established in 1919.

    2. Mussolini took power in 1922 after the "March on Rome" and found many would-be imitators.

    3. Fascism preached the power of the state, aggressive imperialism, and the glory of war.

    4. Mussolini envisioned a revived Roman Empire.

    5. Authoritarian regimes were established in Poland, Hungary, the Baltic states, Yugoslavia, and Portugal.

  B. The Soviet Union came under the control of Josef Stalin (1879–1953), who succeeded Lenin after his death in 1924.

    1. Stalin had secured personal power by 1929 and launched intense purges and show trials.

    2. Georgy Chicherin's establishment of diplomatic relations with European states went in tandem with Comintern activities.

  C. The League of Nations' inability to cope with serious crises became evident.

    1. Japan, whose military dominated politics, attacked China in 1931 in Manchuria.

    2. When an investigation condemned Japan in 1933, it left the league and attacked China again in 1937.

    3. In 1935, Mussolini attacked Ethiopia, a league member.

    4. The league only imposed light economic sanctions on Italy, except for oil, which Italy was still allowed to import.

  D. Memories of the recent world war and inadequate functioning of collective security made effective responses difficult.

  E. This ineffectiveness was compounded by the rise of Hitler and Nazi Germany.

II. Hitler comes to power—1933.

  A. The Great Depression hit Germany very hard, and by 1930 its democracy was crippled.

    1. Even the end of reparations at the Conference of Lausanne in June–July 1932 brought little relief.

    2. In this crisis, the Nazi Party scored a breakthrough election result in 1930.

    3. The party was led by Adolf Hitler (1889–1945), an Austrian, a failed artist, and a war veteran.

    4. Nazi ideology was anti-Semitic and populist, denouncing democracy, liberalism, and the Treaty of Versailles, and promising Germany's restoration to power.

    5. Hitler's foreign policy conceptions were outlined in his ranting manifesto, *Mein Kampf.*

    6. These conceptions included expansion for "living space" (*Lebensraum*) in eastern Europe, a fanatical hatred of Jews, antipathy for the Soviet Union, and hopes for an alliance with Britain.

  B. Hitler became chancellor of Germany on January 30, 1933.

III. Hitler's diplomatic revolution.

  A. Once in power, Hitler engineered a diplomatic revolution in Europe that wrecked the Paris Settlement.

B. Historians debate whether Hitler pursued a blueprint or improvised "expansion without object."

    1. Asserting the primacy of domestic politics, some interpreters argue that Nazi foreign policy was driven by internal crises.

    2. However, Hitler's personal role in shaping foreign policy was key.

C. In the beginning, Hitler benefited at home from continuities between his demands and the long-standing revisionist consensus in German politics, but his aims went far beyond these continuities.

D. Abroad, a key part of his success was his ability to hide his real ideological agenda behind appeals to the rhetoric of traditional diplomacy and modern values: peace, equality, and self-determination.

    1. He was aided by sentiment abroad that Germany had authentic grievances that could be appeased.

    2. The radical reach of his ambitions later became clearer.

E. First, Germany pulled out of the Geneva disarmament talks and the League of Nations in October 1933.

F. Hitler negotiated a German-Polish Pact in 1934.

G. German rearmament and conscription were announced in March 1935.

    1. Great Britain, France, and Italy joined in the Stresa Front to coordinate action, to little effect.

    2. Britain negotiated the Anglo-German Naval Treaty of June 1935, validating Hitler's actions and stunning France.

    3. Hitler supported Italy in its Ethiopian campaign, winning an ally.

H. German foreign policy was increasingly dominated by Hitler's favorite, Joachim von Ribbentrop, an exemplar of the Nazi style of diplomacy: brutal, blundering, and treacherous.

I. Hitler ordered his armies to march into the demilitarized Rhineland in March 1936 and renounced the Treaties of Locarno, without encountering military action.

J. The Versailles Treaty was smashed.

K. In October 1936, the Rome-Berlin Axis was formed, and Germany and Japan signed the Anti-Comintern Pact in November 1936.

L. At a November 1937 meeting recorded in the Hossbach Memorandum, Hitler outlined his further plans.
  1. When conservative officials balked, they were replaced.
  2. Von Ribbentrop was appointed Foreign Minister in 1938.

M. After personally intimidating the Austrian chancellor, Hitler annexed Austria in March 1938.

IV. Responses and appeasement to Hitler's Germany.

A. With Hitler's advent to power, the Soviet Union began to shift its policy to seek cooperation and in 1934 entered the League of Nations.
  1. As Foreign Minister beginning in 1930, Maxim Litvinov (1876–1951) turned to collective security.
  2. The United States recognized the Soviet Union in 1933.
  3. In 1935, France and the Soviet Union signed a pact.
  4. From 1935, the Comintern turned to "popular front" policies to cooperate with non-Communists.

B. The Spanish Civil War, which broke out in 1936, became a proxy confrontation.
  1. Italy and Germany intervened on the Nationalist side led by General Franco, while the Soviets sided with the Loyalists.
  2. France and Great Britain followed a noninterventionist policy.
  3. By 1939, Franco's forces won.

C. Hitler's demands escalated after the propaganda spectacle of the 1936 Berlin Olympics.

D. British conservative Prime Minister Neville Chamberlain (1869–1940) advanced a policy of "appeasement."
  1. The term today has associations that it lacked at the time.
  2. To contemporaries, it signified compromise by meeting justified complaints to avoid renewed war.
  3. It enjoyed popular support at first, although Foreign Secretary Anthony Eden resigned in protest.
  4. France pessimistically followed the British lead.

E. Presenting himself as a defender of minorities, Hitler demanded from Czechoslovakia the Sudetenland, where 3.5 million "Sudeten Germans" lived.
1. Czechoslovakia refused, and war seemed near by September 1938.
2. In a dramatic initiative, Chamberlain flew to meet Hitler and engaged in "shuttle diplomacy."
3. Chamberlain was willing to compromise to avert war "because of a quarrel in a faraway country between people of whom we know nothing."
4. A summit meeting took place in Munich on September 29, 1938, with Hitler, Chamberlain, Mussolini, and French Prime Minister Edouard Daladier (1884–1970), but without the Czechs.
5. The conference assigned the Sudetenland to Germany and Chamberlain returned home with promises of "peace in our time."
6. Contrary to Hitler's promises, in March 1939 Germany occupied the rest of Czechoslovakia.
7. This proved to be a turning point in the evaluation of Hitler's intentions; Britain and France extended guarantees to Poland, the likely next victim.
8. Churchill described appeasement as akin to waiting to be eaten last, and war was only delayed by a year.
9. There is a range of contemporary verdicts on appeasement.
10. Ironically, appeasement would perhaps have yielded real results in the 1920s, with democratic Germany.

V. The unexpected Nazi-Soviet Pact, announced in August 1939, prepared the way for war.

Essential Reading:

Henry Kissinger, *Diplomacy*, pp. 288–318.

Supplementary Reading:

Norman Rich, *Hitler's War Aims: Ideology, the Nazi State, and the Course of German Expansion*, pp. 1–120.

Questions to Consider:

1. Could more vigorous action by the League of Nations have forestalled the descent into chaos?

2. Why did the policy of appeasement toward Hitler last so long?

Lecture Twenty-Nine—Transcript
Europe into Crisis

In this lecture, we will be considering Europe's swift descent into crisis over the course of the 1930s as the promise of the interwar period rapidly ebbed and as the Great Depression of 1929 and a shift toward Authoritarianism and Fascism in European politics began to move the continent toward another plunge into disaster.

I might also mention before we enter into an intensive discussion of the 1930s and this age of dictators that The Teaching Company also offers another course specifically on the record of the dictatorships and the totalitarian ideologies of Communism, Fascism, and Nazism that they represented. This course is also by myself. It's titled, *Utopia and Terror in the 20th Century*. It focuses much more on the ideologies and internal dynamics of these dictatorships. I commend it to the attention of anyone who might have more detailed interest.

This lecture will cover the diplomatic dimension of this darker period from 1929 through the 1930s to 1939. We will track the rise to power of Mussolini in Fascist Italy, Hitler in Nazi Germany, and the calculations of Stalin at the same time in the Soviet Union. We will observe Hitler's aggressive racist ideology in action, preaching as it did domination and the diplomatic revolution that he enacted to dramatically bring his plan into realization as he overthrew the Versailles Treaty and exploited the appeasement policies of the Western democracies before launching, and this will be the conclusion of our lecture, World War II in 1939 after signing a strange sort of treaty, the Nazi-Soviet Pact, an unexpected alliance indeed.

In the immediately previous lectures, we have been looking at the 1919 Paris Settlement and the Treaty of Versailles—with defeated Germany in particular. Then we've looked at how the new system enacted as a result of the 1919 Paris Settlement worked in practice. Debate continues to this very day on how to evaluate the Versailles Treaty, and indeed that will remain a question that sort of hovers in the background throughout the lecture that we are presently engaged in as well—questions like: Was the Versailles Treaty too harsh? Did it provoke reactions that might have been avoided otherwise if it had been milder in nature? Was it by contrast, as some suggest, not harsh enough? Was the problem that it didn't do enough in this regard in order to contain a future rise to power or renewal of power on the part of Germany? Was Woodrow Wilson, whose ideas had done a lot to shape the Paris Settlement, a prophet of new politics who was simply ahead of his time? Or by contrast, was his role ultimately disastrous and ill-considered in its privileging of idealism above the realities of power politics?

We should keep in mind throughout this lecture that many historians do see a direct line between the liabilities or the flaws of the Versailles Treaty and World War II. Others, by contrast, argue that there is no such direct linkage and instead see the Paris Settlement at the end of World War I as the best that could have been achieved under the circumstances. They instead point to flawed decisions after the Paris Settlement as really leading up to World War II. We will essentially be able to make our own decisions in this regard as we observe the slide into Authoritarianism and disorder of the 1930s in this lecture.

The Great Depression from 1929 and its economic crisis compounded instabilities that already had appeared earlier in the European international order because the wave of Authoritarianism that would really take hold in earnest after the great crisis and its onset from 1929 on had actually appeared some time before in Europe, in particular in Italy.

In Italy, Benito Mussolini led the Fascist movement that had been established in 1919 to power, and we note here a somewhat strange phenomenon. Italy had been among the victor powers in World War I, and yet afterwards, especially under the rule of Mussolini would become a revisionist state, one that wanted to overthrow the status quo. In particular here, this paradox of Italy being a victorious power and yet wanting revision, this had everything to do with the sense of many Italian nationalists that Italy had not enjoyed a victorious peace but instead a "mutilated victory," as they called it. This was a sense of bitter disappointment at the outcome of World War I in which many Italian nationalists felt they had not gotten what had been promised to them, as they had been lured onto the side of the Allies and the Entente in this struggle.

Exploiting some of this nationalist bitterness as well as a general sense of crisis, Benito Mussolini came to power in 1922 after a stage-managed "March on Rome" in which allegedly his storm troopers had descended upon Rome and had seized power in a dramatic way. The reality was more prosaic. In fact, back room dealings had helped Mussolini to come to power with the approval of conservative elites. This sort of "March on Rome," this sort of seizure of power that was supposed to be the active will of a radical new movement found many imitators around Europe and elsewhere around the globe—many would-be imitators in part.

Fascism as an ideology was famously incoherent, but some of its values we can isolate. Fascism preached the power of the state and celebrated centralized state power. It also preached aggressive imperialism as a sign of the health of a people as well as the state that practiced that imperialism, and also glorified war. Foreign to our sensibilities, this glorification of war celebrated conflict as a purifier of the national community, a stream-liner of the state and the real patent of future glories.

As the fascists sought future glories, they also looked backwards as well. Mussolini envisioned a revival of the ancient glories of the ancient Roman Empire and looked forward to the day when in a revival of those glories the entire Mediterranean might once again be a Roman realm and the area under the command of the Italian people and the Italian state, obviously with Mussolini himself at the helm. Thus, Mussolini committed his new state to an active and often very aggressive revisionism throughout the region. Sometimes in imitation of the style of the fascist regime, if not all elements of its ideology, authoritarian regimes of various sorts were established in many other European countries in what really amounted to a dark development, a rolling back of what had been an initial enthusiasm for democracy in the immediate aftermath of World War I, so often called a "war to end all wars" and to make the world safe for democracy.

Instead, what one saw now was a wave of authoritarian regimes established in Poland, Hungary, the Baltic states, Yugoslavia, and Portugal as well. Further to the east, the regime in the Soviet Union was also taking its route into a more centralized and ever more effective dictatorship under the control of Josef Stalin, who had succeeded Lenin after that revolutionary's death in 1924. As a result of complicated and tremendously fraught succession struggles, Stalin had in the end managed to secure his personal power by 1929. Through intensive purges and dramatic show trials that made clear some of the ideological energies of the Soviet Union, Stalin further centralized in a really remarkable way power around his own person.

The Soviet foreign policy establishment, its diplomatic core, continued that dual track that we had discussed as characteristic of Soviet diplomacy in this period.

Georgy Chicherin's establishment of diplomatic relations with European states on a formal level went in tandem and in parallel with continuing revolutionary activities by the Comintern, this institution centered on the Soviet Union that aimed to spread revolution worldwide on a more covert plane.

For its part, the League of Nations, which as an international institution had such hopes vested in it, now unfortunately was compiling an increasingly disappointing record. The league's inability to cope with serious international crises became evident in part through its inability to contain the aggressive intentions of someone like Mussolini but then especially in earnest with events in Asia.

Japan, whose military increasingly was dominating internal as well as external politics, set a very aggressive course—this was focused on an attack on China in 1931 centered on Manchuria where the Japanese military aimed to carve out for itself a special sphere of action. How did the league react to this aggressive policy in Manchuria against Chinese authority from the 1930s? Well, an investigation was held, and it condemned Japan in 1993. But effective action remained lacking, and Japan simply reacted by leaving the league and in 1937 continuing to attack China in a vigorous way. Clearly, the league might have spoken up against these actions but was not able to contain them or to really effectively present a reaction that would have rolled them back. This instability, which to many Europeans might have seemed distant and of less concern, soon boomeranged back towards Europe itself when in 1935 Mussolini reached out for that Mediterranean and larger sort of North African and African empire that he hope to establish by attacking Ethiopia.

This attack in 1935 upon Ethiopia by Fascist Italy was especially important because in this case you had one member of the League of Nations attacking another member of the League of Nations. But the League of Nations was only able to muster quite ineffective and very soft reactions; it was only capable of agreeing on imposing light economic sanctions on Italy. Even these light sanctions in punishment for this aggressive action excluded a blockade on oil, which was a very important strategic resource for Italy in its war effort. Other goods were not to be exported to Italy, but oil was not included among them.

How do we account for the strange and disappointing weakness of these sanctions? Well, one anxiety that left collective security behind as a concept had everything to do with the terms of the balance of power. The anxiety of Great Britain and France in particular was that if Mussolini was pressed too hard, he might ally with the new Nazi Germany that we will be discussing in a moment. There were anxieties thus that the balance of power might be disrupted, and in some sense this anxiety did come true because Mussolini and Hitler did make common cause. All of this showed the inadequate functioning of the collective security as an arrangement, which made any kind of effective response to aggression increasingly difficult. This was further compounded by the arrival on the scene of a tremendously aggressive power and one that was difficult for European diplomats to take a proper estimate of from the beginning. That was the rise of Hitler and Nazi Germany.

Let's now examine Hitler's arrival to power in 1933. The Great Depression hit Germany especially hard. The United States had been pounded by the Depression, and Germany was probably in second place in this regard. By 1930, even the German Weimar Democracy, the democratic republic that had been established and its constitution written in Weimar, was already ceasing to function effectively. Even the ending of reparations, which had been such a theme that had created such bitterness over European affairs in previous years, as a gesture towards the anxieties of Germans in this time at a conference of Lausanne in June and July of 1932—so intense was the crisis that even the end of reparations was little noticed at the time, and it's not a coincidence that the Nazi party, a radical new force in politics, was scoring its breakthrough election results precisely in 1930 when the economic crisis was hitting very hard.

This party was led by a man by the name of Adolf Hitler, who was a failed artist from Austria and a veteran of World War I. Some of his fellow veterans had reflected that Hitler had enjoyed World War I just a little bit more than was normal under the circumstances. He championed the new ideology that he was instrumental in giving institutional form to in the Nazi party. Nazi ideology was anti-Semitic. It denounced the Jews as a reason, so they alleged, for all of the woes in German society. It was populist in its energies, breaking with earlier conservative traditions in German politics and also denounced democracy and liberalism as signs of weakness. Part and parcel of the formulaic denunciations of the status quo that the Nazis excelled in was also a denunciation of the Treaty of Versailles in particular. Hitler would often begin speeches with an almost formulaic recitation of the wrongs that had been done against Germany by the Western democracies at the Treaty of Versailles. By implication, by promising to break the Treaty of Versailles, the Nazis promised Germany's restoration to power. All of this was an incoherent but effective package deal in ideological terms.

The Nazis also excelled in propagating the so-called "stab in the back" legend, which claimed that Germany in fact had not lost World War I, but elements within had undermined the German war effort and had led to this unaccountable result of the Treaty of Versailles. Hitler actually laid out in some detail his foreign policy conceptions in a ranting manifesto, *Mein Kampf*—which became one of the most famous if unread books in world history. He later actually regretted having been so candid in all of his manifesto in this regard; if he had to do it over again, he at one point explained he might not have actually divulged all of those intentions. Unfortunately, as it turns out, very few people actually upon reading the incoherent diatribe took it seriously as it probably should have been in this regard.

Hitler's foreign policy conceptions included a radial agenda: expansion for the winning of "living space," the German term was *Lebensraum*, for a future master race distilled out of the German people in their present condition. That "living space" for the master race was to be found in the wide-open spaces of Eastern Europe where the Slavs and other people were to be driven out. Nazi ideology also emphasized its fanatical hatred of the Jews; antipathy for the Soviet Union, which was seen as the mortal enemy of Nazism precisely because it was more vital than the weak democracies; and oddly enough Hitler also placed his hopes on an alliance with the British, whom he saw as a kindred Germanic people.

Hitler became chancellor of Germany on January 30, 1933, as a result of machinations that allowed him to come to power with the approval of conservative and national elites within Germany. Hitler now was able to enact a diplomatic revolution, and we want to focus on this because it truly revealed, as it were, an intuitive kind of evil genius for the manipulation of international politics. Once he was in power from 1933, Hitler engineered a diplomatic revolution. No other phrase is adequate in this regard in Europe, which ended up wrecking the Paris Settlement. Historians continue to debate to this very day about whether Hitler, as he claimed afterwards, was pursuing a blueprint in which all of the details of step-by-step agendas had been thought out in advance or whether by contrast, as some historians on the other extreme have claimed, Hitler was an opportunist who improvised endlessly in sort of a nihilistic pursuit of power for its own sake. A phrase that's sometimes used is "expansion without object." Clearly these are extremes that might very well find the truth landing somewhere in the middle between them. Being ideologically consistent and fanatical might not preclude a certain pragmatism on occasion.

Other interpreters of Nazi foreign policy sometimes look back to one of the themes of our course, the option of considering the primacy of domestic politics. Some of these interpreters argue the Nazi foreign policy and its aggressive energies were in fact driven by internal crises, a regime that was not capable of dealing in any other way with serious domestic and structural problems.

Other historians accent instead Hitler's personal role in shaping foreign policy. I think in this debate one has to emphasize that indeed Hitler's personal role in making the key decisions can't be disputed. Indeed, one doesn't form the impression of someone who is simply reacting, as it were, on a case-by-case basis but rather someone who, though his aims clearly are malicious and driven by fanaticism, are nonetheless ones that he's making in a deliberate way.

In the beginning, as Hitler launched his attempt at a diplomatic revolution, Hitler benefited at home in Germany with undeniable popularity. In fact, as he pursued this foreign policy route from continuities that existed between certain of his demands in foreign policy and something we've already talked about before in the politics of the Weimar regime, a long-standing revisionist consensus in German politics—the aim to revise the Treaty of Versailles. As would soon be clear, Hitler's aims went far beyond those of even many nationalist Germans. Just to give an example, back in the 1920s Gustav Stresemann who had worked for peaceful revision had also been a revisionist but very different from Hitler's aggressive brand.

Abroad, outside of Germany, a key part of Hitler's success was his ability to actually hide his real ideological agenda and long-range goals behind appeals to a kind of rhetoric of more traditional diplomacy as well as modern values. I mean as astonishing as it might sound to us who know Hitler's real record in hindsight, Hitler was able to hammer away at rhetorical themes of seeking peace, equality for Germany among sovereign nations, and the modern value of self-determination. Hitler was also aided in this tremendously effective appeal for all that he was conducting it in bad faith by the sentiment abroad that in fact Germans might have some authentic grievances that might be appeased, might be met in a way that was seen as reasonable compromise.

The recollection of the outbreak of World War I and the way in which a crisis had escalated also stirred anxieties. It further underlined for many people the necessity of somehow finding a way to appease, if it were possible to appease. Hitler alternatively played on fears and hope. In his foreign policy, he alternated between sudden aggressive surprises with on the other hand avowals of peace or what one might call peace offensives on occasion keeping foreign diplomats uncertain of his real intentions. The radical reach of his ambitions would only become clear later.

Germany first simply pulled out of disarmament talks at Hitler's order that were being held at Geneva because they claimed they weren't being treated equally and then pulled out of the league in October of 1933. Hitler then avowed that he was interested in European peace and stability by signing a German-Polish Pact in 1934. Hitler then claimed he was only establishing German equality by rearming Germany and reintroducing conscription, both of which were not allowed under the Versailles Treaty announcing this step in March of 1935. Great Britain, France, and Italy together tried to coordinate action against Germany to contain these moves in the so-called Stresa Front, but it ultimately had little effect. Great Britain, in particular, broke ranks with its powers in this regard by negotiating a naval treaty in June of 1935 that in some sense validated Hitler's actions even in breaking the terms of the Versailles Treaty and left the French stunned and dismayed. Hitler also supported Italy in its Ethiopian campaign and in the process won a Fascist ally.

German foreign policy was increasingly dominated by Hitler's favorite, a tremendously repellant man by the name of Joachim von Ribbentrop whose only qualification for the role of diplomat was the fact that he had earlier been a wine merchant and supposedly had international connections. He was the ultimate "yes man." This was someone who excelled in finding out what Hitler thought in advance and then echoing his opinions back to him. He was an exemplar of the Nazi style of diplomacy. Even the way in which Nazi diplomacy sounds like almost a contradiction in terms is indicative of its brutality, its blundering nature, as well as its treacherousness. He was a man who had a tremendously high opinion of himself and always walked around with his nose in the air. This almost led him once to fall under a train in Paris as a result.

He was spectacularly incompetent and was responsible for one of the most famous diplomatic blunders of history that took place in Britain in 1937 when he greeted the British king not with the polite etiquette that would otherwise have been demanded but instead with an aggressive Nazi salute and shouting of, "Heil Hitler." He was a man who was proud of his treachery. In a sort of mindless way, he would joke about having an entire chest made for all of the treaties that he had broken or wanted to break.

Hitler now set about furthering his agenda by ordering German armies to march into the demilitarized Rhineland in March of 1936 and then renounced the hopeful Locarno Treaty, without encountering any military response on the part of the Western democracies that at this point might have effectively intervened. The Versailles Treaty, as a result, was simply in ruins, smashed, and in October of 1936, the Rome-Berlin Axis was formed. It was rhetorically stronger than a real effective alliance. Germany and Japan on their part as well, signed the so-called Anti-Comintern Pact that pledged to resist Communism in November of 1936.

At a November 1937 meeting recorded in the famous so-called Hossbach Memorandum, notes taken down by a military aid known as Hossbach, Hitler outlined his further plans. Indeed, they actually match what further took place, and in this sense the Hossbach Memorandum is a sort of smoking gun for may diplomatic historians.

When German conservative officials in the government balked at what they heard at this famous meeting, they were replaced.

Ribbentrop, for instance, was now finally appointed formally Foreign Minister in 1938. He had been interfering a long time previously. After personally intimidating the Austrian chancellor, this was another badge of Nazi diplomacy and characteristic of it, Hitler then set about annexing Austria, which he did in March of 1938.

What were the responses abroad to this sequence of confusing actions? With Hitler's advent to power, the Soviet Union began to shift its policy to seek more cooperation even with a capitalist enemy and in 1934 broke its earlier traditions by entering the league of Nations. Maxim Litvinov as Foreign Minister from 1930 now tried to enmesh the Soviet Union in collective security, and indeed the United States, which had long resisted the move, recognized the Soviet Union in 1933. In 1935, France and the Soviet Union signed a pact that in some ways was reminiscent of the pact between Russia and France of the later 19th century. From 1935, the Comintern, which earlier had fomented revolution abroad instead now turned to a strategy of so-called "popular front" policies to cooperate with non-Communists.

A moment of truth came with the Spanish Civil War, which broke out in 1936 and became a proxy confrontation between the forces of Fascism and Nazism on the one hand, and democracy and the Soviet Union on the other, which was a sort of uneasy constellation of forces. Italy and Germany intervened on the Nationalist side, which was led by General Franco, while the Soviets sided with the Loyalists. France and Great Britain for their part followed a sort of irresolute, non-interventionist policy, and by 1939 Franco's forces had won.

Hitler's demands now escalated increasingly after the dismaying propaganda spectacle of the 1936 Berlin Olympics. We think of Olympics as celebrations of peaceful competition. Hitler intended this as a showing off of his new power. British conservative Prime Minister Neville Chamberlain at this point advanced a policy called "appeasement," which had not the negative connotations that the term since has acquired—not for accidental reasons. At the time, it actually had positive connotations. To contemporaries, it signified going the extra mile to seek compromise by meeting justified complaints to avoid the disaster of renewed war. Indeed, appeasement enjoyed popular support at first even though Foreign

Secretary Anthony Eden resigned in protest and people like Churchill were skeptical to say the least.

France, more pessimistic about whether Hitler could be appeased followed the British lead in this. Hitler now presented himself in the strange guise of the defender of the rights of minorities, and he demanded from democratic Czechoslovakia the annexation to Germany of the Sudetenland, where 3.5 million so-called Sudeten Germans, meaning people living in this region of German heritage, were living. Czechoslovakia refused and war between Germany and Czechoslovakia seemed near by September of 1938. In a dramatic initiative of appeasement, Chamberlain flew to meet Hitler and engaged in what we today would call "shuttle diplomacy." Chamberlain was willing to compromise to avert war as he put it "because of a quarrel in a far-away country between people of whom we know nothing." The fact that Czechoslovakia was the only functioning democracy in Eastern Europe or Central Europe at the time made the betrayal that was about to happen all the more bitter.

A summit meeting then took place in Munich on September 29, 1938, with Hitler; Chamberlain; Mussolini; and the French Prime Minister, Edouard Daladier; but the Czechs were not invited. They would have to wait to hear what the future of their country would be. The conference assigned the Sudetenland to Germany appeasing Hitler, and Chamberlain returned home to promises of peace—"peace in our time," in a phrase that later would be regretted. Munich would become synonymous ever afterwards with betrayal and achieving one's own defeat in a moral sense without military action.

Contrary to Hitler's promises of wanting nothing more after the Sudetenland had been annexed, soon thereafter in March of 1939 Germany occupied the rest of Czechoslovakia. This moment of truth of the gobbling up of the rest of the territories proved a turning point in the evaluation of Hitler's intentions abroad, and Britain and France now changed from appeasement to extending guarantees to Poland, Hitler's likely next visit.

Churchill for his part, who is a voice in opposition in this regard, described appeasement as akin to waiting to be eaten last, and war indeed was only delayed by a year. At the time, however, appeasement had been quite popular. Ironically, appeasement might have yielded real results in the 1920s when Germany was still democratic. Stresemann's appeals for a new beginning in European politics might have instead met with the sort of generosity that Hitler ironically had received.

The unexpected treaty, known as the Nazi-Soviet Pact, which was announced on August 23, 1939, now prepared the way for war, and it was an astonishing event. It was instrumental in bringing on the next conflict, World War II, which we will examine in our next lecture.

Lecture Thirty
World War II

Scope:

World War II (1939–1945) was a renewed and perfected "total war," even more intense than World War I and ultimately taking a toll of some 50 million dead. This lecture examines the diplomatic bombshell that paved the way to war: the Nazi-Soviet Pact of August 1939. We outline the scale of Hitler's ambitions for hegemony, culminating at last in the invasion of his Soviet ally in 1941. We turn to discuss the complicated alliance coordination of the United States, Great Britain, and the Soviet Union, including the key conferences in Tehran and Yalta, where the personalities of the wartime leaders Roosevelt, Churchill, and Stalin played crucial roles.

Outline

I.   The Nazi-Soviet Pact of 1939.

   A. A diplomatic bombshell was the announcement of the Nazi-Soviet Pact dated August 23, 1939.

      1. The pact had seemed impossible due to the mutual ideological hatred of the parties, but now apparently it vindicated the Realist interpretation of international relations.

      2. British diplomacy to promote an alliance with the Soviet Union was slow and irresolute but also reflected serious questions about Soviet intentions and the Polish refusal to cooperate.

      3. Stalin signaled his desire to come to terms with Hitler, replacing Litvinov with Vyacheslav Molotov as Foreign Minister in May 1939.

   B. Von Ribbentrop was sent to Moscow to negotiate the treaty between Nazi Germany and Soviet Russia.

      1. Officially, it was a nonaggression treaty, harking back to the Treaty of Rapallo of 1922.

      2. In a secret appendix, central and eastern Europe were divided between the signatories.

      3. Poland and the Baltic states were to be wiped off the map, recalling the 18th-century partitions of Poland.

4. The existence of the secret treaty was denied by the Soviet Union until just before its collapse.

C. Hitler gained the assurance of avoiding a two-front war.

D. Stalin aimed to stay out of the next war to save the revolution (recalling the 1918 Treaty of Brest-Litovsk). Stalin, who trusted no one and decimated those he felt were potential enemies, chose to trust, of all people, Adolf Hitler.

E. Soviet-Nazi cooperation now paved the way to starting World War II.

II. The outbreak of World War II.

A. On September 1, 1939, Hitler attacked Poland.

B. On September 3, 1939, Great Britain and France declared war on Germany.

C. While the role of Hitler seems obvious, there has still been debate on the causes of the war.

    1. The perennially controversial A. J. P. Taylor argued in his 1961 book, *The Origins of the Second World War*, that Hitler was in many ways "an ordinary German statesman" and that mistakes on all sides led to war. This view has not won many supporters.

    2. Another debate centers on the continuity or discontinuity of the Nazi period in German history at large.

    3. Clearly, ideology played a key role.

D. German forces conquered Poland in five weeks, and Soviet forces moved in from the east, partitioning Poland.

E. Stalin sought to solidify control over his sphere of influence.

    1. He gave ultimatums to the Baltic states (Estonia, Latvia, and Lithuania), which were forced to accept Soviet bases and were annexed in 1940; mass deportations followed.

    2. The Soviets executed captured Polish officers at Katyn.

    3. In a disastrous campaign—the Finnish Winter War (November 1939–March 1940)—Soviet forces invaded Finland.

    4. The Soviet Union was expelled from the League of Nations.

F. Although Great Britain and France were at war with Germany, the "Phony War" saw few clashes.

G. Germany overran Denmark and Norway in a swift campaign in the spring of 1940.

H. Germany invaded the Netherlands, Belgium, and France in May 1940.

    1. France fell with alarming speed, in part due to domestic divisions.

    2. In June 1940, the French signed an armistice with Germany.

    3. British forces narrowly escaped from Dunkirk.

I. Some in the British cabinet urged seeking peace, but this was turned down by Winston Churchill (1874–1965), who became Prime Minister on May 10, 1940.

    1. One of Churchill's great strengths was his mastery of persuasive language.

    2. In a dramatic gesture, Churchill urged the union of France and Great Britain.

    3. Britain now endured "standing alone" for 18 months, holding out against the air war of the Battle of Britain.

    4. Churchill worked to bring the neutral United States into the war.

    5. U.S. President Franklin Roosevelt began Lend-Lease deliveries to Britain from March 1941.

    6. On August 14, 1941, Roosevelt and Churchill signed the Atlantic Charter, which laid out common principles, including self-determination.

J. Hitler worked on the reordering of Europe.

    1. Germany, Italy, and Japan signed the September 1940 Three Power Pact of mutual aid; henceforth, they would be known as the Axis Powers.

    2. In the Vienna Award of 1940, Hitler's revisionist ally, Hungary, recovered the bulk of Transylvania from Romania.

III. Operation Barbarossa: Germany's attack on the Soviet Union.

A. Pursuing his ideological long-term goals, Hitler turned to attack his ally, Stalin's Soviet Union.

    1. The attack was delayed by the need to assist Mussolini in his failed invasion of Greece in October 1940.

    2. The attack began on June 22, 1941.

    3. German armies (allied with Romania, Italy, Slovakia, Hungary, and Finland) overran great areas of the Soviet Union.

  B. Behind the lines, the Nazis organized a program of mass murder against the Jews, later systematized as the Final Solution.

    1. Amidst the Holocaust, individual diplomats (Sweden's Raoul Wallenberg and Japan's Chiune Sugihara) worked to save Jews.

    2. The diplomacy of the Vatican and the Red Cross are still debated.

  C. After a counterattack before Moscow in winter 1941 and the German defeat at Stalingrad in early 1943, the Soviets began to drive the Germans back.

IV. The alliance between the West and the Soviets.

  A. Great Britain and the Soviet Union allied in July 1941.

  B. The United States began shipments of materials to the Soviet Union.

  C. The Soviet Neutrality Pact with Japan of April 1941 saved the Soviets from war on both fronts.

  D. On December 7, 1941, Japan attacked the United States.

    1. Showing solidarity, Germany and Italy declared war on the United States on December 11.

    2. Hitler's motive was to tie Japan into the conflict.

  E. The United States was now involved in the European war, allied with Great Britain and the Soviet Union.

    1. The image of the Soviet Union was improved in the United States.

    2. British policy remained more cautious about Soviet motives.

    3. Stalin urgently demanded a second front in the West.

    4. To reassure his allies, Stalin dissolved the Comintern in May 1943.

  F. General Charles de Gaulle (1890–1970) organized the Free French movement from London.

V. Conferences.

    A. Even as the war raged, diplomacy now came into play, not between the warring sides but as coalition diplomacy negotiated at conferences and summit meetings held by the top leaders.

    B. The January 1942 Washington Pact committed the 26 "united nations" associated with the Allies not to make a separate peace with the Axis Powers.

    C. After earlier meetings, Roosevelt and Churchill met at the Casablanca Conference (January 14–24, 1943) and agreed on demanding Germany's unconditional surrender.

    D. At the November–December 1943 Tehran Conference, Stalin, Roosevelt, and Churchill ("The Big Three") met together for the first time.

        1. Stalin's calls for a second front were finally met with the decision to invade northern France and not pursue Churchill's southern strategy to invade through southern Europe.

        2. A secret agreement agreed that Russia and Poland were to be shifted westward at Germany's cost.

        3. Stalin demanded keeping his gains in eastern Europe.

        4. Roosevelt and Churchill worried about Stalin making a separate peace with Hitler.

        5. Roosevelt won agreement on setting up an international organization.

    E. Seeking to pin down Stalin's demands, Churchill flew to Moscow in October 1944, concluding the Percentages Agreement.

        1. This strange encounter established spheres of influence in the Balkans, scrawled on a scrap of paper.

        2. The Soviets were to have most of their influence in Romania and Bulgaria, the British in Greece, and equal influence in Yugoslavia and Hungary.

    F. Events on the ground influenced diplomacy.

        1. U.S. and British forces launched the Normandy invasion on June 6, 1944.

        2. Polish and Russian relations deteriorated over the Katyn Massacre and the failed Warsaw uprising in August 1944.

G. Wartime negotiations climaxed at the Yalta Conference (in the Crimea) between Stalin, Churchill, and Roosevelt (already seriously ill) in February 1945—the most important of the summit meetings.

1. The Allies had reached Germany's borders.
2. The main issue concerned Poland (which received Silesia, Pomerania, and most of East Prussia) and establishing zones of occupation in Germany (Stalin also agreed to enter the war against Japan).
3. Roosevelt pressed his plan for a United Nations and got Stalin's agreement.
4. The leaders signed the Declaration on Liberated Europe, promising national sovereignty and democracy for the future, and Stalin agreed to free elections in Poland.
5. The French were not invited to negotiate but received an occupation zone in Germany at Churchill's urging.
6. Roosevelt announced afterward that Yalta meant the end of spheres of influence and the balance of power, but events soon negated this prediction.
7. Many eastern Europeans see Yalta as emblematic of their consignment to the Soviet sphere; some have viewed it as a Western betrayal.
8. Other scholars respond that Yalta was the best that could be realistically achieved at the time.
9. Tacitly, this left eastern Europe to Stalin, who insisted on friendly governments.

VI. The war ends.

A. The trap closed on Germany and its allies.
1. Mussolini was overthrown and in September 1943, Italy changed sides.
2. Senior Nazis sought to negotiate but were turned down.
3. When Roosevelt died on April 12, 1945, Hitler hoped in vain for a repetition of the "Miracle of the House of Brandenburg" of 1762, which had saved Frederick the Great.
4. On April 30, 1945, Hitler killed himself.
5. On May 8, Germany's total surrender came into effect.
6. After the United States dropped two atomic bombs on Japan in August 1945 and the Soviets declared war, Japan surrendered on September 2, 1945.

B. In the wake of immense destruction and suffering, Europeans awaited a new peace, but one that now would be determined from outside.

Essential Reading:

Henry Kissinger, *Diplomacy*, pp. 332–422.

Supplementary Reading:

John Keegan, *Winston Churchill*.

Norman Rich, *Hitler's War Aims: Ideology, the Nazi State, and the Course of German Expansion, pp. 121–250.*

Questions to Consider:

1. If Britain had negotiated with Hitler in 1940 after the fall of France, as some urged, what would the historical results have been?

2. Why did Stalin choose to ally himself with Hitler?

Lecture Thirty—Transcript
World War II

In this lecture, we will be considering the diplomatic dimensions of World War II. World War II, from 1939–1945, was a renewed and perfected "total war" even more intense than World War I and ultimately taking a toll of some 50 million dead. In our earlier lecture, we considered the European descent into crisis, Hitler's diplomatic revolution—the lead-up, in other words, to World War II. In this lecture, we will examine the diplomatic bombshell, first of all, which paved that way to war, the Nazi-Soviet Pact of August 1939. We will outline the scale of Hitler's ambitions for hegemony culminating at last in the invasion of his own Soviet ally in 1941 and ending that strange alliance. We will then turn to discuss the complicated alliance coordination of the United States, Great Britain, and the Soviet Union including key conferences held at Teheran and Yalta where the personalities of the wartime leaders, Roosevelt, Churchill, and Stalin, would play crucial roles.

I might mention at this juncture that while this lecture will look at the diplomatic dimensions of World War II, The Teaching Company actually offers an extensive course on World War II in its many dimensions by Professor Childers of the University of Pennsylvania, and I commend that to your attention.

First of all, let's begin with a discussion of the Nazi-Soviet Pact. The very name itself, this alliance of seeming opposites and ideological mortal enemies says volumes about its bizarre nature. When it was announced, the Nazi-Soviet Pact dated August 23, 1939, was a diplomatic bombshell. It had seemed to many earlier observers an impossibility due to the ideological and intense mutual hatred of the two parties that now had become allies. Now, however, the very existence of this treaty apparently vindicated the realist interpretation of international relations that we've averted to in earlier lectures, the conception by Realists that power politics will make its own demands and dynamics that are not always ideologically consistent and indeed obey power imperatives first of all. A bit of pre-history to the entire bombshell is useful.

British diplomacy had sought to promote an alliance with the Soviet Union, but the approaches of British diplomats to the enigmatic Soviet Union under the despotic rule of Stalin were slow and irresolute. This was not only a fatal misjudgment prompted by a blinkered ideological view. The very slowness and ambiguity of the British advances reflected serious questions about what it was that Stalin really wanted—that is to say Soviet intentions more broadly, and Poland's refusal to cooperate, which would have been necessary in any unified opposition to Nazi Germany. Poland, with some justification, was anxious that once Stalin was able to move troops through Poland, there was no telling that they would ever be moved out. Stalin signaled his desire to come to terms with Hitler by a subtle diplomatically significant move, and that was replacement of the person who was in charge of the Foreign Ministry. He replaced Maxim Litvinov, who was of Jewish origins, with a new Foreign Minister, Vyacheslav Molotov, in May of 1939 in order to prepare the way for negotiations with the intensely anti-Semitic Nazis.

Joachim von Ribbentrop—that bizarre Nazi diplomat, and the very term "Nazi diplomat" rings strangely to our ears—was sent to Moscow to negotiate the treaty that had been invited by this opening. Officially, this was a nonaggression treaty simply proclaiming friendship, and in certain ways it harked back to the Rapallo Treaty of 1922 when the two outlaw nations or pariahs of the international system defeated Germany as well as the Soviet Russia had made common cause in an earlier period. This agreement, however, was far more far-reaching with significant impact historically. Apart from the protestations of friendship that were to be read by all, there was a secret appendix, secret paragraphs, that were added on to the nonaggression pact. In these secret appendices, central and eastern Europe was to be divided up between Nazi Germany and the Soviet Union in their own spheres of influence. Poland and the Baltic states were to be wiped off the map in a way that recalled the earlier partitions of Poland in that part of the world in the 18th century—a reversion in some sense to these earlier cannibalistic traditions that had marked a previous stage of diplomacy and international politics.

The existence of the secret treaty, which soon would be put into effect and its effects were there for all to see, would be denied by the Soviet Union until just before its collapse in our own times. It was viewed as something that was taboo and would not be admitted. Hitler gained assurance as a result of this nonaggression pact and the division of central and eastern Europe of avoiding what he feared and what had been the fear of many German policymakers in ages previous—the fear of facing a two-front war. What did Stalin hope to gain by this bizarre arrangement? Stalin aimed to stay out of what he was sure would be the next war, and the aim in essence as capitalists powers, and for Stalin, Hitler as well as Great Britain, France, and the United States were all capitalist powers—that was the crucial criterion here. It would be possible for the Soviet Union to stay out of their future collision brought on by mutual competition and thus to save the revolution at all costs. This is logic by the way that we've heard before by a revolutionary regime.

In 1918, Lenin had urged the existential importance of signing the Treaty of Brest-Litovsk even with the harsh demands that the German capitalists were raising at the time in order to just gain a breathing space to save the revolution. Further, Stalin was also pursuing what he felt would be a further guarantee or buttressing of stability. One of the themes of our course is just how elusive and in some cases counter-productive the pursuit of stability above all can be in certain situations. Stalin won "stability" in this case by the accretion of more territory and pushing frontiers forward, but that territorial expansion ultimately, as it turns out, didn't guarantee any more security. It simply allowed Stalin to be distracted from the task of preparing the defense of the Soviet Union by gobbling up more territories and ironically leaving the frontiers even more exposed in that day when his ally Hitler would decide to turn on Stalin and the Soviet Union. Beyond that, one just has to take aboard the craziness of all of this.

Stalin, who was paranoid to the core of his being and was convinced that everyone was out to get him even among the Bolsheviks and the result was mass murder on an enormous scale and deportations to the Gulag prison camps that were being run in the Soviet Union as purges again and again decimated people he felt were potential enemies. This man who trusted no one chose to trust of all people one man, Adolph Hitler, to keep his promises. The insanity of this is truly remarkable. Soviet-Nazi cooperation thus would now pave the way to starting World War II. One might think of it this way—Hitler had a little bit of help from his friends.

Let's turn now to the outbreak of World War II itself. On September 1, 1939, Hitler attacked Poland. This was an attack that began with a lie. The lie was intrinsic to Hitler's political career. The lie was that Poland, in fact, had initiated an attack against Germany and that the Germans were now firing back. Honoring their obligations and guarantees to Poland, on September 3, 1939, Great Britain and

France declared war on Germany, and World War II was now beginning in earnest. While the role of Hitler seems obvious—I mean in some sense this was Hitler's war, there nonetheless has still been debate on the causes of the war, and this probably also speaks volumes about how much historians love to debate. The perennially controversial historian, a man who gloried in controversy and paradox, the British historian A. J. P. Taylor argued in a book that was published in 1961, and you might recall that 1961 was the same year that Fritz Fischer launched a big controversy as a German historian about the origins of World War I. So, 1961 was a bumper crop year in terms of historical controversies. Taylor had argued in his book, *The Origins of the Second World War*, that Hitler if you put aside his domestic policies and aspects of his ideology was in many ways "an ordinary German statesman," following power political imperatives, and that mistakes on all sides led to war. I think you can see the problem immediately with this controversial explanation. Putting aside Hitler's ideology and domestic politics, puts aside a lot that's essential about Hitler, and it needs to be said that this view of A. J. P. Taylor's that was criticized furiously at the time hasn't won very many supporters in the profession.

Another debate centers more broadly on questions of continuity or discontinuity of the Nazi period in the longer scope of German history, and obviously here those who see important continuities argue that Germany had long been militarist even in its Prussian persona that was a precursor to German unification in the 19th century. They point to its expansionist and erratic foreign policy during the German Empire period afterwards and see this as part of a longer continuum. But I think that this needs to be modified or qualified with the emphasis that Nazi ideology now really infused unprecedentedly new hateful energies into whatever continuities might still exist. Ideology thus would play a key role in marking a new era.

For their part now, German forces conquered Poland in five weeks and carved off their areas of partition as they extinguished independent Poland's existence, and then as per agreement, Soviet forces moved in from the east meeting in a very friendly way the German forces at of all places Brest-Litovsk, the same fortress where in 1918 the despotic German dictated Treaty of Brest-Litovsk had been negotiated and then finally signed. It was an odd symbolic meeting but one that spoke volumes nonetheless about this strange partnership.

Stalin for his part in the areas that he now had newly controlled sought to solidify his power in those spheres of influence. He soon gave ultimatums to the Baltic states—independent sovereign countries that won independence after World War I—Estonia, Latvia, and Lithuania. They were forced to accept Soviet bases and were then finally annexed in 1940, mass deportations followed of people who were viewed as potential opponents to the regime. Stalin's paranoia was such that even people who spoke Esperanto or collected foreign stamps were viewed as people with dangerous foreign or international sympathies.

The Soviets also executed great numbers of captured Polish officers at Katyn and threw them into mass graves, and this later would become a serious diplomatic issue in years to come. In a disastrous campaign, Stalin also sought to solidify his control over Finland. In the Finnish Winter War of November 1939 to March 1940, Soviet forces invaded Finland but did very badly in that campaign, which encouraged Hitler to feel that the Soviet Union was a lot weaker than it looked. You will recall, however, an earlier maxim that we had advanced, which was that as sometimes is said, "Russia is never as strong as it appears, nor as weak as it appears." The Soviet Union, as a result of this Finnish invasion of a sovereign country, was expelled from the League of Nations, and although Great Britain and France at this time formally were at war with Germany, this was a strange sort of calm before the storm. It is sometimes called the "Phony War," in which few clashes took place while Hitler now prepared to seize the initiative, which he did when Germany overran Denmark and Norway in a swift campaign in the Scandinavian countries in the spring of 1940.

Then he turned his attentions westward, and Germany invaded the Netherlands, Belgium, and France in May of 1940. France, which had spent so much blood and energy in World War I holding off the German invasion, now instead, fell with alarming speed. Historians view this as being not only a military collapse but maybe even more importantly a psychological and political falling apart. It was in part due to intense domestic divisions within. In June 1940, the French signed an armistice with Germany and now would be under the German sway. British expeditionary forces that had sought to play that perennial balancing role from their position off the continent only narrowly escaped from Dunkirk in an epic withdrawal across the English Channel.

Hitler for his part, now in a symbolically significant act, made a lightning-quick trip to Paris, which now was under German domination and there among the other key tourists sites he wanted to visit, he visited Napoleon's tomb and there in a bizarre sense I guess you would have to say paid his respects to the earlier great conqueror exalting in his triumph and seeing this as the greatest hour of his life.

At this point, the question was how Britain would react. Some in the British cabinet actually urged at this point to seek compromised peace with this overpowering might of Germany, but Winston Churchill who now became Prime Minister just as this war in the west had been unleashed on May 10, 1940, turned down such suggestions. He now sought to mobilize the energies of the British people in order to resist.

One of Churchill's great strengths would be his mastery of persuasive language. He would go on in 1953 to actually win the Nobel Prize in literature for his writings. His ability through famous speeches that pledged that Britain would never surrender, for instance, truly did much by way of tremendous psychological impact. In another dramatic gesture of the times that suggested the gravity of the situation, Churchill urged in the hour of France's greatest peril before its defeat the union, the formal union, of France and Great Britain. This is another really surprising moment. Even in this course as we have been tracing continuities, a moment of discontinuity in this sense—a surprise given the earlier hereditary rivalry between France and Great Britain over the course of the 18th and the 19th centuries. We now see instead a suggestion of union, which came to nothing but symbolically was of significant import.

Britain now would endure a period of "standing alone" for 18 months against Nazi Germany's great might holding out especially during the air war of the Battle of Britain. Churchill now would work to bring the neutral United States into the war as the prime chance for achieving finally a great victory. The United States' president, Franklin Roosevelt, began lend lease deliveries to Britain from March of 1941, hemmed in as he was, restrained by isolationist sentiment in the United States that sought to steer clear of repetition of the gory encounter of World War I.

On August 14, 1941, Roosevelt and Churchill, however, underlined common principles that they shared by signing the Atlantic Charter, as it was called, which laid out common values including the struggle for self-determination and democratic ideas as well. At this point, Hitler was working for his part on the reordering of Europe. Germany, Italy, and Japan signed the September 1940 Three Power Pact of mutual aid, and henceforth would be known as the Axis powers. Europe was also being redrawn at this time, much of it coming under the domination of a greater Germany, as it was called but also allies were being paid off. In the Vienna award of 1940, for instance, Hitler's revisionist ally Hungary recovered lost territories, irredenta, the bulk of Transylvania in particular from neighboring Romania.

Hitler was ready to reverse tact again with an attack upon his own ally, the Soviet Union—so-called Operation Barbarossa. As Hitler now shifted to continue to pursue his ideological long-term goals rather than giving primacy to pragmatism in a short-term approach. Hitler's attack upon his ally was delayed by the need to assist Mussolini in a failed invasion of Greece in October of 1940. The attack itself, against the Soviet Union, began on June 22, 1941, very close in fact to the anniversary of the Napoleonic armies advancing against Tsarist Russia back in 1812. German armies, allied with Romania, Italy, Slovakia, Hungary, and Finland, now soon overran great areas of the Soviet Union. Behind the lines, in line with Hitler's hateful ideology, the Nazi's set about organizing a program of mass murder against the Jewish populations of eastern Europe, men, women and children—what was later given even more systematic form as the "Final Solution" as the Nazis styled it in all of its murderous impact of genocide. Amidst the Holocaust, it's tremendously dramatic and indeed stirring in a human sense to see that there were individual diplomats who worked to save numbers of imperiled Jews in eastern Europe. Examples include Sweden's diplomat, Raoul Wallenberg, who saved Hungarian Jews and in Lithuania the Japanese consul, Chiune Sugihara, who likewise set about a mission of mercy and of salvation.

At the same time, the diplomacy that was pursued by two other institutions, the Vatican, the head of the Roman Catholic church, and the Red Cross in particular, are still being debated by historians because they pursued a traditional policy of neutrality and seeking to work behind the scenes rather than a full confrontation with the power of Nazi Germany in part because of fear of the consequences of retribution that might follow. The debate still continues to this very day.

The Nazi advance and surging into the Soviet Union was finally halted by a counter attack by Soviet forces in front of Moscow in the winter of 1941, and the Germans finally met an epic defeat at Stalingrad in early 1943 after which the tide began to turn. The Soviets began to drive the Germans back. The very invasion of the Soviet Union by its ally, Nazi Germany, now changed the complexion of the struggle in decisive ways and allowed the Western democracies and the Soviet Union to ally in their common interests albeit this would be likewise ideologically a problematic mixture. Great Britain and the Soviet Union allied with one another in July of 1941 when Churchill had heard the news of the attack by Nazi Germany on the Soviet Union. He had said that if Hitler invaded Hell, he would find good things to say about the Devil in Parliament. In this sphere, Churchill—an intense anti-Communist, now set about solidifying a union with the Soviet Union. The United States began shipments of materials to the Soviet Union as it had to Great Britain as well.

The Soviet Neutrality Pact with Japan of April 1941 now saved the Soviets from war on both fronts because Japan was setting about its own program at the time. On December 7, 1941, a date that will live in infamy, Japan attacked the United States at Pearl Harbor. Showing solidarity with this attack, both Germany and Italy soon declared war on the United States on December 11. Hitler's motive in all of this was to tie Japan into the conflict, and it's been called one of his greatest mistakes of the war. Some historians argue, in fact, that it's not clear that he had many other options. Hitler himself was convinced that the United States was going to go to war against Germany in the near future anyhow, and he sought to gain, as it were, the moral advantage, a strange consideration, in terms of being the one who had the initiative by declaring war first. So, the United States now was involved in the European War, allied with Great Britain and the Soviet Union.

Churchill celebrated a "special relationship," as he called it, between the United States and Great Britain. He himself was a sign of this "special relationship" one might joke because he himself was of mixed American and British parentage. There's a story that Churchill actually denied that on a visit to the United States to meet with Roosevelt soon afterwards he had taken a bath preparatory to this meeting, and Roosevelt had entered the room while he was rising from his bath in all of his nakedness. As Roosevelt was about to retreat politely, Churchill had instead announced, dropping his towel, that the Prime Minister of Great Britain has nothing to hide from his friend the president of the United States—no secrets. This was a story that he didn't admit to, but it gets repeated nonetheless because it's symbolic of that "special relationship" between Great Britain and the United States. For its part, the image of the Soviet Union was improved in the United States and Stalin even hailed as "Uncle Joe," a bluff but ultimately honest leader of the Soviets. The reality, of course, was that he was one of the greatest mass murderers in history.

British policy, for its part, remained more cautious toward the Soviets than the American enthusiastic approach. Churchill worried about Soviet motives even as he encouraged this relationship. Stalin, for his part, had an urgent demand, and that was the opening of a second front to the west. To reassure his allies, Stalin also at this time dissolved the Comintern, which had encouraged revolution worldwide in May of 1943. There was also another would be ally, and that was General Charles de Gaulle, who in London was organizing the Free French movement as a way, as it were, of salvaging morally something from the collapse that France had experienced at the start of the war.

Let's turn now to examine crucial diplomatic conferences that were taking place even as the war raged between allies, not between the warring sides. This would be a fight to the finish. Diplomacy, however, now even as war raged came into play as coalition diplomacy—the problematic question of how to coordinate alliances. This was negotiated at conferences and summit meetings, so-called because they brought together top leaders. In January of 1942, the Washington Pact committed 26 "united nations" as they were called—and this is the origin in fact of the institution of the United Nations later in an extended sense—that were associated with the Allies and promised not to make a separate peace with the Axis. After earlier meetings, Roosevelt and Churchill met in January of 1943 at the Casablanca Conference and there agreed once again on a fight to the finish by demanding Germany unconditionally surrender rather than proposing terms.

At the November to December 1943 Teheran Conference in what today is Iran, Stalin, Roosevelt, and Churchill—who came to be called "The Big Three"—met together for the first time. This is truly personal diplomacy. Stalin's insistent, constant calls for the opening of a second front were finally met with a decision to prepare an invasion of northern France not to pursue Churchill's southern strategy, which was to invade through southern Europe, the soft under belly, as it was called, of the continent, which would have been much more in line with the traditional British off-show balancer approach of peripheral attacks upon a continental enemy. A secret agreement, moreover, also agreed at the time that Russia and Poland were to be shifted westward, their frontiers moved at Germany's cost. Stalin, in essence, was very firm about demanding being able to keep his gains in eastern Europe. Roosevelt and Churchill, though perhaps they might have wanted to resist, worried about Stalin perhaps making a separate peace with Hitler if their alliance was not solidified.

Roosevelt managed also to win agreement to setting up an international organization that he hoped might redeem some of the flaws of the League of Nations and be more effective in its international role. Churchill, who was anxious about Stalin's mysterious thought processes, then flew personally to Moscow in a strange sort of meeting in October of 1944 and there concluded the so-called Percentages Agreement. This was probably not Churchill's finest hour. This strange encounter between Stalin and Churchill established spheres of influence in the Balkans.

Now, this is very much something that ran against Wilsonian notions of open diplomacy. Scrawled on a scrap of paper, they agreed different percentages of influence in different parts of this contested part of Europe. The Soviets were to have the most influence in Romania and Bulgaria, the British in Greece, and equal influence in Yugoslavia and Hungary. This in and of itself didn't have much practical effect. It's not even clear what percentages of influence would have meant in practice, but it does speak volumes about the reversion sometimes to an earlier kind of diplomacy, earlier conventions in even this stage.

Events on the ground could also overturn diplomatic agreements. Dramatic events were soon unfolding in the West as the United States and British forces launched the dramatic Normandy invasion on June 6, 1944, opening the western front. Polish and Russian relations meanwhile also deteriorated over revelations of the Katyn Massacre where Stalin's secret police had executed great numbers of Polish officers, the very elite of Polish patriotism; and also the failed Warsaw uprising in August of 1944 when Polish underground fighters had risen up and Soviet forces that were nearing Warsaw halted their advance and didn't come to their aid while the Nazis wiped them out. All of this produced much bad blood between the Poles and the Soviets.

Wartime negotiations then climaxed at the famous Yalta Conference in the Crimea—the location of the Crimean War that we had talked about in a lecture earlier in our course. When Stalin, Churchill, and Roosevelt—who was already very seriously ill and approaching his death—met in February of 1945, this was the most important of the wartime summit meetings. The allies had by now reached Germany's borders. The noose was tightening around Hitler's regime, and the main issue at this conference concerned Poland. Poland was to gain new territories. It received German areas that were carved off, Silesia, Pomerania, and most of East Prussia, and it also agreed as a conference on establishing zones of occupation in Germany. Stalin agreed in turn to enter the war against Japan in the near future.

Roosevelt continued to press his plan for a United Nations and got Stalin's agreement to these further projects. The leaders together signed the so-called Declaration on Liberated Europe, which promised national sovereignty and democracy for the future. Stalin, for his part, agreed to free elections in Poland, a promise that wouldn't be honored. The French were not invited to negotiate at this conference but did receive an occupation zone in Germany at Churchill's urging. Churchill's logic was that in a future balance of power it would be very useful to have the French aboard, as it were, on one's own side.

Roosevelt announced afterwards in a very Wilsonian tone—it's as if Wilson were speaking through him, that this conference, Yalta, had meant the end of spheres of influence and the end of the balance of power. Very quickly, events were to reveal that this prediction was not valid. For their part, many eastern Europeans at the time and to this day continue to see Yalta as emblematic of how their part of the world was consigned to the Soviet sphere. Indeed, some have viewed it as a sign of Western betrayal reminiscent of the Munich conference.

Other scholars, by contrast, respond that Yalta in some sense was the best that could be realistically achieved at the time given that the Red Army had already established possession of much of eastern Europe. Tacitly, this was clear—eastern Europe was left to Stalin who would insist on friendly governments, whatever promises he had made about democracy or self-determination.

We come to the end of the war. The trap closed on Germany and its allies. Mussolini was overthrown, and in September of 1943, Italy changed sides. Senior Nazis sought to negotiate behind Hitler's back but were turned down. When Roosevelt died in April of 1945, Hitler hoped in vain looking back to the history of Frederick the Great that there might be some repetition of the "Miracle of the House of Brandenburg" as in 1762 when a death of another monarch had saved Prussia. That was not to happen, and in April of 1945 Hitler took the coward's way out by killing himself in his bunker beneath Berlin.

On May 8, Germany's total surrender came into effect. Half a world away, the United States dropped two atomic bombs on Japan in August of 1945, and the Soviets declared war. Japan surrendered in September of 1945. In the wake of immense destruction and suffering, Europeans now in a continent in ruins awaited a new peace, but it would be one that would be determined largely from outside. The aftermath and future plans it involved we will examine in our next lecture.

Lecture Thirty-One
Aftermath and Peace Plans

Scope:

This lecture devotes special attention to the immediate aftermath of World War II from 1945 to 1946. No final and comprehensive settlement was worked out as had been the case in Paris in 1919 after World War I, as the victorious alliance, which had already experienced earlier strains, began to drift apart. We trace the outlines of the founding of the United Nations as a successor to the failed League of Nations; the results of the Potsdam Conference held in defeated Germany by the United States, Great Britain, and the Soviet Union; Stalin's reimposition of harsh personal control; and growing tensions between the victorious powers.

Outline

I. The aftermath of World War II.

   A. With the end of World War II in May 1945, Europe was left devastated.

   B. World War II had emphatically proved the end of European global supremacy, already indicated in World War I.

   C. Now, Europeans witnessed the beginning of their continent's division into two blocs, western and eastern, both under the patronage of outside powers that now in practice became European powers.

      1. The Western Bloc would be led by the United States, which now dramatically changed earlier patterns of its involvement in foreign affairs.

      2. The Eastern Bloc was dominated by the Soviet Union, a Eurasian power, inheriting the ambitions of the earlier Russian Empire.

   D. Europe's peoples were marked by displacement; some 30 million refugees lost their homes and around 14 million Germans fled the East.

   E. The "victor powers" were the Soviet Union, the United States, and Great Britain.

F. The Soviet Union was weakened internally, but it also dramatically expanded its territorial control.

    1. The Soviet Union had lost 20 million in the war; another estimated 20 million fell victim to Stalin's terror.

    2. Stalin was left in control of eastern Europe, dominating conquered countries, while the Soviet Union absorbed the Baltic states, eastern Poland, and northern East Prussia (Kaliningrad).

    3. Stalin declared to Yugoslav allies in the spring of 1945: "This war is not like the wars of the past; whoever controls a territory will impose his own social system on it, as far as his army can reach. It cannot be otherwise."

    4. Stalin joked in a brutal Realist fashion about those lacking military power: "The pope? How many divisions does the pope have?"

    5. Even while the war was still going on, Communist regimes were being established in occupied countries.

    6. The key sensitive case was Poland, where Soviets sponsored the Lublin government.

    7. Even in the West, Communist parties forged ahead, gaining a quarter of the vote in French elections in 1945.

G. The United States ended the war with vast power from its mobilization, comprising almost half of world production.

    1. There was no clear U.S. policy vision for Europe—in fact, Roosevelt had assured Stalin at Yalta of a quick American withdrawal.

    2. American leaders had a general intention to create structures for a future liberal political and economic order (for example, the 1944 Bretton Woods Agreement, which set up the General Agreement on Tariffs and Trade, the World Bank, and the International Monetary Fund).

    3. Roosevelt withdrew agreement on the severe Morgenthau Plan (for a deindustrialized Germany) in 1944.

    4. Upon Roosevelt's death in April 1945, he was succeeded by Harry Truman (1884–1972).

H. Great Britain was the weakest of the three victors.

    1. The reality of this relative decline sunk in over a long period.

    2. Churchill's realism and suspicion of Stalin were active throughout the war, reflected in the strategies he had pressed.

I. No comprehensive peace conference took place, as after World War I.

    1. The alliance soon dissolved.

    2. By default, the first postwar years and their improvisation set the stage for a new bipolar conflict.

II. The United Nations.

    A. The plan was a cornerstone of Roosevelt's coalition diplomacy during the war.

    B. The phrase "United Nations" originally signified the alliance against the Axis Powers.

        1. Twenty-six states signed the January 1942 Declaration by United Nations.

        2. The August–October 1944 Dumbarton Oaks conference discussed plans with representatives of the Big Three and China (together, the Big Four).

        3. Following the structure of the League of Nations, the Big Four were to make up a Security Council with a larger General Assembly.

        4. Frictions emerged as the Soviet Union demanded that all its 16 republics receive separate seats in the General Assembly and total veto rights for permanent Security Council members.

        5. At the Yalta Conference in February 1945, the Soviets agreed to three seats and limited vetoes.

    C. The Conference of San Francisco convened on April 25, 1945.

        1. The United Nations Charter was signed by 50 states on June 26, 1945.

        2. In a dramatic shift in diplomatic tradition, French representatives had to battle for parity of status for the French language alongside English.

        3. The United Nations (UN) absorbed functions and some organization of the League of Nations, which held its last meeting in April 1946 before dissolving.

4. It instituted a General Assembly and a Security Council with five permanent members (with a total of 11 members and later, 15 members, including rotating members) and an International Court of Justice at The Hague in the Netherlands.
5. In 1947, an agreement with the United States set the location of UN headquarters in New York City.
6. Nazi atrocities prompted efforts to codify human rights, as in the 1948 Universal Declaration of Human Rights—a document that shows the cumulative nature of human rights diplomacy—and the Genocide Convention of 1948.
7. International law on wartime treatment of prisoners and civilians was elaborated in the 1949 Geneva Conventions.

III. The Potsdam Conference (July–August 1945).
   A. The last summit meeting of the Allies took place 10 weeks after the German surrender, while the war with Japan continued.
   B. Stalin, Truman, and Churchill met at a hunting lodge outside shattered Berlin.
      1. During the conference, elections in Great Britain replaced Churchill with the Labour Party's Clement Attlee (1883–1967).
      2. Truman informed Stalin of the new atomic bomb.
   C. The conference established a provisional settlement for Germany—now divided into four zones of occupation (United States, Britain, France, and the Soviet Union)—and placed Berlin under four-power control, although deep inside the Soviet zone.
      1. The conference determined policy in the zones of occupation (denazify, demilitarize, and democratize), left reparations policy up to individual zones, and created an Allied Control Council.
      2. The conference also agreed on the redrawn German eastern border, validating the expulsions of Germans as a "population transfer."
   D. It resolved that a Council of Foreign Ministers would prepare final peace treaties.

E. After the Potsdam Conference, Allied actions continued to shape occupied Germany.

    1. The Nuremberg Trials began in November 1945, lasting a year and publicizing Nazi crimes against humanity.

    2. The industrial Saar region was split off in 1947 as an autonomous area under French control but then was returned in 1957.

    3. In March 1947, the Allied Control Council abolished Prussia, once a Great Power.

IV. The Paris Peace Treaties of 1947.

    A. The Council of Foreign Ministers convened in Paris on July 29, 1946, and signed treaties with Germany's five allies (Finland, Italy, Hungary, Bulgaria, and Romania) on February 10, 1947.

    B. The Soviet Union insisted on a treaty with Finland, barring it from treaties directed against the Soviet Union (coining the term "Finlandization," a forced neutrality).

    C. No general settlement followed for Germany, which thus became a power vacuum.

V. Stalin reimposes control.

    A. Stalin professed his need for security, but it all depended on how that security was defined.

        1. This need appeared to reflect a primacy of domestic politics.

        2. After the traumatic war and wartime promises of liberalization, Stalin aimed to reassert his personal control.

        3. His precise intentions remain mysterious.

    B. Within the Soviet Union, "punished peoples" accused of disloyalty (including the Chechens) were deported.

    C. Stalin insisted that the Western allies agree to forced repatriations; Cossacks returned to the Soviet Union by Great Britain were executed.

    D. Liberated Soviet prisoners of war were sent directly to Gulag camps.

    E. Deportations from the Baltics continued and a decade-long Baltic Forest War raged.

F. Stalin's Five Year Plan introduced in early 1946 focused on industrialization and military power.

VI. Growing tensions.

    A. Tensions grew with the Soviet occupation of eastern European countries and the breach of Yalta promises.

        1. On May 11, 1945, just after German surrender, Truman halted Lend-Lease aid.

        2. Previously, on April 23, 1945, Truman dressed down Foreign Minister Molotov for not respecting Yalta Agreements.

    B. In March 1946 the Soviets dragged out the promised evacuation of Iran until pressed by the United States.

    C. In July 1946 the Soviets refused the economic union of the German occupation zones as agreed at Potsdam.

    D. Free elections in Poland promised by Stalin were postponed.

    E. In the Balkans, civil war in Greece between royalist and communist forces appeared to threaten increased Soviet influence.

    F. The Soviets pressured Turkey over the Turkish Straits and bases.

    G. George F. Kennan (1904–2005), a diplomat at the American embassy in Moscow, sent his famed "Long Telegram" of February 22, 1946.

        1. This classical Realist addressed "sources of Soviet conduct" as a product of longer-term Russian history.

        2. He outlined "containment," which became U.S. policy by 1948.

VII. The "Iron Curtain" speech.

    A. Out of office, Churchill gave a historic commencement address on March 5, 1946, in Fulton, Missouri.

        1. He announced that an "iron curtain" had descended across Europe "from Stettin … to Trieste," sundering an older cultural unity.

        2. The solution lay in solidarity and, especially, an Anglo-American "special relationship."

        3. Stalin denounced the speech, and the initial public reaction in the United States was poor.

B. Later that year, Churchill urged the formation of a United States of Europe in a speech in Zurich, alongside a Britain with renewed imperial strengths.

C. Spring 1946 was a turning point, ushering in a new period and a slow recognition of the altered international scene for Europe.

Essential Reading:

Henry Kissinger, *Diplomacy*, pp. 423–45.

Supplementary Reading:

Paul Kennedy, *The Rise and Fall of the Great Powers*, pp. 347–95.

Questions to Consider:

1. What advantages did the newly founded United Nations have over the League of Nations?

2. If there had been a peace congress in 1945, as at Vienna in 1815 or Paris in 1919, could a different outcome have been crafted?

Lecture Thirty-One—Transcript
Aftermath and Peace Plans

In this lecture, we will be considering the immediate aftermath of World War II and the peace plans that were abroad at the time. In our previous lecture, we examined the diplomatic dimensions of World War II. In this lecture, we will devote very special attention and a close focus to the immediate aftermath, 1945–1946 and the things that were distinctive about this aftermath of the World War as opposed to what had happened after World War I. No final and comprehensive settlement was worked out, as had been the case in Paris in 1919 when the victorious alliance now, which had already experienced earlier strains during World War II, drifted apart.

We trace in this lecture also the outlines of the founding of the United Nations as a successor to the earlier failed institution of the League of Nations. We look at the results of the Potsdam Conference held in defeated Germany by the United States, Great Britain, and the Soviet Union. We examine aspects of Stalin's reimposition of harsh personal control, his new course in foreign policy as well, and growing tensions as a result between the victorious powers.

With the end of World War II in May of 1945, Europe was left devastated with great parts of the continent in ruins. World War II also had implications that would take more time to really sink in in this devastated and rubble-strewn aftermath. World War II had emphatically proved the end of European global supremacy. This already had been indicated or presaged at the time of World War I when there arose superpowers on either side, but now in earnest this was becoming ever more clearly in focus. Now, Europeans witnessed the beginning of their continent's division into two blocs, a Western Bloc and an Eastern Bloc, both under the patronage of an outside power, what is sometimes called a flanking power on either side, which now in practice became European powers—both the United States and the Soviet Union, which had identities distinct and separate from those of Europe obviously as well for all that they now would function as European powers. The Western Bloc would be led by the United States, which now dramatically changed earlier patterns of its involvement in foreign affairs. You'll recall the default mode of trying to stay away from the tangled and entangling affairs of the old world of Europe.

In some sense there's a very fascinating historical parallel that one might point to here. Just as Great Britain around 1900 was beginning to move out of its splendid isolation, so the force of circumstances would slowly convince American policymakers likewise that they needed to craft a new approach to Europe. For its part to the east, the Eastern Bloc was dominated by the Soviet Union, a vast Eurasian power that inherited the ambitions and some earlier traditions of the earlier Russian Empire but now also with a distinctive ideological stamp of Communism. Europe's peoples were marked by tremendous displacement, the uprooting and homeless that left some 30 million refugees losing their homes. In the process of the redrawing of the map in eastern Europe, some 14 million Germans fled places where in many cases their families had lived for centuries.

The "victor powers" were now the Soviet Union, the United States, and Great Britain. They were to dispose of the future. The Soviet Union itself, as a result of the battering of World War II and the millions of casualties that the Soviet Union had taken as a result of the war, was weakened internally but also dramatically expanded in terms of its territorial control and reach in both direct and indirect control as a result of the war. The Soviet Union had lost 20 million as a result of the war. It's also the case that Stalin's terror took a toll of an estimated 20 million in addition—so, one just needs to imagine the searing results of this for the Russians and the other people of the Soviet Union, both internal terror as well as the terror of war.

Stalin for his part was now left in control of Eastern Europe, dominating conquered countries, while the Soviet Union continued its absorption of the Baltic states to which it now added eastern Poland and northeast Prussia, an area that still today is part of the Russian state, the so-called "Exclave" or non-contiguous territory of Kaliningrad on the Baltic Coast separated from the rest of Russia by other countries.

Stalin declared to Yugoslav allies in the spring of 1945 in really ringing tones that are significant of how he viewed this new stage in foreign policy and international politics, that "This war is not like the wars of the past; whoever controls a territory will impose his own social system on it, as far as his army can reach. It cannot be otherwise." There was precious little here in terms of concert or international cooperation. The notion was that even the peace would in some sense be a continuation of ideological conflict, your own social system imposed on others by other means. Stalin also revealed the brutal nature of his worldview by laughing at or joking at those who lacked military power. In this sense Stalin was showing a brutal Realist side to himself. He at one point when someone had mentioned the moral authority of the pope joked and answered, "The pope? How many divisions does the pope have?"

As it would turn out, in fact, moral power—or moral suasion or influence—does actually figure in foreign affairs as we have seen before in this course and we'll have occasion to see again. In this sense, Stalin's brutal view was probably such that it might blind him to other factors at work in human affairs. Even while the war was still going on and the Red Army had occupied parts of eastern Europe, Communist regimes were being established in those occupied countries. An especially key sensitive case in this regard was Poland. Poland had been the occasion of World War II breaking out. It had been divided by the Nazis and the Soviets in their strange symbiotic partnership; the Soviets for their part now even though they had promised to hold representative elections at some point sponsored a government, which was communist in orientation and owed its loyalties to Stalin's regime, the so-called Lublin Polish government after the city, Lublin, where it was centered.

Even in the West, in countries outside of what Stalin called the reach of his armies, Communist parties were enjoying some really remarkable political successes in part because of the prestige that they had won by opposing the Nazis. Of course, Communists had earlier been allied with the Nazis, but once the invasion of the Soviet Union took place, they were again implacable foes. An example of this new stature was the fact that in French elections in 1945 the French Communist party won an impressive quarter of the vote. Similar results were being scored in some other Western European countries.

For its part, the United States had ended the war with vast accretions of power from its mobilization and the revving up of its industrial energies so that by the end of the war the United States accounted for almost half of world production. We have mentioned the default mode of American foreign policy of seeking to avoid entangling affairs; indeed there was no clear U.S. policy vision for Europe at this time. In fact, in line with that default mode, President Roosevelt had at one point assured Stalin at the Yalta Conference that America intended a quick withdrawal across the Atlantic once the war had been brought to a successful conclusion. American leaders for their part did have some plans, and these involved a general intention to create structures that would give institutional form to a future liberal, political and economic order.

An example of this was the 1944 Bretton Woods Agreement, which set up institutions that are of import to this very day—the General Agreement on Tariffs and Trade, the World Bank, and the International Monetary Fund—as key institutions of a future economic order. Roosevelt, for his part, withdrew earlier agreements that had been advanced on a very severe plan for what would happen to Germany after the war. This was the so-called Morgenthau Plan, which had been created by one of his subordinates, Morgenthau that foresaw a deindustrialized Germany, a Germany broken down into subsidiary parts, which would never again represent a threat even in some future stage. This agreement or initial sympathy for the plan was withdrawn in 1944 because it became clear that it would be necessary just out of self-interest in terms of the burden of looking after masses of people at the center of the continent to somehow revive some more modern conception for a future Germany. When Roosevelt died in April of 1945, he was succeeded by his vice president, Harry Truman, who initiated a quite different and bluffer approach to international politics than the in many ways more aristocratic Roosevelt had championed in his time.

Great Britain, for its part, was the weakest of the three victor powers. It was weaker by orders of magnitude. In some sense, the cost of standing alone and of resisting Nazi Germany had gone far to bankrupt the earlier supreme power of the British Empire. It would take a long time for the reality of this relative decline on the part of British power to really sink in for British policymakers. Churchill's realism and his suspicion of Stalin's deeper motives and future plans had been active throughout the war. This had been reflected in the strategies that Churchill had not with great success, as it turns out, pressed—strategies like trying to approach Europe from the south and this would have had in fact the subsidiary or secondary result of bringing Western allied armies deeper into central or eastern Europe than turned out to be the case. Churchill was pursuing that traditional strategy of Britain as an off-shore balancer and aimed in this sense to be true to those earlier traditions and to meet some of his anxieties of his earlier anti-Communism.

The alliance between these victor powers soon was dissolving, and by default—and this was of crucial importance—this is why we are looking so closely at 1945 and 1946, these first post-war years and the sort of improvisation they saw really set the stage for a new bipolar conflict, which pitted one pole against another pole, the Eastern Bloc against the Western Bloc.

Let's first of all, however, look at some of the vast hopes that were vested in the United Nations. The plan for the United Nations as a new institution was a cornerstone of Roosevelt's coalition diplomacy during the war itself, and in a way that really parallels Woodrow Wilson's approach to his beloved project, the League of Nations, just as Wilson had so Roosevelt too was willing to overlook much and too, as it were, put to the side some key problems or conflicts that were even arising during the war itself hoping that the future institution would be a "clearinghouse" for those problems and resolve them if only the structures could be put in place now.

The phrase itself, "United Nations," actually originally signified the alliance against the Axis. It was identified closely with the victor powers, the 26 states that signed that declaration by the United Nations of January 1942. Planning continued during the war itself. In the August to October 1944 Dumbarton Oaks Conference plans were discussed with representatives of the Big Three, including China, together making up the Big Four, who would really be sort of the steering committee for this further elaboration of plans. In many ways, following the structure and some of the traditions established by the League of Nations that after all had scored some success in its time, the Big Four set up the project or the institutional flowchart of a Security Council which would play its roll as a sort of steering committee with a larger General Assembly along more representative lines giving the United Nations its representative character. Frictions emerged very quickly on key issues that involved these questions of structure. The Soviet Union demanded that all 16 of its separate constituent republics be given separate seats in the General Assembly. This would have given a lot of votes to the Soviet Union, which otherwise would have been represented by one vote. The Soviets also demanded total veto rights for permanent Security Council members, meaning themselves, which would have simply allowed them to dispose as they willed of the decisions that were being made there. At the Yalta Conference that we had already mentioned earlier in February of 1945, the Soviets under Stalin's leadership scaled down some of these demands and agreed to only having three seats in the General Assembly. That's a fact that some people may not know about the Soviet Union—that it held three seats in the General Assembly, and more limited vetoes in the Security Council, which it would use with quite some frequency in the years to come.

The Conference of San Francisco, which was convened on April 25, 1945, really represented the founding then of this institution that had been so long in the planning. The United Nations Charter was signed by 50 states on June 26, 1945, launching the institution. In a dramatic shift in diplomatic tradition, French representatives had to battle for the parity of status for the French language alongside English, and this really showed to the French representatives a bitter sign of shifting cultural power as well.

The United Nations absorbed many of the functions and some of the organization of the league, which in fact had continued formally to exist throughout World War II. The league held its final formal meeting in April of 1946 and then dissolved itself. The chairman let out the hopeful and optimistic cry, the League of Nations is dead—long live the United Nations. The United Nations instituted a General Assembly, and a Security Council with five permanent members, a total of 11 later expanded to 15 members, some of them rotating besides those of the permanent members; and also an International Court of Justice, which was to sit at the Hague in the Netherlands.

In 1947, an agreement with the United States defined the special status of the territory of the United Nations' headquarters in New York. The imposing building there was finished in 1951–1952 and can be toured to this very day.

Nazi atrocities prompted efforts to codify human rights as well. We have talked about this at stages as a crucial part of the Western and European tradition of diplomacy. This was the aim of the 1948 Universal Declaration of Human Rights, which was a document that really spoke volumes about the cumulative nature of human rights diplomacy because in some sense it was a culminating collection of earlier ideas and projects on what human rights should be guaranteed and how and now were given formal status. Whether they would be honored more in the practice or the breach would be a later question. Similarly the Genocide Convention of 1948 wrote a new page in international law by obligating signatory states to step up against the destruction of a group in whole or in part as genocide was defined by that convention—a new international obligation in a sense for intervention. International law on wartime treatment of prisoners and civilians was also elaborated and given fuller explanation and institutionalization in the 1949 Geneva Conventions—this impulse to advance human rights had everything to do with the immensity of suffering and the atrocities of World War II.

Let's turn now to examine a crucial post-war conference, the Potsdam Conference, July to August of 1945. It was post-war in the sense that it took place when the war against Germany had ended while the war with Japan was still continuing. This last summit meeting of the Allies, the last meeting of the main leaders, took place 10 weeks after the German surrender. Stalin, Truman—who had replaced Roosevelt—and Churchill met at a hunting lodge that earlier had been occupied by Kaiser Wilhelm II of the German Empire outside shattered Berlin in the royal complex at Potsdam. You can actually tour the facility that's been preserved. It seems frozen in time almost with the negotiating table still there, the chairs intact, and the flags—really sort of a remarkable monument, as it were, to this conference. This conference, by the way, showed just how much domestic change has an impact on foreign relations because during the conference elections in Great Britain replaced Churchill, whose leadership had been so valuable, with a new leader, the Labour Party's Prime Minister, Clement Attlee. Truman, for his part, used this conference to inform Stalin of the fact that the Americans had acquired a devastating new weapon, the atomic bomb. Stalin seemed completely unphased. He said, good for you essentially. There were some suggestions that Stalin may have known a good deal more about the atomic bomb project than Truman did at the time given the extensive nature of espionage at the time.

The conference itself established crucially a provisional settlement for Germany for now, which would be divided into four zones of occupation. Berlin itself although deep inside the Soviet zone, also a mirror of the larger Germany by being divided into four zones of occupation, of the western powers, the United States, Britain and France—France was included at the insistence of the Western allies and on the other hand the Soviets. The conference also determined policy in the zones of occupation of Germany. It involved the three "d's"—denazification, demilitarization, and the third one doesn't really work quite as well for purposes of symmetry—democratization. This was to be a fundamental remaking of Germany's domestic politics. What it would look like in practice was left an open question because each of the occupying powers was charged with advancing this agenda on their own. Reparations policy was also left up to the individual zones, and an Allied Control Council was created to coordinate over all.

The conference also agreed to changes that would have enormous significance for millions of people. The conference re-drew or agreed on the re-drawing of the German eastern border so that territories that were given to Poland or were assigned to the Soviet Union in the case of Kaliningrad, the northern part of East Prussia, were now given formal approval and the expulsions of Germans that were taking place at the time—what we would today call ethnic cleansing, was presented as "population transfer." In some sense, politicians look back to the tradition of the Treaty of Lausanne of 1923 in which Greek and Turkish populations had been allegedly in a humanitarian and organized way transferred or exchanged. The reality had been a far more brutal one. This was a dark hour in international politics of such population transfers being validated. It was also resolved that a Council of Foreign Ministers of the victorious powers, the Allies, would prepare final peace treaties with all of the defeated powers.

After the Potsdam Conference, Allied actions continued to shape occupied Germany. These included important events like the staging of the Nuremberg Trials. These began in November of 1945 and lasted a year. They were especially useful in publicizing Nazi crimes against humanity and documenting the horrific record that the Nazis had accrued over time. There were other changes as well that are less well known but were significant. The industrial Saar region in Western Germany was split off in 1947 as an autonomous area under French control. It later would be returned in 1957, and it might very well be a significant fact that it got returned avoiding irredenta or the longing for lost territories in the West at least.

In March of 1947, the Allied Control Council also did something, which marks in a course in which we've pursued continuities and parallels a new fact, a striking and startling innovation. In March of

1947, the Allied Control Council simply abolished formally in a legal sense Prussia. Prussia had in the united Germany still retained its identity as the strongest of the constituent parts of Germany. It had been a great power looking back to the earliest lectures of this course. Now, the Allied Control Council, which saw Prussian traditions of militarism as somehow feeding into the Nazi atrocities, a point of view that was disputed by many Germans who had identified with Prussia. The reality was that now this state ceased to exist; it doesn't get much more definitive than that in terms of breaks in the historical tradition.

Let's turn now to the peace treaties that were signed in the absence of a comprehensive settlement of the sort that one had seen in Paris in 1919. These were, again, treaties signed in Paris in 1947, but they did not include a comprehensive settlement or a settlement with defeated Germany. The Council of Foreign Ministers that had been established among the allies convened in Paris on July 29, 1946, and signed treaties with Germany's five defeated allies but not with Germany itself. These included the allied states of Finland, Italy, Hungary, Bulgaria, and Romania. These treaties were signed after negotiations in February of 1947. The Soviet Union in particular insisted, and this was a sign of its pressing for stability, for security as their slogan would have it. The Soviet Union insisted on a particular treaty with Finland, which banned it from adhering to treaties directed against the Soviet Union. In the aftermath, European political observers would coin the term "Finlandization" for this sort of forced neutrality. The way in which a state would suddenly find its foreign policy linked to that of a Great Power, its neighbor, without a more extensive freedom of maneuver or of action. Many Fins consider the notion of "Finlandization" a slur against a very complicated dilemma that their small country without the sort of magnitude of power of the Soviet Union faced in the shadow of a greater neighbor.

It needs to be hammered home again—no general settlement followed for Germany, which thus became a power vacuum in this context. Stalin for his part was reimposing control within his own Soviet sphere. Stalin again and again professed his need for security, but a lot depended on how that security was defined. In Stalin's case, that security looked an awful lot like expansion. This in part appeared to reflect this mania for an ever more expansive definition of security, something that we might subsume under the category of a primacy of domestic politics that we have talked about as one of these alternative debating positions in diplomatic history.

After the traumatic war and promises implicit or explicit made during wartime of liberalization to come, Stalin once the war was over aimed to energetically and ruthlessly reassert his personal control fearing any challenges to his post-war power and legitimacy. His intentions continue to be debated to this very day. Within the Soviet Union, the record was a brutal one. So-called "punished peoples" who were accused of disloyalty were deported in mass with massive losses—these included by the way the Chechens, who were a people in the Caucasus, whose drive for independence would be a phenomenon much seen in the headlines of our own times today. Stalin insisted that the Western allies also agree to forcibly repatriate those he considered to be his subjects who had not proven their loyalty to him. For instance, Cossacks, who had switched sides and had fought on the side of the Axis powers were returned to the Soviet Union by Britain and were executed en mass immediately after their return.

Liberated prisoners of war who had been Soviet soldiers but had come under German captivity were not brought home and honored as people who had sacrificed in the great patriotic war but instead were brought home and shipped immediately to the prison camps because Stalin suspected them of disloyalty. Deportations from the Baltic states had continued and continue now. A decade-long but almost unknown in the West guerilla war continued in the Baltic states of Lithuania, Latvia, and Estonia that had been incorporated into the Soviet Union, the so-called Baltic Forest War lasting into the 1950s and isolated fighters holding out even longer. Stalin's Five Year Plan, the new economic master plan for the Soviet Union, introduced in early 1946 focused both on heavy industrialization and military power. Stalin seemed to have very much in prospect the notion of a future looming confrontation with the capitalist world in line with his ideology.

So, let's examine next growing tensions that occurred at this period. On May 11, 1945, just after Germany surrendered, Truman ordered the Lend-Lease aid to the Soviet Union halted, and this was in line with his much bluffer and more confrontational stance toward the Soviet Union. Previously, in April of 1945 Truman had showed just how undiplomatic in one sense of the term he could be by actually dressing down Foreign Minister Molotov for not respecting Yalta agreements, and Molotov had been outraged and had explained, I've never been talked to like this. Truman just shot back by saying if you kept your promises, you wouldn't have to be talked to like this. For their part, in March of 1946 the Soviets dragged out a promised evacuation of Iran until the United States placed heavier pressure on them to do so. This was a sign of the beginnings of a breakdown of wartime understandings. In July of 1946, the Soviets also refused the notion of economic union of the German zones of occupation, east and west that already had been projected at Potsdam.

Crucially, given its symbolic significance, given the fact that Poland had been the reason the war had broken out in a sense, the free elections that Stalin had promised for Poland were repeatedly postponed. It didn't look good. In the Balkans, civil war in Greece had broken out between Royalist and Communist forces; that appeared so it seemed to Western observers to threaten increased Soviet influence there at a time when the Soviets were also pressuring Turkey that had managed diplomatically to remain neutral through World War II concerning its access to the Turkish Straits and with the demand for bases in Turkey perhaps as well. The American diplomat, as well as diplomatic historian, George F. Kennan, who at that time was a diplomat at the American embassy in Moscow analyzed what he saw as the trend of Soviet foreign policy and sent a famed "Long Telegram" back to Washington on February 22, 1946. This classical realist, as a diplomat and diplomatic historian addressed what he saw as the long-term "sources of Soviet conduct" and saw them as a product of longer-term Russian history, which had continuities with the Tsarist regime.

In one formula associated with Kennan, one needed to ask not just how the Bolsheviks had changed that older state of Russia, but also how Russia might have changed the Bolsheviks, maybe adding to their ideology some longer-term or older traditions of government as well as foreign policy. Kennan would outline a policy called "containment" of hemming in an expansionist power at whatever point it advanced, which we'll talk more about in later lectures, which would become American formal policy by 1948.

I want to close by talking about words, a ringing speech that made history, and that's the "Iron Curtain" Speech. Out of office, Churchill gave a historic commencement address on March 5, 1946 in Fulton,

Missouri at the express invitation of Truman. He announced at this speech that an "iron curtain" had descended across Europe "from Stettin in the [north] to Trieste in the [south]," sundering an older cultural unity of Europe and leaving Europe divided. As far as Churchill was concerned, the solution lay in solidarity, hanging together and especially an Anglo-American "special relationship." As an Anglo-American himself, he was an appropriate person to announce this new doctrine, but as someone who had negotiated the somewhat old-fashioned "Moscow Percentages" agreement during the war, he might not have been the ideal messenger.

Stalin, for his part, denounced the speech, and the initial public reaction in the United States was poor. Few people wanted to hear that a new confrontation was in the offing. Later that year, Churchill would add another element to his recipe for success. He urged the formation of a United States of Europe in a speech in Zurich, Switzerland alongside a Britain, which would stand off apart from the European continent with a renewed imperial power. Churchill's vision of British imperial power, however, was probably out of synch with the realities that now were being revealed. Spring of 1946 would be a turning point ushering in a new period and a slow recognition that a lot had changed in the international scene for Europe. That new reality, which was now dawning, was that of a Cold War, which we'll examine in our next lecture.

Lecture Thirty-Two
The Cold War Begins

Scope:

Earlier tensions and disagreements between the Soviet Union and both the United States and Great Britain now turned into a long-term standoff called the Cold War. This lecture examines Europe in the key years of 1946–1949, as the split between former allies widened, and explores the distinctive crisis diplomacy of the Cold War. Issues included the future of Poland and divided Germany and the civil war in Greece. After the 1947 announcement of the Truman Doctrine, American involvement in Europe extended to the Marshall Plan for economic recovery, the massive and dramatic airlift of supplies in the Berlin Crisis of 1948–1949 and support for the establishment of the Federal Republic of Germany formed out of the western zones of occupation.

Outline

I. Europe in the postwar years (1946–1949).

   A. Because of their crucial importance, we need to look in detail at these postwar years.

   B. Tensions between the Soviet Union and the United States, already present during the war, emerged more clearly in 1945 and 1946 and now took on substantial form.

      1. The Cold War would be a bipolar confrontation lasting some 45 years between two blocs led by the superpowers (earlier Great Powers but on a global scale).

      2. This confrontation was a contrast with the multipolar structure of the European classical balance of power of 1815–1914.

   C. The implications for a Europe struggling for recovery were existential.

      1. Rather than being an arbiter of the globe, Europe now became an arena for conflict and a prize.

      2. In this sense, Europe after 1945 bears a resemblance to Italy after 1494 or German lands after the Treaty of Westphalia.

       3. The abiding dilemma for Europeans would be how to be actors rather than merely acted upon.

  D. Diplomacy also changed under the impact of the bipolar conflict.

       1. Diplomats had to concentrate on managing crises rather than finding comprehensive solutions.

       2. Diplomacy also expanded to include public diplomacy, diplomacy directed at popular opinion through propaganda and culture.

II. Origins of the Cold War.

  A. The term "Cold War" signifies an intense conflict and a rivalry short of direct armed clashes (as opposed to proxy fights).

       1. The term was used first by American financier Bernard Baruch in 1947 and popularized by journalist Walter Lippmann.

       2. No summit meetings took place from 1945 to 1955 between the superpowers.

  B. Some historians argue that the Cold War's origins are to be found much earlier than 1945.

       1. They characterize the United States and Russia as expansive, continental powers with distinctive ideologies.

       2. Some see World War I and the contest between Wilson and Lenin as decisive.

  C. The Cold War lasted four decades after World War II and went through different phases.

       1. From the end of the war to 1946, crucial issues of the Cold War emerged.

       2. In 1947–1949, the Cold War division took shape.

       3. From 1950 to 1962, the Cold War was at its height.

       4. Tensions relaxed until they were renewed in 1979 (known as the "Little Cold War" or "Second Cold War").

       5. After a winding down of conflict beginning in 1985, the Cold War ended with the Soviet Union's fall in 1991.

III. The shifts of 1946–1947.

    A. Important shifts took place between 1946 and 1947.

        1. In 1946, the Soviets turned down an American project for international control of nuclear energy.

        2. Dean Acheson and other American leaders faced a changed perspective, recognizing an ideological conflict recalling the Crusades.

    B. Developments in Poland were key, given that its fate had started World War II.

        1. Although Stalin had promised free elections in Poland, they were postponed, and elections held in January 1947 were rigged.

        2. The result was a Communist-Socialist coalition and a Soviet general as defense minister.

        3. Poland became a Soviet satellite state, alarming the West.

    C. Britain discovered its involvement in the Greek Civil War and its aid to Turkey to be too costly; in February 1947 it informed the United States that it would cease military assistance to Greece and Turkey.

        1. The United States feared Soviet expansion of influence in the Mediterranean and the Middle East.

        2. Was this to be a reopening of the Eastern Question in a new form?

IV. Containment and its European implications.

    A. The British announcement of ceased military assistance led President Truman to a response that dramatically shifted American foreign policy traditions.

        1. On March 12, 1947, before a joint session of Congress, Truman articulated American support for nations resisting armed coercion.

        2. This message came to be known as the Truman Doctrine.

        3. American diplomat George Kennan's famous article in the July issue of *Foreign Affairs*, signed as "X," explained the strategy of containment, although Kennan later saw himself as misunderstood.

        4. Aid flowed, and by October 1949 the royalists had won in Greece.

B. Truman's declaration was coupled with a European Recovery Program (ERP) announced by Truman's new Secretary of State George C. Marshall (1880–1959) on June 5, 1947.

1. Renewed prosperity was seen as a guarantee against destabilization and Communist influence.

2. The aid was offered to all Europe, including states under Communist rule, but Stalin forced them to refuse.

3. The aid was distributed together rather than country by country; this encouraged European cooperation in the Organization of European Economic Cooperation (OEEC).

4. From 1948 to 1952, the plan delivered about $13 billion in aid, contrasting with the Soviet extraction of resources from its sphere.

5. Western European economies revived dramatically, and Communist parties were excluded from power in elections.

6. Stalin revived the Comintern in October 1947 as the Cominform.

V. The Prague Coup of 1948.

A. The Czech Communist Party took power in Prague in February 1948.

B. This event was catalytic among foreign observers, given the record of Czech democracy and appeasement in 1938.

C. In a tragic echo of the 1618 "defenestration of Prague," Foreign Minister Jan Masaryk fell from a window in a suspected murder.

D. The impact of this coup was to hurry Marshall Plan aid approval by the U.S. Congress (which passed in April 1948).

E. In March 1948, Great Britain, France, Belgium, the Netherlands, and Luxembourg signed an alliance, the Brussels Pact, as European defense efforts had been required by the United States as a counterpart to an American commitment.

F. The United States reinstated a peacetime conscription (draft) in 1948.

VI. The 1948–1949 Berlin Crisis and the division of Germany.

    A. The German Problem now took on a different form, divided by the superpowers.

        1. In a striking shift so soon after World War II, the defeated Germans were now reintegrated into the opposed blocs as allies.

        2. Although Germany was to be administered together, in practice the occupiers followed their own policies in their respective zones.

        3. Negotiations over the future of Germany yielded no concrete results.

        4. The British and U.S. zones (and later the French) were fused economically in 1947, and in June 1948 a common currency was introduced.

    B. The first major standoff of the Cold War came over the Berlin Crisis.

        1. On June 24, 1948, Soviet forces blocked access to Berlin, 100 miles within the Soviet zone.

        2. The Western Allies responded with the dramatic Berlin airlift to their sectors of the city.

        3. On May 12, 1949, Stalin lifted the blockade.

    C. On May 23, 1949, the Federal Republic of Germany was established in the West, with its capital in Bonn.

    D. In the Soviet zone, the German Democratic Republic was founded in October 1949.

    E. Both states claimed to be the "true" Germany.

    F. In the Federal Republic of Germany, the new chancellor Konrad Adenauer (1876–1967) launched an independent policy of adhering to the West.

VII. Tito's break.

    A. Within the Eastern Bloc, Yugoslavia under former partisan leader Josef Tito (1892–1980) steered a course increasingly independent of Stalin.

        1. Their break came out into the open in June 1948.

        2. Nationalism's continuing importance was revealed.

        3. The Cold War standoff prevented Stalin from intervening with force.

B. This showed that even in the bipolar division of Europe, there were exceptions and complexities.

VIII. The "Balance of Fear."

    A. The earlier American monopoly on atomic weapons ended with the Soviet explosion of an atomic bomb in August 1949.

    B. The result was a new dynamic: the "balance of fear" as each side now threatened the other with "mutually assured destruction" (MAD).

        1. This threat was also part of a global pattern as the Cold War expanded worldwide.

        2. China came under Communist control in October 1949 and allied with the Soviets in February 1950.

        3. The United Nations was increasingly immobilized by vetoes.

        4. The arms race grew intense and expensive.

        5. Europeans worried about what British historian Arnold Toynbee called "annihilation without representation."

        6. Some Europeans spoke of this conflict as a superpower condominium (a shared dominance over Europe), but other options were obscure.

IX. Debating the Cold War.

    A. Historians continue to debate the reasons for the Cold War.

        1. Contemporary analysis, today called the traditionalist view, argued that Stalin's intentions were key (although their precise nature is debated).

        2. In the 1960s and 1970s in the West, the revisionist school emphasized American motives—in particular economic imperatives, expansionism, and leadership—and viewed Stalin as a traditional statesman with limited goals.

        3. By the 1980s post revisionists saw the Cold War as almost inevitable due to the nature of the state system (bipolarity in place of the earlier balance of power) and the character of both superpowers.

    B. The Cold War was also a new dynamic, with fearsome weaponry of deterrence braking an all-out armed conflict.

C. For Europeans, 1949 had brought increasingly firm lines of division across their continent and posed complex questions about their fate.

D. Idealized images of alleged stability or perfect alliance solidarity are inaccurate.

Essential Reading:

Henry Kissinger, *Diplomacy*, pp. 446–72.

Supplementary Reading:

Reynolds, David. "The Origins of the Cold War: The European Dimension, 1944–1951," *The Historical Journal.*

Questions to Consider:

1. Could the Cold War have been avoided? If so, how?

2. Was the division of Germany inevitable? What were the other options?

Lecture Thirty-Two—Transcript
The Cold War Begins

In this lecture, we will be witnessing the opening of a new era in the diplomatic history of Europe that we have been following over this long, long stretch of time—the opening of the Cold War. In our previous lecture, we concentrated on the immediate aftermath of World War II. We had examined the hopes that then were raised for a durable sense of stability and something other than conflict on the European continent, but we had already also seen the rise of frictions and tensions. In this lecture, we will follow how those earlier tensions and disagreements between the Soviet Union on the one hand and the United States and Great Britain on the other now turned into a long-term standoff called the "Cold War." This lecture will examine Europe in the key opening years of that conflict, 1946–1949, as the split between these former allies widened, and we will explore the distinctive crisis diplomacy of the Cold War that evolved.

Issues included the future of Poland, the future of divided Germany, and the civil war in Greece. We will see how after the 1947 announcement of the Truman Doctrine a new phase in America's involvement in Europe opened, which extended to the proposal of the Marshall Plan for economic recovery on the continent. We will survey the massive and dramatic airlift of supplies in the Berlin Crisis of 1948–1949 and crucial support for the establishment of the Federal Republic of Germany, a democracy formed out of the western zones of occupation. Because of the crucial importance of this turn, we need to look in some detail at these post-war years in particular.

Tensions between the Soviet Union and the United States—which we have already indicated in earlier lectures—had been present in embryo in a sense during the war, not yet full-fledged but already there in their beginnings. These had emerged more clearly in 1945 and 1946, as we surveyed in our previous lecture, and now took on substantial form. They needed to be confronted. The Cold War would be a confrontation different than ones that we have surveyed in our earlier survey of the balance of power. This would be a bipolar confrontation pitting two powers, not a multiplicity of powers but two powers, against one another over the course of more than 45 years, two blocs led by the individual superpowers.

We might ask what is the definition of a superpower? Well, analysts continue to argue to this day about an adequate definition of a superpower. The very word "super" is meant to indicate the global scale, the larger scale of the might exercised by one of these powers that implicitly supersede the earlier Great Powers. We might think of them as Great Powers on a global scale in essence.

This bipolar confrontation was a stark contrast with the way in which European politics had been structured before. It was a stark contrast in particular with the multi-polar structure of that European classical balance of power, the middle part of our course, that had endured with obviously some problems but from 1815–1914 as a classical balance of power in structure. For Europe, as it struggled for recovery, the implications of this bipolar conflict were existential, and we need to stop for a moment to just take them aboard—what a profound shift this would be for a European continent and peoples that made up Europe who now understood their status and what it meant to be a European in these times quite differently than before. Where earlier Europe had been the arbiter of the globe—think of the state of European power around 1900—Europe now in a startling reversal instead became an arena for conflict and in some sense a prize of the conflict as well in the face-off of the Cold War.

There's a sense in which we have seen a phenomenon like this before. If you think all the way back to the very first lectures of our course, you will recall that Italy after 1494, after the disaster of invasions that followed one after the other by the new monarchies of Europe from the north, had gone from being at least to some extent a self-contained political world with all of its achievements and balance of power to being an arena for conflict. So too, Europe after 1945 bore a resemblance to that Italy after the disaster of 1494 from the start of our course. One might even venture another comparison to the German lands at the center of Europe after the Treaty of Westphalia in 1648 when the weakness of that part of Europe had been institutionalized as a power vacuum, which Great Powers could descend upon, could intervene in, according to the dictates of the balance of power.

Europe now felt a dramatic shift in its status, and as a result the abiding political dilemma in international politics for Europeans would be essentially this—how to be actors, how to be active agents rather than merely being acted upon from outside. With atomic weapons in particular, the existential stakes of being, as it were, the hostage of this Cold War situation, this confrontation, were especially acute. Diplomacy also changed under the impact, under the pressure, of this bipolar confrontation. Diplomats had now in particular to concentrate as a very important part of their job, their vocation, on managing crises rather than being able to find comprehensive solutions. Rather than being able to resolve once and for all some particular issue, management of these outstanding issues now came to the fore. Diplomacy also under the impact, I guess you could say, of the total nature of this confrontation, which was not just military, not just political, not just economic, but also cultural, social and ideological in nature. Diplomacy also expanded in the very sense of what it was that made up diplomacy. One now spoke increasingly of something that already had been in some sense presage but now came into its own—public diplomacy in which one tried to address vast audiences, not just the elites, not just the counterparts in the high world of diplomacy and diplomatic elites but rather populations at large, trying to affect popular opinion, public opinion through propaganda, culture and other routes of getting one's message, as it were, "over the heads" of the elite of the opposing side.

We first should consider the origins of the Cold War. The "Cold War" term itself has a history. What is a "Cold War?" A "Cold War" signifies intense conflict and existential rivalry, yes, but short of direct armed clashes, short of the all out confrontation in violent, immediate, active violence, which if it had taken place we might very well not be talking about today in this course. This would have been World War III and might very well have spelled the end of civilization. Now, the Cold War doesn't preclude the possibility of in more peripheral areas, or marginal areas, on the flanks there being proxy conflicts—that's to say struggles in which there are representatives of the opposing sides, but something short of that total intense sort of conflict that World War I and World War II had so obviously represented.

The term itself, the "Cold War," was used precisely in this period first by American financier and statesman Bernard Baruch in 1947 and had then been popularized by the writer and indeed the founding editor of the *New Republic,* Walter Lippmann. This was part of a public discourse about the change that people could see unfolding before them in this period; it was marked by icy relations between the superpowers. No summit meetings, none of these gatherings of the heads of state, took place from 1945–1955 in this particular icy period, and certainly there have been analysts of diplomacy who have questioned the utility or the efficacy of summit meetings as such. But the very absence of them putting that debate aside indicates something of the intensity of that ideological confrontation.

Some historians—and historians always love to do this, to point out that there's a past, there's a history involved here, there's a more remote antecedent that one always has to look to—argue that in fact the Cold War, even though it emerges into full bloom, as it were, in this period, actually has origins that are going to be found much earlier. Some historians point to the very identity and national self-understanding of the United States or of Russia in which case both countries, it's pointed out, are or have been in the past expansive, endowed with a certain dynamism that makes them move and expand territorially, continental powers above all pursuing this expansion with distinctive ideologies and a sense of themselves that's different and in some sense places them apart from the mainstream of European political tradition in this regard and the conviction that they are both exceptional.

Well, some historians don't go quite as far back as that to the founding, as it were, the deeper origins of these states and instead see the contest that took place during World War I between the visions of the future of someone like Woodrow Wilson in the case of the United States or someone like Lenin in the case of the Soviet Union as being already a premonition of the future clash of the Cold War. They sometimes posit World War I as a time in which people were being invited to make a choice. You could choose Wilson, or you could choose Lenin—very different visions of the future but ones that promised to break down and abolish the way traditional, international politics and diplomacy had been done.

It's sufficient to have mentioned these debates and to then consider that the Cold War was of remarkably long duration lasting four decades after World War II without thankfully ever tipping over into active conflict. In this time, and here we just want to, as it were, indicate the longer-term trajectory we will be following in some of our remaining lectures, it went through different phases. The Cold War was not monolithic throughout, always the same; it changed over time. From the end of World War II to 1946, as we already mentioned in our previous lecture, crucial issues of the Cold War emerged. They were in the process of appearing and really being taken aboard in ordinary consciousness. In 1947–1949, the period we are looking at in particular in this lecture, the Cold War division took shape in earnest, and the very fact that the name of the Cold War comes from this period speaks volumes. From 1950–1962 then, the Cold War was at its height some historians consider. After 1962— and this has much to do with the sort of brinksmanship of the Cuban Missile Crisis—tensions then relaxed for a period. But then they were renewed again in 1979 with the onset of what is sometimes called the "Little Cold War" or the "Second Cold War," a renewed period of revived intensity. Then, closer to our own times, after a winding down of conflict from 1985 in a fascinating process that we will explore in a later lecture, the Cold War then ended with the collapse of the Soviet Union in 1991.

Let's then having indicated this longer trajectory pull back and consider the shifts of 1946–1947 as a key moment as well. Important shifts were taking place. In 1946, the Soviets turned down emphatically an American project for international control of nuclear energy. Dean Atchison, Secretary of State Marshall, and other American leaders in this period faced a changed perspective—I mean they actually were changing their minds themselves about the approach of this new era in international relations. In the case of Atchison, he saw himself recognizing, or believed that he saw, an ideological conflict ahead that actually recalled a far earlier age, the Crusades, and their period of intensity except the issues now were not religious but ideological, secular issues in this regard. As we have been at pains to point out in recent lectures, developments in Poland, in particular, were key to registering shifts and the onset of the Cold War because Poland and its fate had been instrumental in the start of World War II. It was bound to be an important issue.

Although Stalin had promised free elections in Poland in earlier negotiations between the allies, these were postponed and postponed, and elections when they were finally held in Poland in January of 1947 were rigged and accompanied by intimidation of the opposition. The result, not surprisingly, of these elections was a Communist/Socialist coalition and a Soviet general as defense minister of Poland—how convenient. Poland became a Soviet satellite state in a process of absorption into the Soviet sphere of influence that alarmed the West. Britain, for its part, now made a discovery that was dismaying to those who still thought as Churchill did in terms of revived and revitalized imperial roles for Britain to play in the future. Britain now discovered what an immense cost had been demanded by its efforts in World War II, and there was a moment that brought all of this into focus. There would be later moments in this tragic, at least to the minds of contemporaries like Churchill, tragic development that we will survey later, but one instance here was of particular significance.

When Britain discovered that its involvement in the Greek civil war that had broken out in the aftermath of World War II and its aid to Turkey, which was coming under Soviet pressure was too costly—it simply couldn't be born by the more straightened resources of a Britain that now was scrambling to somehow put itself on to a peacetime footing. In February of 1947, in a communication that dismayed American policymakers because it struck them with such surprise, the British informed the United States that Britain would have to cease military assistance to Greece and Turkey in the near future. The United States for its part now feared that the result of a British withdrawal would be Soviet expansion of its influence in the Mediterranean and the Middle East. Given the background of the themes that we have already surveyed in this course, the anxiety is understandable that this might be a reopening of the Eastern Question in a new form: the Middle East and its future but now in the context of this ideological conflict not the classical balance of power of Europe in the 19th century.

We turn now to examine the response, which increasingly was crafted by Western policymakers: containment. We want to look in particular at its European implications. The British announcement led President Truman to a response that dramatically shifted many long-standing and deeply held, deeply embedded American foreign policy traditions. On March 12, 1947, before a joint session of Congress, Truman articulated American support for nations resisting armed coercion; this was directed in particular at the situation in Greece and Turkey. This message came to be known as the Truman Doctrine, and it needs to be noted in all fairness to Truman that this was not his name for the doctrine but rather one that came to be attached with it.

In the process, another very important intellectual contribution was given by that American diplomat George Kennan, who we already mentioned as someone who had been thinking through the sources of

Soviet conduct in this initial period of the Cold War. Kennan wrote an article that one might say really shifted history; it's not often the case that articles would have such a catalytic effect. In this case, Kennan's famous article in the July issue of *Foreign Affairs* of that year signed not by his own name but rather with a mysterious pseudonym "X" explained and outlined a strategy of containment. That was the application of counter pressure, in some sense a balancing in terms of balance of power, against an aggressive and expansionist ideological force like the Soviet Union. Kennan himself would later say that he had been misunderstood in precisely how this was to be achieved through indirect force rather than military confrontation. But at the time it seemed to people that here was an agenda being laid out with some clarity.

Aid now flowed from the United States, and by October of 1949, the Royalist forces had won in Greece. Truman's declaration was not just a bellicose statement, however. It was also a case of actually someone putting money where his mouth was because this declaration of the Truman Doctrine was coupled with the announcement of the European Recovery Program, also known by its acronym as the ERP by Truman's new Secretary of State, George C. Marshall, on June 5, 1947. Marshall was so self-effacing that few people noticed it at the time, at the immediate aftermath of the announcement in the speech of this vast new program of American aid to Europe for recovery, but a certain group of people certainly did. Those were European leaders in western Europe who saw this as a lifeline.

From the American perspective, renewed prosperity in what was now a continent in ruins was seen as a guarantee against destabilization and in particular Communist influence and encroachment. Aid was offered to all of Europe. The aid was open to east as well as west including states under Communist rule. But Stalin, who from his perspective and his concerns felt that American aid was surely be accompanied by American influence, forced the eastern European states to refuse that aid. There are many cases were eastern Europeans look back wistfully and think of the alternative history of what might have been if they had been allowed to participate. The aid, and this was a crucial aspect of how the aid was dispersed, was distributed together rather than country-by-country. The European interlocutors of the European Recovery Program— which comes to be called the Marshall Plan instead, identified very closely with its initiator—were instructed that they had to come up with comprehensive and cooperative schemes in how this aid would be used and distributed. This in turn had the crucial implication of forcing European statesmen to put national hatreds and antipathies aside and instead encourage European cooperation.

Indeed, institutionalized in the OEEC, the Organization of European Economic Cooperation, the record was a striking one. From 1948–1952, the plan delivered on the order of $13 billion in aid, and it's been calculated that represents in today's dollars about $100 billion in American dollars contrasting with the record of the Soviet extraction of resources and reparations from its own sphere of influence in eastern and central Europe also apparently on the order of $13 billion—but not being put in, being extracted or taken out in order to rebuild the Soviet Union. This has been called one of the most important and magnanimous examples of foreign aid deployed in international politics in recorded history. Western European economies revived dramatically, and as had been the expectation of American policymakers, Communist parties that had done well in the immediate aftermath of the war were excluded from power in elections as a result.

Stalin responded by reviving what had been the Comintern, this organization to encourage revolution worldwide, in October 1947 as Cominform, or the Communist Information Bureau. It needs to be pointed out, it needs to be stressed, that the remarkable recovery of European economies, the economic miracle of western Europe as well as Germany, was not due solely to Marshall Plan aid. In fact, what sometimes has been suggested is that it was the psychological impact of knowing that America was standing by and, as it were, had not retreated across the Atlantic that really in some sense allowed sort of a safety net in terms of experimentation and bold initiatives in international cooperation among western European politicians.

We need to turn now, however, to a crisis that had enormous symbolic significance and thus was politically catalytic as well: the Prague Crisis of 1948 when the Czech Communist Party took power in a coup in Prague, the capital of Czechoslovakia in February of 1948. This event had crucial significance because it shocked foreign observers, not so much because there hadn't been other Communist takeovers in eastern Europe. That was the order of the day. What was different, however, was the record that Czechoslovakia had as a democracy in the interwar period for all of its problems, and there were certainly serious domestic problems, and—this is what made especially the case of Prague neuralgic was the appeasement in 1938 that had seen the sellout of Czechoslovakian sovereignty.

There was also another tragic historical echo—an echo to events much, much earlier in our course. If you think back to the Thirty Years' War, which began with a "defenestration of Prague," the throwing out of a window of the Prague castle of emissaries of the Holy Roman Emperor in 1618. This had a tragic echo in 1948 when the Foreign Minister, Jan Masaryk, fell from a window in extremely suspicious circumstances that many suspect was a murder committed in the context of this coup to eliminate this democratic politician. The impact of this coup and the shock that it represented for these psychological and symbolic reasons was to hurry along Marshall Plan aid approval by the U.S. Congress in April of 1948.

Sometimes in sort of the rosy hindsight it appears as if in retrospect there had been total unanimity on projects like the Marshall Plan in the context of the Cold War with the orientation just monolithic. That was emphatically not the case. Quite to the contrary, there were very strong voices criticizing the Marshall Plan aid at a time when the United States had its own problems and concerns at home. But it makes the achievement all the more remarkable I think that there was just this domestic resistance.

In March of 1948, there was another response. Great Britain, France, Belgium, the Netherlands, and Luxembourg together pooled their energies to sign an alliance that came to be known as the Brussels Pact, signed in Brussels, Belgium, which was to be a European defense effort. The United States had seen this as a counterpart to the American commitment, and if the Europeans were going to stand on their own feet in terms of speeding along economic recovery, not dependent but as contributors, so too in military terms the expectation of this Brussels Pact was that Europe was contribute to its own defense—an imperative for American policymakers. The United States also for its part reinstated the draft but this was an institution of peacetime conscription in 1948.

Another event that would loom up very large as a crisis was the Berlin Crisis of 1948–1949 and the division of the Germanies that was sped along as a result. The German Problem now took on a different form because Germany now was not an overpowering might that needed to be contained but rather was an area divided by the superpowers, a partitioned power. In a striking shift so soon after World War II, the defeated Germans were now being courted by both sides. They were now being reintegrated into the opposed blocs as allies both to the east and the west. Although Germany according to the initial agreements of the occupying forces was to be administered together in practice the occupiers follow their own policies in the zones, and the result was an increasing growing apart of those occupying forces. Negotiations over the future of Germany on the part of the victorious allies yielded no concrete results. Thus, out of frustration with this lack of progress in negotiations, the British and American zones—and later the French too—after some resistance were fused economically in 1947 in order to speed recovery and in June of 1948 introduced a common currency much to the fury of the Soviets who saw this as a move away from earlier agreements.

The first major standoff of the Cold War thus came over, in this tense context, the so-called Berlin Crisis. In reaction to these western moves, on June 24, 1948, Soviet forces blocked access to the divided city of Berlin, which was 100 miles within the Soviet zone, but in some sense precisely because it was partitioned between the four occupying allies was a mirror image on a small scale deep within the Soviet zone of the larger Germany. The Western Allies responded neither with a passive acceptance nor with crashing through Soviet barricades, which might have brought on World War III, but rather— and maybe here one sees American character at work—with a technological fix; the Western Allies responded with a dramatic Berlin airlift over the blockade shuttling supplies to the city. The result was striking as so-called "raisin bombers" carrying food as well as raisins and candy for the children of Berlin flew in in a striking record of one every few minutes, and not without losses either, in order to supply what had been the capital city of an enemy until quite recently. In the context of public diplomacy, a real cultural and public relations catastrophe, Stalin, whose heavy hand in this was condemned and frightened, on May 12, 1949, lifted the blockade.

Soon thereafter, on May 23, 1949, in the West the Federal Republic of Germany was established. Its capital was situated not in Berlin, which obviously was in the Soviet zone but instead, in the sleepy university town of Bonn on the Rhine. In the Soviet zone, the

German Democratic Republic, as it was called, was founded in 1949 in answer. Both states claimed to be the one "true" Germany in ideological terms. In the Federal Republic of Germany, the new chancellor, Konrad Adenauer, already advanced in years but striking in his determination launched an independent policy of adhering to the West and resisting German isolation in the coming confrontation. We also need to mention another striking development: the break of the Yugoslavian leader, Tito, from the Eastern Bloc.

Within the Eastern Bloc, Yugoslavia, which had been liberated from Nazi control by partisans led by Josef Tito, steered a course that was increasingly independent of Stalin. Their break came out into the open in June of 1948. Stalin condemned Tito as a heretic, but in the process, Nationalism's continuing importance was revealed as Yugoslavia wanted to chart its own political path. The Cold War standoff, however, prevented Stalin from intervening directly. This revealed that even in the Cold War confrontation there was room for maneuver—limited but nonetheless there. It showed that even in the bipolar division of Europe there were unexpected complexities, but the overarching reality was a "balance of fear." The earlier American monopoly on atomic weapons ended with a Soviet explosion of an atomic bomb in August of 1949. Now, both sides had this fearsome, new military technology.

The result was a new dynamic, the "balance of fear," as it was called at the time, which threatened to replace earlier patterns of a balance of power entirely. Each side now threatened the other with the prospect of annihilation; this came to be called by the initials M.A.D., a very appropriate name standing for the words "mutually assured destruction," the certainty that both sides would manage to destroy each other regardless of who began. This was also part of a global pattern as the Cold War extended worldwide.

China came under Communist control in October of 1949 and allied with the Soviets in the following year. The United Nations, which earlier was supposed to be a venue for cooperation, was increasingly immobilized by vetoes. The arms race grew intense with enormous expenses; many Europeans worried about what the British historian Arnold Toynbee called at the time—and this was really sort of whistling past the graveyard with a kind of grim humor—the prospect of "annihilation without representation," meaning no European voice in the apocalypse that might soon be looming. Some

Europeans indeed bitterly spoke of this as not a Cold War conflict that they were involved in but rather a superpower condominium of Europe, a shared dominance over Europe, but what other options were on the table remained obscure at best.

I want to close by just examining some of the debates that center on the Cold War among historians, debate that continues today. At the time, contemporary analysis, which today is termed the traditionalist view, tended to argue that Stalin's intentions were key—that Stalin was the prime mover although what the precise nature of his plans were still remains debated today. In the 1960s and the 1970s a new revisionist school shifted the analysis to American motives—in particular economic imperatives and American expansionism, as it was styled—and American leadership while Stalin was viewed as a more traditional statesman with more limited goals. By the 1980s, however, a new school of post-revisionists saw the Cold War as almost inevitable due to the nature of the state system, the bipolarity that had emerged in the place of the earlier balance of power and the ideological character of both superpowers. The Cold War was also obviously a new thing, a new dynamic, with fearsome weaponry of deterrence breaking, as it turns out, in what was fortuitous the possibility of an all out arms struggle.

For Europeans, 1949 in particular brought increasingly severe lines of division across their continent and posed questions about their future fate. In our own post-Cold War world, we sometimes hear idealized images of the Cold War, a nostalgia for its alleged stability, or the perfect solidarity that allegedly had cemented alliances. These, as I hope has been made clear, are idealized images that are inaccurate. We need instead to have a closer analysis, a far more hard-headed analysis of the Cold War that we will pursue further in our next lecture.

Lecture Thirty-Three
Blocs and Decolonization

Scope:

This lecture covers two processes growing apace in the period from 1949 to 1956. On the one hand, Europe as a key arena of the Cold War stand-off was increasingly polarized into separate blocs to the East and West, configured into the military alliances of NATO and the Warsaw Pact. We discuss challenges to this division of Europe and important exceptions. On the other hand, European powers simultaneously underwent decolonization (a process that could be fast or slow, negotiated or contested), losing most of their once huge imperial holdings around the world, with a profound psychological impact on political self-understanding.

Outline

I. Europe from 1949–1956.

    A. This period brought a redefinition of European status in the world.

        1. On the one hand, it became clearer still that the United States and the Soviet Union were European powers, as their frictions elsewhere had implications in Europe.

        2. On the other hand, rapid decolonization was a reverse scramble away from empire and Europe's earlier global power.

    B. The American role in Europe was marked by an insistence on European contributions.

        1. U.S. policy focused on uniting and leading rather than imperial policies of "divide and conquer."

        2. The "special relationship" between the United States and Britain was celebrated but complex.

        3. Even solidarity did not preclude tensions among allies.

    C. Germany, at ground zero of the Cold War division, was a crucial issue, and the institutionalization of the blocs into military alliances raised the prospect of German rearmament. As well, Germany's economic potential was now being revitalized.

1. The policy of the Federal Republic of Germany was led by its new chancellor Konrad Adenauer in office from 1949 to 1963.
2. The former mayor of Cologne, this Catholic politician had opposed the Nazis.
3. As chancellor, Adenauer pressed a foreign policy to reinforce German democracy in an international context of reconciliation with France, firm orientation toward the West, and restored sovereignty.
4. Neither German state recognized the other.

D. Anxieties about Soviet advance and German revived power spurred military pacts among Germany's western neighbors (known as "double containment").
1. Britain (breaking with splendid isolation) and France promised mutual aid, directed against any future German threats.
2. In the Treaty of Brussels on March 17, 1948, Great Britain, France, Belgium, Luxembourg, and the Netherlands established a self-defense agreement.

II. The North Atlantic Treaty Organization (NATO).

A. The Berlin Crisis of 1948–1949 prompted the further cementing of the western alliance.

B. On April 4, 1949, the North Atlantic Treaty was signed by the United States, Canada, Great Britain, France, Belgium, Luxembourg, Norway, Denmark, Italy, the Netherlands, Portugal, and Iceland.
1. It was committed to collective self-defense; an attack on one was considered an attack on all.
2. It has been called the most successful peacetime alliance in history (it was later joined by Greece and Turkey in 1952 and the Federal Republic of Germany in 1955) and was a new phase in U.S. foreign policy.

III. The Western Bloc.

A. The impact of the Korean War (1950–1953) was significant even in Europe.

B. German rearmament (despite French anxieties) went forward as a result of the tension of the Korean War, pressed by U.S. Secretary of State Dean Acheson (in office 1949–1953) in September 1950.

C. This experience prompted western Europeans to seek a counterweight to their American ally.

D. One French proposal was to embed Germany's military revival in European institutions such as a European army, but France itself ended up rejecting it in 1954.

  1. In the aftermath, Britain stationed forces on the continent to assure French security.

  2. In March 1952, to prevent German entry into NATO, the Soviets dispatched the "Stalin Note," suggesting superpower withdrawal from a neutral Germany.

  3. Adenauer and the United States rejected the proposal as "Finlandization," and its real significance is still debated.

  4. The Federal Republic of Germany joined NATO in 1955 and regained much of its sovereignty.

E. In May 1949, the Council of Europe was established in Strasbourg, France, with representatives sent from national parliaments.

F. Britain remained wary of integration with the European continent.

G. French Foreign Minister Robert Schuman proposed in 1950 to coordinate German and French coal and steel production under one institution in a plan drafted with French businessman Jean Monnet.

  1. This led to the establishment of the European Coal and Steel Community (ECSC) of 1951, with six members: France, Germany, Italy, Belgium, the Netherlands, and Luxembourg.

  2. A small beginning to a larger task, it avoided the biggest debates at first.

  3. German and French economic revivals were linked.

  4. The ECSC would be the foundation for later projects, especially the European Common Market of 1957.

  5. In 1954 the Western European Union was established as a European defense organization when Italy and Germany joined the Treaty of Brussels.

IV. The Communist Bloc.

A. In 1953 Stalin died, and changes took place in eastern Europe.

B. By 1958, Soviet leadership was taken over by Nikita Khrushchev (1894–1971), who mixed confrontation with the West with the rhetoric of "peaceful coexistence."

    1. His 1956 Secret Speech condemned Stalinism and provoked reactions abroad.

    2. Khrushchev was ejected from leadership in 1964.

C. As a counterpart to the Marshall Plan, COMECON (the Council for Mutual Economic Aid) yoked eastern European economies to the Soviet patron.

D. When the Federal Republic of Germany entered NATO, the Soviets set up the Warsaw Pact in May 1955.

    1. Dominated by the Soviet Union, the pact included Poland, Czechoslovakia, Hungary, the German Democratic Republic, Bulgaria, Albania, and Romania.

    2. Its crucial operations involved attacking its own members.

E. Unrest in the Eastern Bloc was forcibly suppressed.

    1. The June 1953 Berlin Workers' Rising was crushed.

    2. In October 1956, revolt broke out in Hungary over demands for independence, and the Red Army withdrew.

    3. Soviet forces returned to crush the revolt and a quarter million Hungarians fled.

    4. The United States and its allies did not intervene in eastern Europe.

V. The Austrian Surprise of 1955.

A. Austria, which had been divided into zones of occupation, was unexpectedly reunited.

B. On May 15, 1955, the Austrian State Treaty was signed in Vienna's Belvedere Palace.

    1. Austria was required to become neutral, which Austrians celebrated as "active neutrality."

    2. One explanation suggests the Soviet intent was to convince the Federal Republic of Germany not to join NATO.

    3. The result was a temporary break in tensions.

C. After a decade of no summit meetings since 1945, in July 1955, the heads of state of Great Britain, the United States, France, and the Soviet Union met at the Geneva Summit.

VI. Decolonization.

    A. From the end of World War II to 1960, European empires were shed.

    B. This was a reflection of several factors: reduced European world power, the loss of the legitimacy of the very concept of Imperialism (already criticized in the 19th century by liberal thinkers), the growth of Nationalism beyond the West, and the anti-Imperialist ideologies of both superpowers.

    C. The United Nations took over the trusteeship of some colonies.

    D. Struggles over independence also intersected with Cold War conflict.

    E. France sought to hold on to its empire to reinforce its status, but the result was a series of wars and retreats.

        1. War in Indochina starting in 1946 led to French withdrawal in 1954, replaced by U.S. involvement in Vietnam.

        2. France fought a fierce war in Algeria from 1954–1961 before recognizing Algeria's independence in 1962 after the loss of Morocco and Tunisia.

    F. The British Empire receded step by step, a process hurried by the costs of World War II.

        1. In 1947 India and Pakistan became independent, followed by Ceylon, Malaya, Cyprus, and Malta.

        2. Britain departed from the Palestine Mandate in 1948, and Israel declared its independence.

        3. Egypt gained its independence in 1952.

        4. British colonies in Africa gained their independence one after another.

    G. Other European colonial powers also reluctantly gave up their holdings.

        1. The Dutch lost Indonesia after fighting in 1948.

        2. One of the oldest powers, Portugal, resisted giving up its colonies until the 1960s.

VII. The 1956 Suez Crisis.

    A. A moment of truth about Europe's new status was offered by the Suez Crisis of 1956.

B. Egyptian leader Gamal Abdel Nasser (1918–1970) had seized power after a revolution in 1952 and sought advantage from Cold War competition.

  1. After Western loans were withdrawn, Nasser responded by occupying the Suez Canal (then under private ownership) on July 26, 1956.

  2. France, Britain, and Israel coordinated military action against Egypt, beginning with an Israeli attack in October and followed by landings of British and French troops.

  3. Both the Soviets and the United States condemned the action as an echo of 19th-century "gunboat diplomacy," and it was stopped.

C. The Suez Crisis revealed the changed status of European powers, now dwarfed by the superpowers.

Essential Reading:

Henry Kissinger, *Diplomacy*, pp. 473–567.

Supplementary Reading:

David Reynolds, "A 'Special Relationship'? America, Britain and the International Order Since the Second World War," *International Affairs*, 62.1 (Winter 1985–1986), pp. 1–20.

Marc Trachtenberg, ed., *Between Empire and Alliance: America and Europe during the Cold War*.

Questions to Consider:

1. What were the potentialities and limits of the "special relationship" between Britain and the United States?

2. What made NATO effective as an alliance?

Lecture Thirty-Three—Transcript
Blocs and Decolonization

In this lecture on blocs and decolonization, we will examine two processes growing a pace in the period from 1949–1956 in this lecture. On the one hand, we will see the consolidation of European division of the continent into opposed blocs of alliances following on the process of the Cold War, which we had considered in our previous lecture. On the other hand, we will also follow at the same time the loss of Europeans' once huge imperial holdings around the world, their earlier empires, with a profound psychological impact on political self-understanding as a result of this decolonization.

In general, one might consider the overall theme of this lecture as the way in which this period would bring a redefinition of European status in the world. On the one hand, it became clearer than it had been even before that the United States and the Soviet Union were European powers. They were located on the flanks of this system but now were very actively intervening in Europe. Their frictions elsewhere around the globe in the conflict between them would have implications in Europe. On the other hand, at the same time, rapid decolonization would be in essence a remarkably quick reverse scramble away from empire and would see the retreat of Europe's earlier position of global dominance. Think about the position of Europe in the world around 1900 by contrast.

The American role in Europe was a fascinating one. It was marked by insistence on a Western European contribution to the common cause of defense. In this sense, U.S. policy focused in a remarkable way on uniting and leading Western Europeans, rather than what might have otherwise been imperial policies followed by earlier empires based on the maxim of dividing, conquering, and accenting frictions, here instead the aim was to achieve unity and solidarity in that sense. When we speak of solidarity, one very particular and special case was that of the American relationship with Britain—the so-called "special relationship," which was celebrated but also a quite complex relationship between those two countries.

Winston Churchill, who famously was in some sense the very embodiment of that "special relationship" by being of mixed British and American parentage, had once famously said that in this "special relationship" the Americans and the Britons were allies or friends who were, as he put it, divided by a shared language. I think this joking maxim actually brings into view very vividly the sort of ways in which even with a shared English language there could still be misunderstandings or friction over issues that were not based on misunderstandings but a keen understanding of issues that divided the two partners. In particular, the division by a shared language was made clear in a case that Churchill talked about—the way in which Americans and the British discovered, as a result of misunderstandings during negotiations that they held, for instance, diametrically opposed meanings for the phrase, "to table something," to table a proposal. In American usage, to table a proposal meant that one hadn't arrived at a solution and it needed to be put to the side and maybe returned to later to see if agreement could be found. In British usage, this key term from diplomacy and negotiation, to table something, meant the exact opposite—to present it for discussion in the hope of being able to achieve negotiated settlement or compromise. Such misunderstandings and frictions would be even a part of this otherwise quite amicable relationship. This is a key point to consider throughout as we discuss Cold War tensions. Solidarity and a firm alliance did not preclude tensions existing between allies.

A very key example of precisely the way in which issues could arise even on the part of an alliance bloc concerned Germany, let's turn to that case next. Germany was truly at ground zero of Cold War division. Germany was a crucial issue in the Cold War, and its very division had led to the incorporation of Eastern Germany into the Eastern Bloc and Western Germany into the Western Bloc as states institutionalizing their division into these blocs of military alliances. In the Cold War context, German potential military power was a very important part of the calculation of resources that one or another bloc might be able to mobilize, and this raised the prospect of German rearmament as being something that both sides could deploy, something that truly a worrying prospect to many of Germany's neighbors, both to the east and to the west. There was a sense also in which this had an economic dimension. Germany, in this period in the west the Federal Republic of Germany, was undergoing what was called with some justice an economic miracle. Germany's economic potential was now being revitalized and really coming into its own in this period. Germany, in this sense, had a lot of economic muscle that was truly being refurbished.

Here we see coming into focus a paradox of the period. German economic predominance in Europe tended over the course of the late

19th and early 20th century and indeed throughout the 20th century to proceed faster in times of peace. This very natural phenomenon of the vast resources as well as the hard work of the German population producing German economic predominance on the continent was actually a natural process that tended to be interrupted by the two world wars and their bids for German hegemony. To the contrary, times of peace had hurried that process along, and this was a paradox that in some sense the world wars had slowed down an otherwise natural progression of German economic dominance on the continent.

At this time, the policy of the Federal Republic of Germany was being led by a very important and striking politician, the new chancellor, Konrad Adenauer, who was in office from 1949–1963. At this point, when he really comes into his own as chancellor of Germany, he had already had a long political career behind him. In this sense, he bore some resemblance to Winston Churchill, who had years in the wilderness and seemed to many people to be beyond his political prime at precisely the moment when he was about to re-enter and play a critical role, a pivotal role, in the history of his own nation, so too with Adenauer. Adenauer has been a Catholic politician who had early been the mayor of Cologne and during the Nazi period had opposed the Nazis. As chancellor of the new German democracy, the Federal Republic of Germany, Adenauer pressed and advanced a foreign policy whose aim had key domestic as well as international implications that reinforced one another.

To reinforce German democracy at home, Adenauer felt that it was imperative to find a new international context for the German democracy based on reconciliation with France, an earlier hereditary enemy, now in some sense following the rapprochement or mutual approach that Stresemann, the remarkable German Foreign Minister of the interwar period, had already advanced. He aimed for reconciliation with France on an entirely new basis. This was part of a larger aim of firm orientation of the Federal Republic of Germany toward the West, linking it to alliance systems of the West and not hovering in a sort of middle space between East and West in some sort of complicated balancing act. He also hoped that as a result of tying Germany in, Germany's sovereignty might increasingly be restored in the Federal Republic of Germany. This was a strange Cold War context in which the reviving Federal Republic of Germany, on the one hand, and the German Democratic Republic under Communist control in the East didn't recognize one another but rather were the very embodiment of Cold War division down the center of the continent. Germany's neighbors, at the same time, looked on with some anxiety at German rearmament, which we will be talking about briefly in a moment, as well as the continuing challenge of what Soviet intensions might be.

These double worries, anxieties about Soviet advance on the one hand and German revived power, spurred a series of military pacts among Germany's western neighbors that really amounted to a "double containment," a way of meeting anxieties both about the Soviet Union on the one hand and a revived German power at the center of the continent on the other. First, Great Britain and France pledged mutual aid against any future German threats. Here one sees, incidentally, a further moving away from the earlier traditions of British splendid isolation off the continent. This was a foundation upon which one built in the Treaty of Brussels of March 17, 1948 when Great Britain and France, who had already joined together in this sense, were now joined by Belgium, Luxembourg, and the Netherlands in the establishment of a self-defense agreement, which in part was motivated by worries about some revival of German power in the future.

Let's turn now however to the key alliance structure that we should consider: NATO. The Berlin Crisis of 1948–1949 that we had mentioned in a previous lecture prompted and urged the further cementing of the western alliance. Stalin's aim of splitting the cohesion of the West through this crisis produced a contrary result and was a blunder in that sense. On April 4, 1949, the North Atlantic Treaty, as it was called, was signed by the United States, Canada, Great Britain, France, Belgium, Luxembourg, Norway, Denmark, Italy, the Netherlands, Portugal, and Iceland—a collection of the states of western and central Europe committed to the goal of collective self-defense. It was formally promised that an attack on any one of them was to be considered an attack that had been waged on all of them. Collectively, each and every one would be responsible for the security of every member of the alliance.

NATO has been called the most successful peacetime alliance in history, and one of its features would be its growth, its expansion. It was later joined by Greece and Turkey in the sensitive region to the southeast of Europe in 1952, and then by the Federal Republic of

Germany in 1955 as part and parcel of this process of bringing the earlier enemy—now the new German democracy, the Federal Republic of Germany—into the fold, which was accomplished with the joining by the Federal Republic of Germany of NATO in 1955.

This also incidentally was a new phase in American foreign policy as well—the joining of a peacetime alliance that really committed the United States to an active engagement far across the Atlantic. There was a joke at the time that was advanced by Lord Ismay, the first secretary general of NATO and one usually doesn't think of first secretary generals as comedians, but he uttered a joke that's gone down in historical records as actually expressing a core of truth. Ismay joked that the point of NATO, its real aim apart from the formal alliance structure that had been outlined in the treaty, was the following: to keep the Americans in, the Russians out, and the Germans down. Keeping Americans in meant keeping America engaged overseas so it didn't retreat into a default mode of isolation. Keeping the Russians out meant containing the Soviet Union from any advance it might envision, and keeping the Germans down was a continued expression of the anxieties of what a revived German power at the center of Europe might involve.

Let's examine how events in the Cold War, distant as they might be, would have an impact on Europe and the Cold War there. The impact in particular of the Korean War from 1950–1953 was significant. It's been called sometimes the forgotten war. In this case, its results would be marked. German rearmament went forward as a result of the increased tension of the Korean War. As the Americans mobilized to fight in Asia, the result was that they tried to mobilize all the resources that were even potentially to be disposed of in Europe. German rearmament thus was encouraged by the U.S. Secretary of State Dean Acheson, over the anxieties of the French and other European neighbors. The experience of in some sense feeling that they had to give way in the face of this American pressure prompted western Europeans among themselves to start to seek some institutional counterweight to their American ally's desires. This didn't mean a break in the alliance. We have been at pains to point out that even in alliances there can be friction. There certainly can be differences of interest and perspective. The intent was rather to find some institutional way of mobilizing what influence Europe might have in this contest.

One proposal, a really striking one, was to embed Germany's new military revival in European institutions. Initially, the French proposed the institution of a European army that would have German participation, but then French anxieties kicked in and the French themselves, who had been instrumental in proposing this project, rejected it in 1954. This was, in some sense, an idea perhaps ahead of its time. In the aftermath of this back and forth of proposals for how to really weave and involve Germany in this web of obligations, Great Britain for its part stationed forces on the continent to assure French security, to in some sense reassure French policymakers that Great Britain was standing side by side. This too you will appreciate was a break with the earlier tradition of not staying engaged on the continent in times of peace. Eventually, German entry into NATO by 1955 would provide the reassuring structure and institutionalization that many Europeans felt was necessary, especially Germany's neighbors.

At the same time as this was viewed with a sense of reassurance in the west, the reaction in the east was quite contrary. Stalin was anxious about what German entry into NATO might mean, and in March 1952, in a bid to prevent Germany's joining of NATO, the Soviets dispatched the so-called "Stalin Note," which was really a diplomatic bombshell at the time. It suggested that both superpowers, the United States as well as the Soviet Union, could withdraw from both Germanys and instead leave at the center of Europe a neutral Germany—one which would not be a part of the blocs but rather would remain outside their scope. Both Adenauer, for the Federal Republic of Germany, and the United States rejected this proposal fearing that the result would be not greater stability but rather the "Finlandization" or that's to say the domination of a neutral Germany by the Soviets. The real significance of this "Stalin Note" is still debated today. Was this a missed opportunity for earlier German unification? Historians still debate the issue.

The Federal Republic of Germany moved ahead to join NATO in 1955 and regained much of its sovereignty as a result. There were other institutional innovations that were taking place at the same time that we want to note. In May of 1949, the Council of Europe was established in Strasbourg, France, in that area close to the German border that earlier had been so contested and fought over where representatives were sent from national European parliaments to engage in an institutionalized form of negotiation and common discussion that would lay the groundwork and establish the precedence for later European cooperation. Britain, however, remained wary of being fully integrated with the continent in projects like this and would remain in a role no longer that of total splendid isolation but a wary position nonetheless.

It was the French who took the initiative. The French Foreign Minister, Robert Schuman, proposed in 1950 a step that looked modest at first but would have large significance in the long run. He proposed that one might join together to coordinate German and French coal and steel production under one institution. This was the result of a plan that had been drafted by the French businessman Jean Monnet, and it had the strategic significance of linking or binding together the production of what in military terms are key strategic resources, coal and steel—necessary for heavy industry. This led to the establishment, when it was agreed to follow this initiative, of the European Coal and Steel Community, the ECSC—and acronyms will be very important in this ongoing institutionalization of European unity—in the year 1951 with six members: France, Germany, Italy, Belgium, the Netherlands, and Luxembourg. This was but a small beginning to a larger task of building on this institutional beginning. It avoided the biggest debates at first by focusing on small details on which agreement could be found. In that sense, it was a diplomatic master stroke. Henceforth, German and French economic revival would also increasingly be linked. So, there were shared interests evolving. That institution, the ECSC, would be the foundation for later, larger projects, especially the so-called European Common Market of 1957, which we will discuss more in our next lecture.

The 1954 establishment of the Western European Union was seen as a European defense organization building on earlier initiatives when Italy and Germany, which earlier had been feared but now were welcomed, joined the Treaty of Brussels. We might ask, so we have a fuller picture of Europe as a whole, what was happening in the east at this time. Let's turn to the Communist Bloc. In 1953, Stalin had died, and changes took place in eastern Europe. By 1958, Soviet leadership was taken over by Nikita Khrushchev, who mixed confrontation with the west with rhetoric of "peaceful coexistence"—shifting in a sort of volatile way between these tropes. In his famous Secret Speech of 1956 to Communist party activists, he had condemned Stalinism and what he terms its excesses. This provoked reactions abroad as many people hoped that change or liberalization might follow. Khrushchev's bumpy record in statesmanship and political life led finally to his being ejected from leadership in 1964.

As a counterpart to the Marshall Plan that was taking hold in western Europe, the Soviet's organized COMECON, the so-called Council for Mutual Economic Aid, which tended to yoke eastern European economies to the larger Soviet patron and its interests. In another sort of mirroring of developments in the West, when the Federal Republic of Germany entered NATO in 1955, the Soviet's responded by setting up the Warsaw Pact in that year. Dominated by the Soviet Union, this military alliance, the Warsaw Pact, included Poland, Czechoslovakia, Hungary, the German Democratic Republic, Bulgaria, Albania, and Romania.

It needs to be said that its record was not a very distinguished one. Its crucial operations mostly involved attacking its own members who were seen as straying from Communist orthodoxy because unrest in the Eastern Bloc when it arose was very forcibly suppressed. In June of 1953, for instance, in the eastern part of Berlin, the Berlin Workers' Rising was crushed by a regime that claimed to be representing the workers. In October of 1956 in an event that really captured the attention of contemporaries, a revolt broke out in Hungary with demands for independence being raised. The Red Army at first withdrew but returned to crush the revolt, and a quarter million Hungarians would flee to exile. Many of these rebels in the Eastern Bloc looked to the United States and the western allies for assistance and help, but the Cold War division meant that the United States and its allies were wary of intervening in eastern Europe at this time.

I want to focus now on a surprise—I mean in terms of this otherwise quite rigid structure something that leaps out at us as an exception. That is the way in which Austria, which earlier had been divided into zones of occupation just like Germany to the north, unexpectedly was reunited in 1955. The Austrian State Treaty was signed in May of 1955 at Vienna's Belvedere Palace—which initially had been built by Prince Eugene, who had in the days of the Habsburgs driven the Ottomans almost out of Europe. In that setting, Austria signed a treaty in which it was required to become neutral. Austrians celebrated this "active neutrality," the price at which they had won independence and reunification. One explanation that historians advance suggests that the Soviets were at this time trying to convince the Federal Republic of Germany to the north not to join NATO. Whatever the explanation was, this attempt to court public opinion if that was the correct interpretation, the result was a welcome break in tensions at least temporarily, so that after a decade of no summit meeting from 1945–1955, it now was possible in 1955 for heads of state of the United States, the Soviet Union, France, and Great Britain to meet at the Geneva Summit and to at least begin negotiations at that level again.

I want now to turn to examine the fascinating and crucial process of decolonization. From the end of World War II to about 1960, European empires that had been gathered up so quickly at the end of the 19th century in that scramble for empire of high Imperialism were just as rapidly given up, shed, abandoned. This was a reflection of several factors, the reasons behind this process. One might point to reduced European world power. One might mention the loss of legitimacy of the very concept of Imperialism, which now was seen as something not desirable and indeed had already been criticized in the 19th century by European liberal thinkers as a phenomenon as we mentioned in earlier lectures. One needs to mention also as a factor the growth of Nationalism and a self-assertive confidence beyond the West by non-Western peoples as well as the fact that both superpowers that now were looming over the world scene in the superpower confrontation, the Cold War, themselves possessed anti-Imperialist ideologies. Whether these were always honored in practice is another question. The United Nations at this period as an institution took over trusteeship of some colonies so there was an institutional framework to hurry along the process.

It needs also to be mentioned that many struggles over independence in the non-Western world also tended to intersect with the Cold War conflict. Nor was this a process that was seamless and smooth. In fact, some countries resisted the process. France, for its part, sought to hold on to its empire as a way of reinforcing its hopes for a revived Great Power status in Europe, but the result, in fact, was a series of wars and retreats. The French War in Indochina from 1946 finally led to French withdrawal by 1954. The French presence then was replaced by American involvement, which led to the protracted Vietnam War. France also, closer to home, fought a fierce war in Algeria in Northern Africa from 1954–1961 before finally recognizing its independence in 1962 after the loss of Morocco and Tunisia also as older colonies.

The British Empire for its part receded step by step, a process that was hurried along by the crushing costs of winning World War II. We have already seen how the abandonment of earlier involvement in Greece and Turkey had been part and parcel of this sense of retrenchment, of pulling back. Britain quickly pulled out of India and Pakistan, which became independent in 1947 at sort of breakneck speed followed also by independence for Ceylon, Malaya, Cyprus, and Malta. Britain also departed from the Middle East, the Palestine Mandate in 1948, and Israel declared independence. Egypt gained its independence in 1952 after having been a key possession of the British imperial system. British colonies elsewhere in Africa soon gained independence one after another.

Other European colonial powers also reluctantly gave up their holdings. The Dutch, for instance, lost Indonesia after fighting in 1948; and in an odd sort of coming full circle, one of the oldest colonial powers, Portugal, whose trading empire went back to the very start of our course in our earliest lectures, still resisted giving up its colonies for a long time into the 1960s. In some sense, in full circle, Portugal with the oldest empire was among the last to give up its empire.

I want to close by examining a key event, which, is some sense, was a moment of truth. This was 1956 Suez Crisis that revealed things that some Europeans had, perhaps, wanted to repress in their own consciousness about their new status in the world. A moment of truth about Europe's new status in the world was offered by this moment of truth of the Suez Canal Crisis in 1956. The crisis as it unfolded went thus: The Egyptian leader, Gamal Abdel Nasser, had seized power after revolution in Egypt in 1952. He sought advantage in the Cold War competition by in some sense finding which side it would be most profitable in terms of aid and alliance to align himself with. After a period of balancing, when Western loans were withdrawn, Nasser responded by occupying the Suez Canal—which at this point, even as a crucial geopolitical linkage east of Suez, was now under private ownership. The seizure of the canal took place on July 26, 1956. At this point, European statesmen had a precedent in mind that made them very anxious. One of the themes of our course has been how policymakers often look to the past for models or patterns in international behavior that they feel they have to respond to. In this case, whether appropriately or not, the precedent that was vivid to their minds and their memories was the 1930s and the way in which Hitler had managed to score one diplomatic success after another finally breaking the Versailles Treaty itself in its entirety through the result of not meeting resistance and instead meeting appeasement. Whether appropriately or not, the anxiety was that this sort of activism—this sort of self-assertion on the part of Nasser—might portend just this sort of pattern.

European policymakers responded vigorously. Britain, France, and Israel together coordinated military action against Egypt. This military action began with an Israeli attack in October and then landings of British and French troops by way of intervention. The reaction of the superpowers was unexpected from the perspective of the Europeans, and it was harsh. Both the Soviets and the United States under President Eisenhower vigorously and loudly condemned that action. It seemed to them too much an echo of the "gunboat diplomacy" of the 19th century when European Imperialist powers had wrought their will upon the world, the non-Western world, in the scramble for colonies and the flexing of Imperialist power. The result was intense pressure focused on Great Britain, France, and Israel. In the case of the United States, in violation of earlier sort of mythologized "special relationship" with Great Britain, in fact, both political as well as economic pressure was put on Britain in order to force it to back down.

As a result of all this pressure, indeed the intervention was stopped. The European powers withdrew in humiliation and reeled psychologically from the impact of this moment of truth. The Suez crisis and the decisive role of the superpowers had revealed in a flash and decisively the changed status of European powers that now truly were seen as dwarfed by the overarching superpowers, the United States and the Soviet Union. The question that obviously arose and the psychological impact of this moment of truth was how to respond, and a very creative response to this new situation of otherwise seeming helplessness would be to build something new. It would be the ongoing project of European unification as a way of building a creative response and a response that we will be turning to precisely in our next lecture.

Lecture Thirty-Four
The European Project

Scope:

In response both to the changed status of Europe after a half century of destructive tensions and world wars, as well as its location as ground zero of the Cold War conflict or a future World War III, European political leaders sought to craft a new departure from the competitive politics of statehood inaugurated at the long-ago Treaty of Westphalia in 1648. This lecture surveys the European project of unity from 1957 to 1980 (later culminating in today's European Union) in the midst of the perilous experience of the Cold War. We examine surprising French-German cooperation, the impact of the Cuban Missile Crisis, détente, German approaches to eastern Europe (*Ostpolitik*), and the unsuspected significance of the Helsinki Accords of 1975.

Outline

I. The European project.

    A. Spurred by the 1956 Suez Crisis, western European statesmen sought to institutionalize unity in the face of their reduced status.

    B. The Treaty of Rome was signed in 1957, creating the European Economic Community (EEC), known as the Common Market, the predecessor to today's European Union (EU).

        1. Six countries united: France, Germany, Italy, Belgium, the Netherlands, and Luxembourg.

        2. Britain did not join at first, stressing ties to the Commonwealth and its "special relationship" with the United States.

        3. Later, after two rejections in 1963 and 1967, Britain joined in 1973, along with Ireland and Denmark; Greece joined in 1981, and Spain and Portugal joined in 1986.

    C. In 1967 the EEC, the European Atomic Energy Community, and the ECSC were fused into the European Community (EC), which became the EU in 1992.

    D. The United States supported European unity efforts.

E. Tensions emerged between contrasting Atlanticist and Europeanist visions.

    1. Atlanticists saw the United States and the NATO alliance as key.

    2. The Europeanists hoped for a European identity that transcended national boundaries, with the United States only as an important ally.

F. Trade and economic issues were also contentious.

II. Crises.

    A. In this period, another series of Cold War crises made painfully clear to western European statesmen the division and world situation and gave further momentum to European unification as an escape from junior partner status.

    B. In the Berlin Crisis of 1958–1959, Khrushchev set a six-month deadline to resolve the status of the city but then let the deadline pass.

    C. In August 1961 the German Democratic Republic built the Berlin Wall, sealing off the city, but no intervention followed.

    D. In the most dangerous episode of the Cold War, the Cuban Missile Crisis of October 1962, a standoff arose between the United States and the Soviet Union over the stationing of missiles in Cuba.

        1. The crisis was resolved with the Soviet removal of missiles, followed by the American removal of missiles from Turkey.

        2. A telephone "hotline" was established between Washington and Moscow to avert crises, underlining the importance of technology and communications to diplomacy.

        3. The crisis reminded Europeans of their position between the superpowers.

    E. Middle Eastern crises also indirectly affected Europe.

        1. After the defeat of Arab forces in the Six Day War in 1967, Egypt and Syria attacked Israel in the Yom Kippur War of 1973.

        2. Arab oil-producing countries set up an embargo on shipments to Europe and the United States, setting off an "oil shock" and inflation.

3. European economies, dependent on the Middle East for 80 percent of their oil, were stunned.
4. News of arms shipments to Israel through NATO led to friction between the United States and its European allies.

III. European relationships.

    A. Even as European unity advanced, relations between states in Europe still were very significant.

    B. In France, General de Gaulle returned to power in 1958 with the collapse of the Fourth Republic, as civil war threatened to break out over the Algerian conflict.
      1. De Gaulle established the Fifth Republic and ruled as president until 1969.
      2. In 1962, De Gaulle recognized Algerian independence.
      3. His foreign policy sought to assert an independent role between the Cold War blocs, symbolized by France's nuclear strike force beginning in 1960.
      4. He expressed suspicion toward the United States and Great Britain (excluding it from the Common Market) and invoked a "Europe of fatherlands."
      5. French-German reconciliation was a keystone; Adenauer was his ally and the Elysée Treaty of January 1963 sealed their partnership.
      6. De Gaulle underlined French independence by removing French forces from NATO command in 1966, although France remained a member.

    C. The Warsaw Pact invaded Czechoslovakia in 1968 when the pact felt reformist leaders were moving too far and too fast.
      1. After Khrushchev was deposed in 1964, the leadership eventually devolved to Leonid Brezhnev (1906–1982).
      2. When reformist leaders replaced hardliners during Czechoslovakia's Prague Spring, the Warsaw Pact invaded in August 1968.
      3. This was called the Brezhnev Doctrine, which urged intervention whenever Communist regimes might be overturned—a reversal of Metternich's doctrine of intervention.

IV. Thaws.

    A. Remarkably, around the tense time of the Cuban Missile Crisis, the Vienna Convention on Diplomatic Relations was negotiated in the spring of 1961 by a U.N. conference. The convention led to a landmark agreement on diplomatic rules, the privileges and immunities of diplomats, and treaty-making.

    B. Other treaties were signed to lessen tensions: the Nuclear Test Ban Treaty (July 1963), the Outer Space Treaty (January 1967), and the Nuclear Nonproliferation Treaty (July 1968).

    C. The period of 1969–1979 was marked by détente, or a lessening of tensions.

        1. In the United States, President Nixon (in office from 1969 to 1974) and Secretary of State Henry Kissinger (in office from 1973 to 1977) pursued an opening to China starting in 1971, at first using "ping-pong diplomacy."

        2. The result was a relationship that balanced against the Soviet Union—a classic strategy of Realists.

        3. As a political scientist, the German-born Kissinger had studied Metternich and diplomatic history.

        4. Kissinger won the Nobel Peace Prize in 1973 but has also been severely criticized.

    D. A separate variant of this détente was the *Ostpolitik* ("Eastern Policy") of West German social democrat, Chancellor Willy Brandt (1913–1992), in office from 1969–1974.

        1. Brandt, a former mayor of West Berlin, launched his policy in October 1969 to create *Wandel durch Annäherung* ("change through mutual approach") in the relationship with the Eastern Bloc.

        2. Some have seen this as a counterpart to Adenauer's Western linkage.

        3. In treaties with the Soviet Union and Poland, he recognized Germany's borders and acknowledged the German Democratic Republic; in 1973 both states joined the United Nations.

4. In December 1970, he fell to his knees before the Warsaw Ghetto monument in Poland, a symbolically charged gesture.

5. In 1971, he received the Nobel Peace Prize, but Germans were divided on his policy.

6. Brandt resigned in 1974 when it was learned that one of his assistants was an East German spy; spying was a dramatic element of the Cold War conflict.

E. A series of international agreements was negotiated.

    1. The 1972 SALT I Treaty and the 1979 SALT II Treaty set limits on missile technology.

    2. The Conference on Security and Cooperation in Europe opened in Helsinki in 1972; force reduction talks opened in Vienna in 1973.

    3. The culminating event of détente was the Helsinki Conference of 1972–1975.

    4. Its Final Act was signed on August 1975 by 35 states, recognizing the borders of Europe and guaranteeing human rights.

    5. Critics expressed anxieties about this underwriting of permanent European division, but the treaty produced unexpected results as human rights activists in the Eastern Bloc mobilized.

F. In spite of these agreements, the Soviets advanced their power through increased stationing of missiles, naval construction, and expansion in the non-Western world.

    1. When U.S. President Jimmy Carter came to office in 1977, his administration faced this challenge.

    2. Carter's national security advisor was Zbigniew Brzezinski (b. 1928), who like Kissinger, was a Realist and of European birth.

V. A Return to turmoil in 1979.

A. The Iranian Revolution, led by Ayatollah Khomeini (1900–1989), produced the declaration of an Islamic Republic in February 1979.

    1. Breaking traditions of diplomatic immunity, revolutionaries occupied the U.S. embassy in Tehran in November 1979, holding hostages there for over a year.

    2. To show their break with Western conventions, Iranian diplomats to the present day do not wear ties.

B. In December 1979, Russia invaded Afghanistan.
   1. Western leaders were alarmed.
   2. Western sanctions were applied and the 1980 Moscow Olympics were boycotted.

C. Détente was now clearly over and a new phase of the Cold War began, one that would bring astonishing results.

Essential Reading:

Henry Kissinger, *Diplomacy*, pp. 568–761.

Supplementary Reading:

John Lewis Gaddis, *The Cold War: A New History.*

Questions to Consider:

1. What were the bases of the new French-German relationship, beyond the amity of Adenauer and De Gaulle?

2. Was Brandt's *Ostpolitik* an expression of Realism or Idealism?

Lecture Thirty-Four—Transcript
The European Project

In this lecture, we will be considering the different dimensions of an accelerating movement toward European unity, European cooperation, to be institutionalized in a way that we are calling here the European project to denote that sense of the imperative importance of institutionalizing European identity and pooling power in a sense. In our previous lecture, we looked at the linked phenomena of the formation of blocs to the east and the west and decolonization. In this lecture, we will examine the response to that new situation in the European project, the response really both to the changed status of Europe after a half century of destructive tensions and world wars, as well as its location as ground zero of the Cold War and perhaps even of a future World War III, as it was feared at the time.

In response, European political leaders sought to craft a new departure moving away from the competitive politics of statehood that had been inaugurated at the long-ago Treaty of Westphalia in 1648 that we had considered in earlier lectures—the establishment of a sovereign state system working with the balance of power. In this lecture, we will survey the European project of unity from 1957–1980. The project later culminates in the European Union of today that we will discuss more in a later lecture. In the very midst, in the very context, of the perilous experience of the Cold War, we will examine in particular surprising French and German cooperation, another historical departure, and the impact of the Cuban Missile Crisis—though it's far away, the reverberations are felt in Europe. We will examine the trend towards détente, an attempt to lesson Cold War tensions through negotiation, and in particular the German approach to détente and attempts to improve relations with eastern Europe in what was called *Ostpolitik,* or Eastern politics. We will close by examining the unexpected significance, the surprising significance of the Helsinki Accords of 1975.

Let's begin by examining some of the original context and the roots of the European project. To a great extent, spurred by the existential facts that were revealed by the 1956 Suez Crisis, western European statesmen sought to institutionalize their unity in the face of their reduced status. Konrad Adenauer, the German chancellor, had famously said at the time to his French counterparts that after the

Suez Crisis and the humiliation it represented, "Let Europe be your revenge." In some sense, this was to be a creative response that would give Europeans a new status and a new role to play, not simply that of being subordinate to an American ally across the Atlantic.

The outcome of these creative efforts was the Treaty of Rome. The Treaty of Rome was signed in 1957, and it created the European Economic Community, which was popularly known as the Common Market, the predecessor to today's European Union. There have been changes of names to indicate the increasing cohesion and the evolution of these units, and the key countries that were engaged in this first stage involved six—the countries of France, Germany, Italy, Belgium, the Netherlands, and Luxembourg that already had been linked in earlier ventures like the Coal and Steel Community that we had mentioned in our earlier lecture.

You will note that among those countries there was a prominent exception, one that was missing, and that was Britain. Britain did not join at first because British policymakers tended at this time rather than seeing themselves as bound up in a community of fate with the European continent to see themselves as in some sense linked with Europe but still having a multiplicity of other ties and other dimensions to the policies that they wanted to follow and the role that Britain should play.

In particular, British policymakers stress ties with the Commonwealth—that's to say other members of the Commonwealth that had evolved out of the earlier empire in which the Sun would never set; in particular what British policymakers celebrated as the "special relationship" with the United States, the American ally. This was a complicated relationship, as we have been at pains to stress earlier. It was sometimes thought of in terms that are especially revealing and in fact say something about the role that precedent or earlier precedent might play in the mind of statesmen even in quite modern times.

In this case, the precedent was an ancient one. Some British policymakers phrased it to themselves thus—that Great Britain was in a position to play Greece to America's Rome. What they meant by that in a reference to Classical times was that America was clearly a vigorous and mighty military power, which had energy and dynamism. It was in that sense like the Roman Empire as they styled it in this parallel to ancient times, and if that was the case, then Great Britain, which was an even older power and whose power had diminished relative to that of the new superpower, America, resembled Classical Greece to their minds. It was old, sophisticated, wise in the ways of international politics, and might, it was hoped, pass along or transmit some of that knowledge and perhaps at key moments play a restraining role to rein in a tempestuous and younger actor on the international scene. As later would be revealed, the Americans didn't necessarily see things in quite these terms, and it's sometimes been suggested that the "special relationship" was more special to the British than to the Americans at this time.

The result, the implication of British steering of a different route—which did not plunge immediately into the initiatives for the European unit—was that Britain's later decision to move towards a closer relationship with the continent, which broke with the earlier concepts of its splendid isolation or its offshore role, was a troubled one. In fact, when Britain tried to join this evolving European unit, it was rejected twice, in 1963 and 1967. French policy—which suspected that Britain might be in some sense a Trojan horse for American influence—was key in these cases of rejection. Britain finally won its application for admission in 1973. It was admitted along with Ireland and Denmark. Greece then would join the European community in 1981, and Spain and Portugal would join in 1986. It was an expanding area of cooperation in this regard.

Later, in 1967, another important step was taken. The EEC, the European Atomic Energy Community, and the ECSC were all fused together into the European Community, as it came to be called, the EC, which then in 1992 was renamed the European Union. Throughout these efforts for European unification, it's fascinating to observe the American role. The United States rhetorically supported and aimed to encourage European unity efforts as a way of encouraging European contributions to common defense as well as European stability; this is different from the role of "divide and conquer" that imperial powers have played otherwise in the historical past. There's a cautionary note here as well. There probably were moments when American policymakers who didn't like directions that European unification was moving in might have thought to themselves, you have to be careful what you wish for in this regard.

It's necessary to keep in mind here that tensions indeed would emerge between contrasting visions on both sides of the Atlantic about how western solidarity should evolve. The two competing visions are sometimes called "Atlanticists," as opposed to "Europeanists" or European concepts. It's necessary just briefly to define what these meant. Atlanticists saw the United States and the NATO alliance and its umbrella of security, as it were, as really being key, and the overarching identity one of western solidarity institutionalized in these terms.

The Europeanist conception, by contrast, saw the United States as an important ally but one that was not essential in their vision to what they hoped would be an evolving sense of European identity—one that transcended national and state boundaries to instead become something far more durable, and not Atlanticist but Europeanist in this sense. We need to keep in mind even as we talk about the cohesion of alliances or the cohesion of blocs that there could be conflicting conceptions or plans for the future playing a role nonetheless. That's simply the complicated reality one has to take aboard, and at the same time similarly trade and economic issues could remain contentious throughout this whole period so that there were mutual anxieties on either side about trade relationships between the Americans and the Europeans institutionalized in this way even as they were cooperating otherwise.

It was a period also marked by important crises; we want to turn to these next. In this period, another series of Cold War crises hammered home again, as if the point needed further emphasis to western European statesmen in particular that the division of their continent and the world situation at large was such that Europe needed to further its momentum or speed along its momentum for European unification to escape from what otherwise would be a perennially junior partner status in terms of the Cold War confrontation. Let's just take a few examples of these crises and see how they would stress or underline this point repeatedly.

In the Berlin Crisis of 1958–1959, the Soviet leader, Khrushchev, set a six-month deadline to resolve the status of the city. In some ways, this harkens back to in the decade previous to the crisis concerning Berlin that Stalin launched. In this case, the crisis and tension grew but Khrushchev let the deadline pass. It was a reminder of the fact that there were still unsettled issues right at the center of the continent. This was again emphasized in August of 1961 with events that took place in Berlin again, when the German Democratic Republic, the East German state, built the Berlin Wall, which sealed off this divided city between the east and the west, but no intervention followed on the part of the allies. The tense standoff remained in this case, and all of this then built to what amounted to the most dangerous episode of the entire Cold War: the Cuban Missile Crisis of October of 1962.

This was a standoff that arose between the United States and the Soviet Union concerning the stationing of missiles in Cuba. The crisis itself was ultimately resolved after times of tremendous tension and anxiety by a compromise settlement: the Soviet removal of missiles from Cuba followed then by American removal of missiles from Turkey that were stationed close to the borders of the Soviet Union. The very mutual sense of anxiety and just how close the confrontation brought both sides to the potential devastation of a conflict of World War III led to both initiatives for an attempt at lessoning of tensions and fascinating diplomatic innovations. I want just for a moment to consider some of the latter.

A "hotline," as it was known, a telephone link that established immediate direct contact between Washington and Moscow was set up as a result of this conflict. Its aim was to be able to avert crises, to be able to initiate communication immediately on matters of mutual concern so that God-forbid misunderstanding and miscalculation would play less of a role. What one sees here is a further underlining or an emphasis on the importance of technology and communications to the immediate human contact of diplomacy.

I might just here as a provocative sideline note that there's actually a fascinating debate that centers on this question of the role of communications in the business of diplomacy for the modern period. How did the advent of instantaneous communication affect diplomats? How did, in particular, the introduction of the telegraph, then later of the telephone, and in our own times the split second communication by e-mail—how did all of this change the role of the diplomat? The relationship, the question, is not a straightforward one. In fact, just consider the sort of evolution we have seen in the course of our lectures.

We will recall that in a much earlier lecture when we considered the 18th century, there had been the case of the lead up to the negotiation of the Treaty of Belgrade of 1739 between the Austrians and the Ottomans when a horrific blunder and miscalculation led to a treaty that the Austrians were not quite happy with because the diplomat they had sent over across to the enemy lines had not been a position to hear about developments that took place on the battlefield afterwards. He had been given powers to negotiate that were remarkably extensive, and so one might think that diplomats in an age of instantaneous communication have lost a lot of those powers—that they're subject to their superiors calling them and telling them what to do.

The debate is actually fascinating because there are historians who instead say that the affect has been the opposite. The very ability to communicate instantaneously, they argue, has actually made the role of the individual negotiator even more important precisely because in the absence of anxieties about the cutting off of communications, diplomats no longer, as they were in the past, are handed long lists of imperatives or orders about how you should do this in case this happens, this in case this happens—instead paradoxically modern communications and the ability to check back in some sense might have given a larger scope of action to individual diplomats. This is a debate that's likely to continue. It's obviously a fascinating one with tremendous practical implications as well.

Returning to the question of the immediate Cuban Missile Crisis and its aftermath, obviously the anxieties were worldwide, but Europeans in particular were reminded during the Cuban Missile Crisis of their position between the superpowers. The very fact that they were being, as they felt, negotiated over their heads, just as the missiles might be flying over their heads if the conflict turned hot, accented the perils of Europe's position of weakness in this regard.

Likewise, crises that also unfolded in the Middle East had an affect on Europe indirectly—we might note the fascinating reality that the very term we still use to this very day, the "Middle East," actually harkens back to earlier times of Imperialism in the 19th century. It was called the Middle East precisely because for the British the Near East, or this eastern Mediterranean, was the middle of an imperial continuum that went to the Far East, India, as a crucial possession. The Middle East was strategically important precisely because it was in the middle, but in this day after World War II, the significance was no longer the same as it had been in the days of Imperialism.

Just to cite a few examples of how this played out in practice: after Arab forces had been defeated in the Six Day War in 1967, there was renewed conflict when Egypt and Syria attacked Israel in the Yom Kippur War of 1973. Arab oil-producing countries then in reaction set up an embargo on shipments of oil to Europe and the United States; this had a traumatic affect on European economies in particular setting off an "oil shock" and inflation. European economies were stunned because they depended for 80 percent of their oil on the Middle East. This was the significance, very different from that of imperialist times, of resources flowing from the Middle East rather than it being a strategic lynchpin on the route to India.

The result was that their policies had to take into consideration their exposed position and their interest in the Middle East economically. News of arms shipments to Israel through NATO led to friction on the part of the Americans with the European allies.

At this key moment, it's also, even as we have been talking in terms of blocs and the project of European unity, it's important not to lose sight of an older reality—the fact that relations between states in Europe still remained quite significant. Let's look at a few of those first in the west and then in the east of Europe. General Charles de Gaulle, who had played an important role in the resistance during World War II, returned to power in France in 1958 after the collapse of the Fourth Republic and at a key moment when civil war was threatening to break out over the Algerian Conflict, a part of decolonization. De Gaulle, for his part, established the Fifth Republic and ruled as a strong president until 1969. He was able, out of the strength of his position and his personal prestige, to do what probably few other politicians could have at the time, which was to recognize Algerian independence in 1962 and draw that conflict to a close.

De Gaulle's foreign policy sought to carve out a new role for France and to in some sense give reality to the vision of French grandeur that he had famously announced in his memoirs as really a part of his very heart and soul. De Gaulle's foreign policy sought to assert for France an independent role between the Cold War blocs, between East and West, and this was powerfully symbolized by France's nuclear strike force that had been established by 1960. De Gaulle expressed suspicion towards the United States and Great Britain, and as we have mentioned earlier worked to exclude Great Britain from the Common Market on several occasions.

His conception was one of a "Europe of fatherlands," as he put it, in which France would play a key role as an arbiter and leader of other European powers. The keystone of this conception and its appeal was French and German reconciliation—in some sense continuing the work of Stresemann, that remarkable German diplomat of the interwar period. In this work of French-German reconciliation, de Gaulle's partner was the German politician Konrad Adenauer. Germany would, in Adenauer's conception, function as an ideal partner, which wasn't stated explicitly, but a junior partner in some sense while France played a key directing role. The signing of the Elysée Treaty of January 1963 sealed this partnership with far-going projects for cooperation in foreign affairs as well as economic. De Gaulle's independent foreign policy in this regard could be quite controversial with his other allies, in particular irking the United States. De Gaulle underlined French independence by removing French forces from NATO command in 1966, although France remained a member of NATO formally.

We want now to shift to examine events in eastern Europe and how the relations between the states could still matter a lot. In particular, we see a pattern of continued intervention by the Soviet Union along with its allies in cases where the Soviet Union grew anxious about the continuance of its influence. The Warsaw Pact thus invaded Czechoslovakia—which had been a member of the Warsaw Pact—in 1968 when it was felt that reformist leaders in Czechoslovakia were moving too far and too fast.

Events played out like this: Khrushchev had been deposed in 1964 and the leadership of the Soviet Union had eventually devolved to Leonid Brezhnev, a very conservative, hard-line figure. When reformist leaders in Czechoslovakia replaced hard-liners in a reform movement known as the "Prague Spring," the Warsaw Pact reacted by invading in August of 1968. This invasion and the quelling of the reform movement in Czechoslovakia was an expression of what came to be called the Brezhnev Doctrine—named after the Soviet leader, Leonid Brezhnev—which urged intervention by Communist regimes led by the Soviet Union whenever Communist regimes in its influence or in its bloc might be overturned. If it seemed that a state was slipping away from Soviet influence or its Communist regime, intervention was said to be justified. Here we see in a strange sort of reversal of historical patterns that Metternich's doctrine of intervention to quell revolution was now being put on its head and instead if revolution rhetorically, so at least the trope went, being reversed or threatened, the Soviet Union should intervene to restore the revolution.

At the same time as we have talked about crises, we also want to keep in mind that in this complicated dance as it were, of the diplomacy of the Cold War there were also periods of thaws. These thaws or lessoning of tensions, a sort of melting of some of the worst Cold War icicles in conflict, came in the form of a fairly constant negotiation in an attempt to probe areas of agreement that might be found perhaps on questions that were subordinate or not of the first order but as a hopeful sign. When we think all the way back to the start of our course and consider the masterful French diplomat, Cardinal Richelieu, who had championed the concept of permanent diplomacy, of always being in negotiation and in conversation. I think Richelieu, if brought back into our contemporary times, might have recognized something of that sort of venture that he had endorsed in his day. Just as an example, it was precisely around the tense time of the Cuban Missile Crisis, as it was unfolding, that the Vienna Convention on Diplomatic Relations was negotiated in a conference that was hosted by the United Nations.

It took place in the spring of 1961, so a little bit earlier, and it represented a landmark agreement on codifying diplomatic rules, the privileges and immunities of diplomats, and how one wrote treaties and conducted negotiations. In some sense this was an extension of the sort of agreements that we had already seen at the Congress of Vienna in 1815 and institutionalized later in the course of the 19th century but with key differences. This U.N. conference now was not just European in scope but in line with our concept, one of the important themes of our course, of the expansion of these earlier European patterns of diplomacy to an increasing scope. We see here that it involved the globe now and all of the countries represented in the United Nations.

Other treaties were also signed at this time to lesson tensions, and while we can't go into details, one might mention the 1963 Nuclear Test Ban Treaty, the 1967 Outer Space Treaty, and the 1968 Nuclear

Nonproliferation Treaty, all of which were intended to lesson tensions and to constrain aspects of the arms race.

The period then of 1969–1979, that decade, was marked by détente, in essence an attempt at lessoning or a downgrading of tensions. Much of this had also a Realist subtext. In the United States, President Nixon and Henry Kissinger, who served as the Secretary of State from 1973, pursued an opening to China; this was launched in 1971. The first ventures, the first contacts, were called by the somewhat whimsical name "ping-pong diplomacy," which didn't actually involve diplomats playing ping-pong but rather the sending of sports teams in a form of cultural or athletic exchange as the first opening of channels of communication that later could flower into much larger negotiations on larger issues. The result of this "opening to China," as it was called, was a relationship that grew up between the United States and China, which balanced off against the Soviet Union in spite of ideological affinities or differences on either side. This was really a classic strategy of realists given institutional form.

As a political scientist, the German-born Henry Kissinger had actually studied Metternich and diplomatic history of this period. Kissinger would go on to win the Nobel Peace Prize in 1973, but he also has been severely criticized for particular aspects of his foreign policy. More broadly, Kissinger's realist tradition has often been quite foreign to American public opinion, which often has instead tended to emphasize the appeal to ideas and values mobilized to such powerful effect by Woodrow Wilson in an earlier stage that we have discussed in previous lectures.

In this lecture, it would be worthwhile to shift the focus from détente in general, and in particular American practice of détente, to examine instead a European and in fact specifically German variant on détente. This was the so-called *Ostpolitik* that translates into "Eastern Policy" of the German social democratic, Chancellor Willy Brandt, who was in office in Germany from 1969–1974. Willy Brandt was a former mayor of West Berlin so he had experienced the front lines of the Cold War itself, who launched his new policy in October of 1969 to create what was called "change through mutual approach." That's a little bit clunky translation of the original German, *Wandel durch Annäherung* but it captures some of the notion of breaking some of the earlier patterns of the Cold War by initiating a new relationship with countries of the East Bloc.

Some historians have seen Brandt as essentially opening up to the east in a way that was a counterpart to the firm Western linkage that Konrad Adenauer, an earlier German leader in the Federal Republic had launched in his day. The result was new treaties with the Soviet Union and with Poland putting their relationship on a new and friendlier basis, the recognition of Germany's borders, which had been a sensitive issue as well, and an acknowledgement of the existence of the German Democratic Republic, which earlier had not been acknowledged diplomatically as a German state to the east.

In 1973 then, both states also joined the United Nations; this seemed to be part of the fruit of *Ostpolitik*. Symbolism was very important as part of the language, the rhetoric, of *Ostpolitik*, and a crucial symbolic moment came in December of 1970 when Brandt on a visit to Poland fell to his knees before the Warsaw Ghetto monument in Warsaw, Poland, in a symbolically charged gesture of historical acknowledgement and of regret for the fraught history of Germany relations with eastern Europe. In 1971, Brandt received the Nobel Peace Prize for his efforts, but many Germans remain divided on his policy and whether it was well-advised or whether it might not be going too far.

Then in 1974, Willy Brandt unexpectedly had to resign when it was learned that one of his own assistants, his own advisers, turned out to be an East German spy. This might be a moment to just briefly mention the way in which this points up the role that spying played as a dramatic element of the Cold War conflict. To cite but one example out of many, the Cold War was brought home to a lot of people in 1978 when the Bulgarian dissident writer Georgi Markov, who was living in exile in London, was assassinated in London with a poison-tipped umbrella, precisely the sort of cloak and dagger killings that were so prominent as a part of the Cold War conflict. Even fictional spies like James Bond, who made his first appearance in 1953, dramatized some of the Cold War aura around espionage, and incidentally the sophisticated British spy working in tandem with an American CIA spy who may not be very smart but has vast material resources at his possession is sort of an echo of some myths about the "special relationship."

A series of international agreements were also negotiated in this period of détente. These included the 1972 SALT I Treaty that set limits on missile launchers and other technologies and then the

SALT II Treaty signed in 1979. The Conference on Security and Cooperation in Europe also opened in Helsinki, Finland, in 1972, and force reduction talks also ran in Vienna in 1973. The culminating event of détente with surprising effect was the Helsinki Conference of 1972–1975. What was surprising about it? Well, its final act was signed at last in August of 1975 by 35 states, and it recognized the borders of Europe in some sense for stability. Borders were to be acknowledged and seen as permanent, not to be changed, and at the same time, a series of guarantees of human rights were signed by all of the signatories.

At the time, there were a lot of people who criticized the Helsinki Accords. They were anxious that this underwriting of permanent European division might in some sense be stability won at too high a cost precluding peaceful change some time in the future. But ironically, the treaty over the long haul produced some unexpected results because human rights activists in Communist countries of the Eastern Bloc actually mobilized demanding the very rights that had been promised by the signatories of the Helsinki Accords, the Soviet Union, in particular, in spite of all of the repression and punishment that they experienced. In spite of these agreements, the Soviets at this period continued to advance their build up of military power with increased stationing of missiles, naval construction and expansion in the non-Western world.

When President Jimmy Carter came to office in the United States in 1977, his administration would face this challenge, and indeed Carter's national security advisor was Zbigniew Brzezinski, like Kissinger a Realist but here of the Democratic Party and of European birth as well in this Realist tradition.

I want to close by examining the return to turmoil in 1979. The Iranian Revolution led by Ayatollah Khomeini produced the declaration of an Islamic Republic in 1979. Breaking traditions of diplomatic immunity, Iranian revolutionaries occupied the U.S. embassy in November of 1979 and held hostages for over a year. In a tradition that endures to this very day, Iranian diplomats do not wear neckties. They want to show their break with Western conventions, and it's felt that the necktie looks too close to a Christian cross in symbolic form. This just accents a new kind of revolutionary Islamic diplomacy that the Iranians see themselves as advancing.

Another event was taking place at the same time that seconded instability, and that was the Russian invasion in December of 1979 of Afghanistan. Many Western leaders were very alarmed at this renewal of the Cold War. The German chancellor at the time, Helmut Schmidt, asked, "Is this the new Sarajevo?" thinking back to 1914 and the escalation that the assassinations in Sarajevo had produced. Western sanctions were applied and the Moscow Olympics boycotted. Détente was clearly now over, and a new phase of the Cold War began. One that would end with astonishing results: the fall of the Berlin Wall and the end of the Cold War, which we will explore in our next lecture.

Lecture Thirty-Five
The Fall of the Wall

Scope:

With unexpected rapidity, the Communist states of eastern Europe and the Soviet Union collapsed near the end of the century. This lecture, covering the years 1980–1991, discusses the deeper causes leading to this startling transformation. It introduces the new generation of leaders on both sides of the Cold War divide—British Prime Minister Margaret Thatcher, American President Ronald Reagan, and Soviet General Secretary Mikhail Gorbachev—and discusses the negotiations that followed a renewed stage of the Cold War. The dramatic internal consequences of a shifting international scene included the liberation of eastern European countries and German reunification, in spite of the anxieties that these sudden changes could produce.

Outline

I. The outcome of increased tensions.

    A. From 1980, the "Second Cold War" unfolded as tensions again increased between the superpowers and the blocs.

    B. The outcome was a startling one: the unexpected (and unexpectedly peaceful) collapse of the Soviet Union by 1991.

    C. In the background, European unification efforts continued.

        1. In 1987, the Single European Act (SEA) resolved that by 1992 a single market should be established for movement, capital, services, and goods in western Europe.

        2. This Europe, however, did not include all of central or eastern Europe.

    D. It is important to note that even as western European countries and the United States were allies, trade conflicts and friction on political issues were nonetheless present.

II. New leaders.

A. In Great Britain, Margaret Thatcher (b. 1925) became Prime Minister in 1979.

   1. She was the first woman to lead the government of a European Great Power.

   2. Her role and conservative policies earned her the nickname "Iron Lady."

   3. When Argentina invaded the Falkland Islands in the south Atlantic in 1982, Thatcher's response was energetic, and the invasion was repelled.

B. In the United States, Ronald Reagan (1911–2004) took office as president in 1981.

   1. In relations with the Soviet Union, his plan moved away from containment or coexistence to an active promotion of change.

   2. Reagan referred to the Soviet Union as "the evil empire."

C. Soviet leadership experienced a changing of the guard.

   1. When Brezhnev died in 1982, he was succeeded by two elderly successors who soon also died.

   2. The Afghan War dragged on, becoming the Soviets' Vietnam War.

   3. A younger Communist, Mikhail Gorbachev (b. 1931) became party secretary in March 1985 at the age of 54.

D. There was also unexpected change in the Vatican, where a new Polish pope was elected in 1978.

   1. Karol Wojtyla (1920–2005) became Pope John Paul II.

   2. His papacy was marked by personal diplomacy, energetic travel, and the advocacy of human rights; it had a catalytic effect on eastern Europe.

E. Apart from the world of state leaders, another institution emerged in 1980 in Poland that played an important role: the independent trade union Solidarity.

   1. Solidarity was led by an electrician, Lech Walesa.

   2. After Soviet warnings, Poland declared martial law in December 1981 and cracked down.

3. The Solidarity movement, together with the stances of dissidents in eastern Europe and groups calling for respect for the human rights promises of the Helsinki conference, was a crucial catalyst for change.

III. The new Cold War.

A. The origins of renewed Cold War tensions went back to the late 1970s, when the Soviets installed new SS-20 missiles and increased their naval power.

1. These medium range missiles could reach anywhere in Europe and promised Soviet supremacy in nuclear weapons in Europe.

2. In spite of large demonstrations opposed to NATO's Euromissile stationing, missiles were deployed by 1984.

B. The forward stance of the United States also came into play.

1. Reagan's 1985 State of the Union address proposed what came to be called the Reagan Doctrine: support to anti-Communist insurgents in Afghanistan, Angola, and Nicaragua.

2. Reagan announced plans for the Strategic Defense Initiative ("Star Wars") in March 1983.

3. The Soviet Union was already spending an estimated 20 percent of its GDP on defense (although it was perhaps only half as wealthy as the United States) and now faced the prospect of an accelerated high-tech arms race.

IV. Gorbachev—the True Believer.

A. As a committed Communist, Mikhail Gorbachev, general secretary beginning in March 1985, sought to reform the Soviet Union and take it back to its Leninist origins.

1. He was representative of a new generation.

2. His policies of g*lasnost* (openness) and *perestroika* (restructuring) implied a retrenchment in foreign policy.

3. His reform project faced challenges from those who wanted more or less change.

B. Gorbachev ended Soviet involvement in the Afghan War in 1989.

C. Gorbachev also rejected the Brezhnev Doctrine of intervention to maintain Communist regimes in satellite states.

D. To western European audiences, Gorbachev urged the idea of a "common European home."

V. Summits.

    A. Summit diplomacy (in which state leaders met in person) changed the roles of traditional diplomats.

    B. Gorbachev and Reagan met in Geneva, Switzerland, and Reykjavik, Iceland.

    C. At the third meeting in Washington D.C., in December 1987, the Intermediate-Range Nuclear Forces (INF) Treaty was signed to eliminate medium-range nuclear missiles.

    D. Succeeding Reagan as president in 1989, George H. W. Bush supported Gorbachev's program.

VI. Climax—1989.

    A. Demands for political freedom and independence from Soviet control rose throughout eastern Europe, beginning in the satellite states and then spreading into the inner empire.

    B. A chain of events in 1989 showed accelerating change.

        1. In Hungary, political parties were legalized, democratic groups won elections, and borders were opened.

        2. In Poland, Solidarity was legalized and won elections.

        3. In Czechoslovakia, mass demonstrations led to a new government headed by dissident Vaclav Havel in what was called the "Velvet Revolution."

        4. In East Germany, experiencing a hemorrhage of citizens (many fleeing to embassies of the Federal Republic of Germany), the Berlin Wall was breached by crowds on November 9, 1989.

    C. German Reunification.

        1. Prime Minister Helmut Kohl (b. 1930) and Foreign Minister Hans-Dietrich Genscher (b. 1927) lobbied for international approval.

        2. The Soviets at first opposed NATO membership for a united Germany, and Germany's European neighbors to the east and west expressed concerns about the increase in German power.

3. In May and June of 1990, the "Two Plus Four" conferences met in Ottawa, including the United States, the Soviet Union, Great Britain, France, and the two German states.
4. The occupying powers gave up their rights.
5. United Germany would be part of NATO but without nuclear weapons; the Soviets were promised economic aid and gradual withdrawal for their forces.
6. In an accord signed in Moscow on September 12, 1990, by the World War II allies and the German states, the unified Germany was promised full sovereignty.
7. The country was united on October 3, 1990.
8. Inevitably, Germany would play a new foreign policy role different from its understated earlier role as an economic giant and a political dwarf.

VII. The Paris Accord.

    A. In November 1990, the Soviets, the United States, and 22 European states gathered in Paris for an accord that in essence ended World War II.

    B. The host was the Conference on Security and Cooperation in Europe.

    C. The accord recognized European borders and reduced conventional forces stationed in Europe.

VIII. The fall of the Soviet Empire.

    A. With stunning rapidity, the Soviet Union, founded in 1922, collapsed in 1991.

    B. Countries earlier controlled by Moscow gained independence, continuing the trends of decolonization seen earlier in Europe.

    C. The impetus now spread further than Gorbachev's team intended—to the Soviet Union itself.

        1. A dramatic scene took place on August 23, 1989, in the Baltic states: a mass protest against the 1939 Nazi-Soviet Pact with two million people holding hands across 600 kilometers in three countries (Estonia, Latvia, and Lithuania).

2. When the Baltic states moved toward independence in March 1990, Gorbachev threatened consequences and a blockade.
3. As events unfolded, Gorbachev was awarded the 1990 Nobel Peace Prize.
4. The Gulf War of 1990 was also part of the international political background at the time.
5. In January 1991, Soviet storm troopers attacked in Lithuania and Latvia, killing unarmed civilians.
6. As Gorbachev shifted back to hard-line support, his rival Boris Yeltsin (1931–2007) was elected president of the Russian Republic.
7. U.S. President George H. W. Bush urged a moderation of demands for self-determination.

D. In August 1991, a coup was launched in Moscow by members of Gorbachev's own government while he was vacationing on the Black Sea.
1. Yeltsin rallied opposition to the coup, which quickly collapsed into disarray.
2. On Gorbachev's return, his power base had evaporated.
3. In December 1991, the Soviet Union was officially dissolved and a Commonwealth of Independent States was organized to include Russia, Ukraine, and Belarus; the commonwealth later included Armenia, Kazakhstan, Kyrgyzstan, Tajikistan, and Uzbekistan.

E. Unexpectedly, Soviet collapse proceeded with little armed conflict.

IX. New challenges.

A. In some sense the legacies of World War II as well as the 45-year Cold War were brought to an end, but a new structure needed to be established.

B. Eastern European countries emerging from dictatorship and command economies now faced tremendous problems on their own, among which was the difficulty of building up their own diplomatic corps.

C. By 1991, central and eastern Europe's map had been redrawn. What implications would that have for a more complete European identity?

Essential Reading:

Henry Kissinger, *Diplomacy*, pp. 762–803.

Supplementary Reading:

Timothy Garton Ash, *In Europe's Name: Germany and the Divided Continent*.

Questions to Consider:

1. Was the collapse of the Soviet Union inevitable once Communist regimes elsewhere in eastern Europe fell?

2. Does the fall of Communism and its aftermath tend to support Realist or Idealist theory?

Lecture Thirty-Five—Transcript
The Fall of the Wall

In this lecture, already closer to our own times, we will examine the fall of the Berlin Wall, the collapse of the Soviet Union, and how diplomacy struggled to simply keep up with these dramatic changes on the ground. In our earlier lectures, we have examined the Cold War as a series of crises and as a process of negotiation with hopes for détente. In this lecture, we will see how with unexpected rapidity the Communist states of Eastern Europe and the Soviet Union itself would collapse near the end of the 20th century. This lecture will cover the years 1980–1991, and we will discuss the deeper causes that led to this startling transformation.

It will look, first of all, at a new generation of leaders on both sides of the Cold War divide including Thatcher, Reagan, and Gorbachev. We will discuss the negotiations that followed a renewed stage of the Cold War. The dramatic internal consequences of a shifting international scene that would follow would include the liberation of Eastern European countries, German reunification in spite of the anxieties that the sudden change could produce, and an unfamiliar new post-Cold War world.

Let's begin by setting the stage. From 1980, a new phase in the Cold War had begun to unfold, the so-called "Second Cold War," or "Little Cold War," as tensions again increased between the superpowers and their respective blocs. Yet, the outcome ultimately of this increased intensity of the Cold War would be a starting one, the unexpected and unexpectedly peaceful collapse of one of the superpowers, the Soviet Union, by 1991. In the background, as the Cold War itself underwent this period of increased intensity and then entered its end stage, we need to keep in mind that European unification efforts were continuing and probably played some role in impelling the sort of change that was happening in Eastern Europe at the time.

In 1987, the Single European Act, the SEA, resolved that in the near future, by 1992 in fact, a single market should be established for movement, capital, services, and goods in Western Europe—but it's important to keep in mind that even as we're talking about this as an example of European unification, this future Europe would be mostly Western, mostly prosperous, and would not include all of Central or Eastern Europe. I think that there were people who had anxieties in this period that they were being left out of the European project as the train might be leaving the station. It's important also to note that even as the Western European countries and the United States were allies in the Cold War conflict, there were nonetheless conflicts and friction over issues like trade or political issues at the same time.

Let's turn now to examine a new generation of leaders, in some cases involving pretty dramatic change. In Great Britain, Margaret Thatcher became Prime Minister in 1979. She was the first woman to lead the government of a European Great Power. We earlier had seen women monarchs like Catherine the Great or Maria Theresa who had played very important roles. Here was the first woman exercising that representative role in a democratic system. Indeed, Thatcher's advent on the scene probably is also the reflection of a larger phenomenon, the growing role of women in international diplomacy as such after World War II. Margaret Thatcher's role and often-controversial conservative politics earned her the nickname, the "Iron Lady." In foreign policy, Thatcher denounced what she saw as the Suez syndrome, an exaggerated timidity in the use of power after the humiliations of the Suez crisis of 1956, and she aimed to shake off some of those impediments in the exercise of British power so that when Argentina invaded the Falkland Islands in the south Atlantic in 1982, Thatcher's response was energetic and the invasion was quickly repelled.

In the United States, Ronald Reagan took office as president in 1981 and soon partnered with Thatcher in vigorous foreign policy initiatives. In relations with the Soviet Union, Reagan's planning from 1983 moved away from earlier notions of containment or coexistence to an active promotion of change, and Reagan famously referred to the Soviet Union as "the evil empire." Soviet leadership at this period also experienced a remarkable changing of the guard that we now know with the historian's perfect hindsight would be fateful. When Leonid Brezhnev, who already was well along in years, had died in 1982 after the invasion of Afghanistan, he was followed by two elderly successors in quick succession. In some sense a leadership crisis was hitting the very pinnacle of the Soviet establishment as well at a time when the Afghan War was dragging on with Soviet troops bogged down in what some considered was the Soviets' equivalent of the Vietnam War experience that the United States had undergone.

Finally, in March of 1985 in a leap of generations, the Central Committee appointed a younger Communist, Mikhail Gorbachev, to become party secretary at the relatively youthful age of 54 given the advanced ages of other party leaders. There was also at the same time—and this is really a remarkable larger generational transformation that we see across the board—an unexpected change in the Vatican as well where a new Polish pope was elected in 1978 after a long period of Italian popes. Karol Wojtyla became Pope John Paul II, and his papacy would be marked by a very active use of personal diplomacy as well as public diplomacy and appeals to public opinion. His papacy was marked by energetic travel around the world and advocacy of human rights that, as we will see shortly, would have a catalytic effect on Eastern Europe and the dynamics of that scene.

At the same time, and here was another Polish connection, apart from the world of state leaders another institution was emerging in 1980 in Poland, which would go on to play a very important role as sort of a catalyst for dynamic political transformations that would have international ramifications. That was the establishment in what was a Communist state of an independent workers' union, the independent trade union known as Solidarity, led by an electrician, someone of working class origins, Lech Walesa.

After Soviet warnings in line with the Brezhnev Doctrine, of not moving away from revolutionary and Communist regimes, Poland, on the part of its Communist leadership, declared martial law in December of 1981 and cracked down on the Solidarity movement. Events were playing in a subterranean way a really dynamic role under the surface, below this sort of repression. The Solidarity movement, and when one adds to that also the stances of dissidence in Eastern Europe, in particular groups calling for respect for the human rights promises that the Soviet Union and other Communist regimes had just made at the Helsinki Conference, together would be a crucial catalyst for dramatic changes in eastern Europe.

First, we need to examine the revving up of Cold War tensions once again in that renewed "Second Cold War." The origins of the renewed Cold War went back to the later 1970s when the Soviets had installed new SS-20 missiles on the European continent at a time when they were also increasing their naval power and in 1979 also invading Afghanistan. The medium-range missiles that the Soviets had stationed could reach anywhere in Europe and promised Soviet supremacy in nuclear weapons in Europe.

In spite of large demonstrations by protestors opposed to NATO's stationing in answer so-called "Euromissiles," that is to say intermediate-range missiles that were intended to balance the ones that the Soviets had just deployed, NATO missiles in fact were, in spite of these protests, deployed by 1984. Further tensions also arose or were accented by the forward stance of the United States in the Reagan administration. Reagan's 1985 State of the Union Address proposed what came to be called the Reagan Doctrine, which moved beyond containment to active support for anti-Communist insurgents in key places around the world including Afghanistan, Angola, and Nicaragua. Reagan also announced plans for the strategic defense initiative, which was nicknamed "Star Wars" in March of 1983—that is to say a space-based system to defend against incoming missiles. When one adds together this increase of tensions as well as the promise of a more aggressive American policy in this regard, it presented a real challenge to the Soviet Union at this period.

The Soviet Union was already spending an estimated 20 percent of its GDP on defense. Those numbers are still the object of debate, but it's clear that the percentage was a very large one and much larger than what the United States was spending in this period at a time when the Soviet Union was—and again the statistics are debated—perhaps half as wealthy as the United States in terms of GDP. Now, added to that tremendous crushing burden of spending on defense, the Soviet Union seemed to also be facing the prospect of an accelerated high-tech arms race. It was at this crucial crossroads moment that Mikhail Gorbachev, as general secretary from March of 1985, came on the scene. He would play a very important role in terms of foreign policy, though one that sometimes was perhaps misunderstood in the west even as his efforts at reducing the Cold War were appreciated because Gorbachev most definitely didn't seek to, as it were, destroy the Soviet Union. He rather sought to reform it and from his perspective as a committed Communist believer to take it back to its authentic, original Leninist origins.

What was crucial about Gorbachev was that he was representative of a new and younger generation. He advanced policies that promised dynamic and really fundamental change in the Soviet Union as part of this renewal. These policies were titled *glasnost*, which can roughly be translated into English as openness, as well as the policy of *perestroika*, or restructuring. These would have crucial domestic effects in terms of opening up discussions on earlier taboo subjects like Stalinist repression, but in foreign policy they also had a very important implication. What was implied was retrenchment or a stepping away from some of the vast implied promises of support to satellite regimes that had been the order of the day before.

Within the Soviet Union, Gorbachev's reform project would face challenges both from those who wanted more change as well as less change, and in some sense he was unable to satisfy these conflicting sets of demands. But in foreign policy fundamental change was wrought. Gorbachev first ended Soviet involvement in the Afghan War by 1989. Gorbachev also in an authentic and important change rejected the Brezhnev Doctrine of intervention such as had been seen repeatedly in satellite states in Eastern Europe to maintain Communist regimes in satellite states.

Instead, Gorbachev in what we see increasingly being deployed a very personal diplomacy that seeks to engage public opinion, in this case worldwide but especially in European audiences, Gorbachev instead urged putting international politics on a new footing moving away from the Cold War instead urging the idea of as he put it a "common European home." What that would mean in precise detail wasn't entirely clear, but it sure sounded like something new and attractive to many western Europeans.

It was precisely at this time that a more personal diplomacy was engaged in the form of more summit diplomacy. Summit diplomacy, which means the meeting of top state leaders in person at often very celebrated and publicity-drenched meetings, changed the roles of traditional diplomats—it needs to be mentioned that not all diplomats were very happy with this development of being relegated to the sidelines, as it were, while a personal diplomacy with all of its potentials as well as perils, the opportunity perhaps to misspeak or to be outmaneuvered by one's adversary or partner in these negotiations, was quite real.

Gorbachev and Reagan met repeatedly in Geneva where they sought to pursue arms control and then in Reykjavik, Iceland, where they raised expectations as a result of their conversations dramatically for the prospect of not just limiting weapons but in fact cutting armaments as such. Indeed, at a third meeting in Washington in 1987 the Intermediate Range Nuclear Forces Treaty, the INF Treaty, was signed that actually eliminated medium-range nuclear missiles that had been such an object of contention so recently. This was seen as a very hopeful departure from earlier patterns. Reagan was succeeded as president in 1989 by George Bush, who supported Gorbachev's program, in an act of international cooperation.

I want to turn now, however, to the climactic events of 1989 when diplomats and leaders would in some sense be scrambling to keep up with mass movements of revolutionary import on the ground. Demands for political freedom and independence from Soviet control rose throughout eastern Europe beginning in the satellite states on the margins of the Soviet system and then spreading into the inner empire of the Soviet Union's republics itself. This was not a process that had been thought out far in advance. Instead, at a crucial point Gorbachev and his advisors saw themselves improvising and having to contend with the press of events. Throughout it all, some diplomats actually retained a sense of humor. Gorbachev's advisor on foreign policy, Gennady Gerasimov, joked at this time that they were replacing the Brezhnev Doctrine with something called the "Sinatra Doctrine," and in fact this was named after the singer, the American singer, Sinatra himself. Instead of as with the Brezhnev Doctrine telling others how they should run their countries, the "Sinatra Doctrine" implied that "they could do it their way," and indeed the Eastern Europeans would set about doing it their way.

As climactic events unfolded, a chain of events in 1989 showed just how much acceleration was taking place, just how much change was the reality of the day. Moving along, we see that in Hungary, first of all, political parties were legalized. Democratic groups won elections, and borders were opened. This was a testing of the limits. It showed indeed that the limits had changed. In Poland, the Solidarity Trade Union was legalized and won elections. One sees country after country here in sort of an international chain reaction was being affected in the East Bloc. In Czechoslovakia, mass demonstrations led to a new government headed by the dissident Vaclav Havel, a playwright and intellectual who was released from prison and soon found himself as leader of the new Czechoslovakia in the smooth "Velvet Revolution," as it was nicknamed at the time.

In East Germany, the situation was probably unique. East Germany was experiencing a hemorrhage of German citizens who were fleeing to embassies of the Federal Republic of Germany in other East Bloc countries where they would present themselves, be given the citizenship that was theirs by constitutional right in the Federal Republic of Germany, and as a result of diplomatic immunity would be able to travel from these embassies to the west experiencing their liberation in this sort of circuitous way. Crowds that didn't want to wait actually breached the Berlin Wall in East Berlin itself on November 9, 1989, and this was a true challenge of sort of the people at large taking politics into their own hands. The results, however, of this remarkable event of the fall of the Berlin Wall would have international ramifications because the issue of how and even whether Germany should be reunified at the center of the continent, another German revolution as it were after the one of 1871, was one that had international ramifications. Thus, Prime Minister Helmut Kohl and his Foreign Minister, Hans-Dietrich Genscher, worked very actively in precisely this period behind the scenes to lobby for international approval for German reunification. It was a tremendously torturous diplomatic process that we can only sketch in sort of its broad outline.

The Soviets at first, while ready to consider the notion of a united Germany, opposed NATO membership for such a united Germany. Germany's European neighbors both to the east and the west often expressed concerns about what would be an increase of German power as two German states, east and west, would be fused into one, larger in population, economic, and military potential. But these diplomatic negotiations finally bore fruit. In May and June of 1990, the so-called "Two Plus Four" conferences met in Ottawa, Canada. They were called "Four Plus Two" because they included the United States, the Soviet Union, Great Britain, and France—that was the "4" part of the equation—and the two German states. This was to be a negotiation in which all of the parties that were involved were engaged in the negotiations rather than let's say the Germans simply waiting to hear what their fate might be. In an act thus of diplomatic departure, the occupying powers gave up their earlier rights as victors that had followed from World War II and agreed that the united Germany would be part of NATO but in a concession to Soviet anxieties would not have nuclear weapons. The Soviets for their part, as an exchange for their spirit of compromise, were promised economic aid—which they badly needed—and a gradual timetable for withdrawal of Soviet forces from East Germany rather than an immediate one.

An accord was then finally signed in Moscow on September 12, 1990, by the allies of World War II and the German states in which the unified Germany was promised that it would then have full sovereignty enjoying in line with the conventions of the Treaty of Westphalia that we have talked about in 1648 that founded the state system. It would enjoy the full sovereignty that independent states are said to enjoy and the functioning of that state system. Indeed, Germany was then united on October 3, 1990. Inevitably, this new Germany, the larger Germany, would play a new and larger foreign policy role very different from its deliberately under-stated earlier role in foreign policy.

Germany's earlier role, especially the role of the Federal Republic of Germany in the West has sometimes been called that of an economic giant because of its vast economic resources and productivity but on the other hand an economic giant that was also playing the international political role of a dwarf because this Federal Republic of Germany tended to follow rather than lead in foreign policy initiatives always beset with the anxiety of re-awakening fears about German power and what German independence might mean in terms of its international role harkening back to the disaster of World War II. Inevitably, Germany's neighbors asked themselves what would then new Germany be like in terms of its foreign policy role? And the answer inevitably and strikingly would be a new role given its new position in a new post-Cold War world.

Finally, just by way of a sense of closure in our earlier conversations about World War II, we will recall that World War II with Germany had not formally been ended. That at last was ended with the Paris Accord, almost an afterthought to these dramatic events. In Paris in November of 1990, the Soviets, the United States, and 22 European states gathered for the signing of an accord that in essence finally formally ended World War II. The host was the Conference on Security and Cooperation in Europe, and the accord recognized again European borders and also reduced conventional forces stationed in Europe in a sign, it was hoped, of a more peaceful future.

Events, however, had not stopped their momentum. We need to pass to the next act in the end of the Cold War, the surprising, indeed shocking, fall of the Soviet regime. With stunning rapidity, the Soviet Union, founded in 1922, collapsed in 1991. As countries that earlier had been controlled from Moscow gained their independence in what earlier had been an imperialist relationship, what one now saw was a continuation you might say of trends of decolonization that we had seen earlier in Europe affecting earlier imperial powers like France, Great Britain, or even Portugal. Now, that process hit the Soviet Union in earnest.

The impetus, which earlier had worked its way out through eastern Europe with the "Sinatra Doctrine" of eastern European countries going their own way now spread further than Gorbachev had intended to the Soviet Union itself. A dramatic scene, which underlined the way in which masses were now participating in international politics in a sense took place on a fateful anniversary, August 23, 1989. August 23, 1939, had been the date of the Nazi-Soviet Pact that had divided up eastern Europe. Now, in the Baltic countries, in 1989 on the anniversary of that fateful pact, two million people, protestors, came out to hold hands across 600 kilometers, across three countries, crossing borders in a sign of peaceful protest against an act of diplomatic injustice of the recent past.

When the Baltic states continued to move towards popular demands for independence from March 1990, Gorbachev for his part didn't know quite what to do and threatened severe consequence and blockade. This was a time of tremendous tension. Even as these events were unfolding, Gorbachev was awarded the 1990 Nobel Peace Prize in recognition of his earlier international role. There was also war on the horizon. The Gulf War of 1990 was part of the international context at the time, and it was not clear how events would now unfold. The answer at least in the short-term unfortunately was violence. In January of 1990, Soviet storm troopers attacked in the Baltic states in Lithuania and Latvia killing unarmed civilian protestors. As Gorbachev shifted back toward a more conservative hard-line stance, his rival within the new Russian politics, Boris Yeltsin, was elected president of the Russian Republic. For his part, the American president, George Bush, in Kiev, Ukraine, actually spoke to crowds urging that their demands for self-determination and independence be moderated—think of what a contrast this was to an earlier role of someone like Woodrow Wilson who had championed self-determination at the time. An unkind commentator at this point described Bush's speech as the "chicken Kiev speech."

Events trundled along with startling rapidity. In August of 1991, a coup was launched in Moscow by members of Gorbachev's own government while he was vacationing on the Black Sea. As famous news photos of the time remind us, atop a tank, Boris Yeltsin now rallied opposition to this coup, which quickly collapsed into disarray because the plotters lacked the confidence and sense of willingness to use force that would have been necessary to bring it to success. When Gorbachev returned from his arrest, his power base as he slowly discovered had evaporated, and in December of 1991, the Soviet Union was officially dissolved. In its place, a looser Commonwealth of Independent States was organized that included Russia, Ukraine, and Belarus—later also Armenia, Kazakhstan, Kyrgyzstan, Tajikistan, and Uzbekistan. It included, thus, many post-Soviet states, not the Baltic states—which now gained their independence.

Unexpectedly, the Soviet collapse proceeded with little armed conflict. In addition to this being a fact that we should be very grateful for, it remains in some sense a great puzzle of this entire process of why it didn't tip over into violence as one might have suspected. Clearly, the restraint on the part of those who were protesting and agitating for change played a key role.

We want to conclude by examining some of the new challenges that were in a sense the outcome of this changed, dramatically changed, international scene for many Europeans. In some sense, at long last by 1991 with the collapse of the Soviet Union at this point many of the legacies of World War II as well as that long, long, 45-year Cold War confrontation were finally wrapped up and brought to an end. But this raised as many questions as it answered. A new structure would need to be established in the aftermath of these astonishing events with both domestic and important international diplomatic consequences.

Eastern European countries emerging from dictatorship and command economies now faced tremendous problems on their own. In terms of diplomacy, one problem that they were confronted with immediately was the difficulty of building up their own diplomatic cores, and thus it was that countries like the Baltic states as they won their independence often had, as some other European diplomats felt, ridiculously young Foreign Ministers or ambassadors who were now engaged in international politics, sort of testimony to the dramatic change and revolution indeed that those countries had undergone in their international status and regained independence.

The key question that we want to pose for the purposes of our course that was posed by 1991 was this—Europe's map by 1991 had been redrawn in its central and eastern parts in particular at a time when the west was moving toward an increased European identity and consolidation. The tremendous upheaval that had been witnessed by 1991 would have crucial implications for a more complete European identity, not limited just to the prosperous west but extending eastwards as well. How Europe responded to this new post-Cold War scene and its challenges right up to the present day in our own times will be the important topic of our next lecture.

Lecture Thirty-Six
Post–Cold War to the Present

Scope:

This concluding lecture of our course covers the years from 1991 to the beginnings of the 21st century, including the expansion of NATO and the European Union, renewed violence in the Balkans, and Russia's search for an international role. We end by considering key questions of tremendous import for the future of our world: What is the current trajectory of the European Union project and what challenges does it face? What dynamics now guide relations between Europe, the United States, and the world at large? Is Europe now entering a fundamentally new stage in its experience of statecraft, or do the historical dynamics of war, peace, and power still apply?

Outline

I. A new European reality.

    A. With the end of the bipolar order of the Cold War, Europe faced the challenge of constructing a new order, a task that continues today.

    B. After the Cold War ended in 1991, hopes rose for new roles for international institutions earlier hampered by tensions, including the United Nations and regional cooperative organizations.

    C. The collapse of the Soviet Union left the United States as the world's sole superpower; Realist theory predicts challenges to balance supremacy.

    D. At the heart of the European Union project is the imperative to avoid another war in Europe.

II. The European Union.

    A. The 12 members of the European Community signed the Maastricht Treaty in 1992.

        1. Formally titled the "Treaty on European Union," it called for economic and monetary union, as well as the development of common foreign policy.

        2. The new unit was named the European Union.

B. The European Union continued its expansion.

    1. Austria, Finland, and Sweden joined the European Union in 1995.

    2. In 2004, the European Union admitted 10 countries, many of them from the former Eastern Bloc: Poland, Hungary, the Czech Republic, Slovakia, Slovenia, Estonia, Latvia, Lithuania, Malta, and Cyprus; and in 2007, Bulgaria and Romania were admitted.

    3. Currently, the European Union has 27 members.

C. European integration has proceeded at different paces.

    1. In 1999, the Euro was introduced in a dozen countries.

    2. In the March 1995 Schengen Accords, free movement across borders was agreed upon by some EU countries.

    3. In 2004, a Constitutional Treaty was drafted calling for closer union, but it was rejected by French and Dutch voters.

    4. An important issue is the prospect of membership for Turkey, which remains uncertain.

    5. In 2007, the EU's population was 494 million, larger than that of the United States.

    6. Simultaneously, the EU is experiencing challenges with an aging population, growing multicultural populations due to immigration, and uneasy encounters between the secular character of the European population and the Muslim immigrant population.

D. How much sovereignty are European states willing or able to give up?

E. Is a common European identity evolving?

F. A key question remains how the relationship between the European Union and the United States will evolve after decades of American urgings for European unity.

III. NATO expansion.

A. NATO was a key institutionalization of American-European cooperation during the Cold War, but some questioned the need for it after the Cold War's end.

B. NATO expanded in eastern Europe, testifying to a felt need for continued security.

    1. In April 1999, the Czech Republic, Poland, and Hungary were formally admitted to NATO.

2. In its fifth and largest round of expansion, NATO accepted Estonia, Latvia, Lithuania, Bulgaria, Romania, Slovakia, and Slovenia in March 2004.

IV. The Yugoslav War as a test.

    A. As the Communist federal state of Yugoslavia unraveled, a series of wars broke out in 1991 concerning its future, sometimes called the "Wars of Yugoslav Succession."

        1. The Yugoslav leader Tito died in 1980.

        2. Slobodan Milosevic (1941–2006) became head of the Serbian Communist Party in 1987, replacing Communist orthodoxy with a nationalist Greater Serbia ideology.

        3. When Slovenia and Croatia declared independence in June 1991, Serbian forces attacked and captured a third of Croatia.

        4. In December 1991, Germany unilaterally recognized Slovenia and Croatia.

        5. Early in 1992, many European states and the United States recognized Croatia, Slovenia, and Bosnia-Herzegovina.

        6. In spite of this, Serbian forces took 70 percent of Bosnia.

        7. Ethnic cleansing describes the policy of terrorizing different ethnic groups into fleeing through murder, rape, and devastation.

    B. Luxembourg's Foreign Minister Jacques Poos declared, "This is the hour of Europe," but resolute action lagged.

        1. In July 1995, Serbian paramilitaries overran the U.N. "safe haven" of Srebrenica, guarded by Dutch peacekeepers, and killed 7,000 Bosnian Muslims.

        2. In 1995, Bosnian and Croatian forces counterattacked and NATO launched air strikes.

        3. The Dayton Accords were negotiated in Ohio in November 1995, and a peace was signed in December 1995 in Paris.

    C. War broke out again in the summer of 1999 over Kosovo.

        1. In an instance reflecting the primacy of domestic policy, Milosevic pursued antagonisms that steadily shrank the Serbian state.

        2. The earlier autonomy of Kosovo (with its large Albanian population) was revoked, and clashes took place.

3. When ethnic massacres of Albanians took place, NATO bombed Yugoslav positions from March to June 1999 without UN approval.

4. In a sea change, Germany took part in the operation under the Social Democratic leadership of Chancellor Gerhard Schröder (b. 1944) and Foreign Minister Joschka Fischer (b. 1948).

5. In June 1999, Milosevic gave in and withdrew Serbian forces.

6. In 2000, Serbian protests ousted Milosevic, who was put on trial for war crimes and died in custody in 2006.

V. Russia.

A. The role of Russia remains a crucial one in Europe.

B. Under Yeltsin, Russia underwent a difficult transition.

1. Yeltsin's government sought to join Western structures.

2. From 1994, Russian forces waged a brutal war in the region of Chechnya until a ceasefire in 1996.

C. In 1999, Yeltsin appointed Vladimir Putin (b. 1952), a former KGB officer, as Prime Minister; Putin became Yeltsin's successor as president.

1. Putin launched the Second Chechen War in September 1999.

2. He called the breakup of the Soviet Union the "greatest geopolitical tragedy of the 20th century" and sought a renewed role for Russia as a Great Power.

3. Russia's aggressive foreign policy, buoyed by oil wealth, worried its neighbors.

VI. Looming issues for Europe and the world.

A. From the 1970s to September 11, 2001, and on to the present day, fears of terrorism continue to present challenges to the world.

1. Diplomats have often been targeted by terrorism.

2. The effectiveness of diplomacy in confronting rogue states (states fired by aggressive ideology or dictatorship) or terrorist groups remains unclear.

B. American-European relations are a key question in international politics.

    1. While French politicians have spoken of resisting American "hyper-power," this has not found institutional expression.

    2. While NATO allies generally cooperated in the war in Afghanistan that began in 2001, disagreements arose over the Iraq War launched by U.S. President George W. Bush (b. 1946) in March 2003.

    3. Among the disagreements were serious divides among the European states.

C. Robert Kagan's *Of Paradise and Power: America and Europe in the New World Order* (2003) provocatively argues that in some sense America and Europe increasingly inhabit separate universes with different values.

    1. Current U.S. defense spending is roughly double that of European defense spending.

    2. The European unity project has been motivated by the avoidance of war.

    3. As diplomacy's reach has spread to a wider range of international topics, other differences in values concern initiatives on environmental issues, the 2002 International Criminal Court, and multilateralism versus unilateralism.

D. Some commentators have argued for a refounding of American-European relations in a new Concert of Democracies, harking back to Metternich's guidance of Europe.

VII. Abiding issues, changes, and challenges.

A. Over five centuries, Europe's state system has been marked by tremendous changes. The earlier state system of Europe expanded to encompass the world and has changed in the process, with Europe no longer being the center.

B. An overview of major changes since 1500 is striking.

    1. From the Renaissance, European states crafted patterns of diplomatic exchange and communication.

    2. In answer to hegemonic challenges and religious war, Europe's state system was restructured in the 1648 Treaty of Westphalia.

3. Great Power states claiming sovereignty dominated the international scene (and, through imperialism, the globe) in shifting alliances and coalitions, first against French bids for hegemony, then against German advances.

4. World War I destroyed the traditional balance of power system of Europe and European supremacy as non-European powers rose, joined the system, and came to dominate it during the Cold War after World War II.

5. With the end of the bipolar confrontation of the Cold War, will the expanded state system be restructured again?

6. Clearly, stability is elusive in a world of constant change, and future questions are pressing.

C. Whither Europe and European identity?
1. The balance of power, once key, is now rejected.
2. In a speech, German Foreign Minister Fischer said that the:

> core of the concept of Europe after 1945 ... is a rejection of the European balance-of-power principle and the hegemonic ambitions of individual states that had emerged following the Peace of Westphalia in 1648.

3. Some suggest that the European Union represents a vindication of the decentralized and diverse structures of the Holy Roman Empire before 1648.
4. European identity is still under construction.

D. We have also seen the expansion of diplomacy as a vital theme.
1. Diplomacy has opened out to broader participation beyond narrow elites and circles of crowned heads.
2. Besides states, nongovernmental organizations (NGOs) and corporations play roles in contemporary diplomacy.
3. Fundamentally, public involvement in and knowledge of foreign affairs, whether by taking out a passport to travel or by understanding the past and present, is perhaps also a diplomatic act of participation and promise for the future.

4. This is an undertaking open to all of us: to seek to understand the scourge of war, the profound gift of peace, and the potentialities and perils of the use of power.

Essential Reading:

M. S. Anderson, *The Rise of Modern Diplomacy 1450–1919*, pp. 291–3.

Supplementary Reading:

Robert Kagan, *Of Paradise and Power: America and Europe in the New World Order.*

Questions to Consider:

1. What is the main source of European strength, potential, and vitality today?

2. What do you see as the main challenge facing Europe today?

Lecture Thirty-Six—Transcript
Post–Cold War to the Present

In this concluding lecture in our course, we will have the satisfaction of bringing the diplomatic trajectory that we've been charting over so many lectures right up to the present day. In this lecture, we will examine the years from 1991 to our own times. We'll look at some particular crucial events like the expansion of NATO and of the European Union, renewed violence in the Balkans, and Russia's search for an international role in the aftermath of the end of the Cold War, which we examined in our previous lecture. We'll then take stock of where we are today. We'll end by considering key questions that are of tremendous significance for the future of our world. These will include: What is the current trajectory of the European Union project, which is today still under construction? What challenges does it face? What are its prospects? What dynamics now guide relations between Europe and the United States and the world at large? Is Europe perhaps now entering a fundamentally new stage in its experience of statecraft, or do the older historical dynamics of war, peace, and power still apply?

Let's first begin by sketching in the new European reality that came with the end of the earlier bipolar order of the Cold War that had endured for decades. With the end of the Cold War, Europe faced the challenge of constructing a new order; in some sense this is a task that still is continuing today. After the Cold War ended by 1991 with the collapse of the Soviet Union, many hopes arose for new roles to be taken on by international institutions in some sense now coming into their own after earlier being hampered by Cold War tensions. That included the United Nations, for instance, or regional cooperative organizations that it was felt could now step into the breach. The collapse of the Soviet Union so unexpected, and blessedly so relatively free of larger violence, also had another effect: It left the United States standing as the sole superpower. If we consider realist theory—that important school of international politics that we had talked about throughout this course—realist theory on the basis of the imperatives of power politics has a prediction about what happens in cases like this when there is a sole superpower. It predicts challenges—challenges on the part of less formidable powers perhaps but uniting in order to balance off against the supremacy of a sole superpower. It's an open question whether such challenges are emerging today or might emerge in the future. To date, they haven't emerged with quite the same force that realist theory might otherwise have insisted they would.

A fascinating departure in terms of the international system has to be noted as well from the outset. At the very heart of the project of European unification as it is still under construction today, at the very heart of that vision of the European Union, is a crucial imperative: to avoid war in Europe again. That has had affects on precisely how war and peace have been thought about in the present European context.

Let's pass to talk about this construct, this emerging institution, the European Union. The 12 members of the European Community, as it was called before, signed the Maastricht Treaty in the Netherlands in 1992. Formally, this Maastricht Treaty was titled the "Treaty on European Union." It called for an ambitious list of innovations, economic and monetary union, as well as the development of a common, shared foreign policy among the members of this new unit that was to be named the European Union. The European Union saw, as one of its purposes, its expansion in order. After it had consolidated stability within and a great measure of cooperation among nations that pooled their sovereignty in order to achieve a greater unification, it continued its expansion as a way of extending that stability.

In 1995, Austria, Finland, and Sweden joined the European Union. There was a long hiatus while Eastern European countries clamored for entry and hoped to be admitted to the European Union, but it was a process that took a long time and probably also frayed tempers in the process. At long last after an extended pause, in 2004 the European Union admitted 10 countries in a large expansion, many of them from the former Eastern bloc that earlier had been under Soviet domination. These included the countries of Poland, Hungary, the Czech Republic, and Slovakia. These countries, the Czech Republic and Slovakia, had undergone a remarkably peaceful "Velvet Divorce," as it was called allowing for both of them to become independent rather than fighting a Civil War as might have been the case in less happy circumstances over the issue. The newly-admitted countries also included Slovenia; the Baltic states of Estonia, Latvia, and Lithuania; and also Malta and Cyprus. Then, in 2007, Bulgaria and Romania in southeastern Europe also joined so that currently the

European Union has experienced a large expansion and by today has 27 members.

European integration, the process of coordinating within the context or the framework of the European Union has proceeded however at different paces rather than being uniform across the board. In 1999, the Euro, for instance, a common currency, was introduced in a dozen countries, but some who are members of the European Union have not accepted the Euro and have retained their national currencies. Similarly, in the so-called Schengen Accords of March 1995 free movement across borders was agreed to by some but not all European Union countries; it has to be said that the experience of traveling in countries within the so-called Schengen Zone, in which the free movement has been guaranteed by this accord is a dramatic departure from how we thought about statehood in the past. Countries that have agreed to this free movement under the Schengen Accord now have opened their borders for travel without passports, and while they retain travel restrictions on the outside of their area, on the frontiers of the Schengen Zone, within one sees absolutely free movement of this sort. This is part of a commitment to in some sense a downgrading of nation-state identity, which now instead emphasizes other kinds of identities within the new Europe including regionalism, a sense of shared interests for instance in the areas in the French-German borderlands or on the German-Polish border rather than the exclusive dictates of Nationalism as had been the case in earlier decades or indeed centuries.

A constitutional treaty was drafted in 2004 to move the entire European Union toward a more perfect union for a close association, but it met a fateful reverse when it was rejected by French and Dutch voters. Conversations and negotiations continue to this very day about how one might advance institutional movement toward closer union after this reverse concerning a European constitution. There's also a very important issue, which also looms up for the policy makers of the European Union, which given our long survey of centuries of European diplomatic history we can really appreciate in its depth and its significance. That is the question of whether Turkey, which hopes to become a member of the European Union, will be admitted to membership.

Turkey, as we will recall, has been a European power. It's played a very important role in European history. That role, however, over the course of several centuries had often been an adversarial one as the Ottoman Turks represented a Muslim civilization at its height with all of its formidable power and challenge to earlier periods of European history. The arguments in favor of Turkish membership are that Turkey might in that sense be the very embodiment of the extension of this European model for stability domestically and in foreign affairs. But, many Europeans also have anxieties about whether Turkey belongs in its own concept of what it means to be European and long-standing traditions that condition self-identification as a European. The question remains for now an open one.

The European Union has already scored a tremendously expansive record. In 2007, the European Union's population was 494 million, making it larger as a political unit than the United States. At the same time, one needs in all candor to note that simultaneously the European Union is also experiencing challenges within that are sure to have implications for its diplomatic policies and foreign policy without. Those include: looming demographic problems with an aging population and the impact that will have on economic productivity, as well as growing multi-cultural populations due in great measure to immigration from outside that are changing the landscape in Europe in ethnic terms. An added dimension concerns religion and this is of some significance. We had earlier in our lectures in this course mentioned the important way in which after the experience of the religious wars with the Treaty of Westphalia in 1648, religion had not been excluded but had in some sense been moved to the side as a central issue in diplomacy. Now, religion returns as a very important and key issue as a European population, much of it a very secular character, uneasily encounters intensely religious Muslim immigrant populations and raises questions about how the future will unfold.

There are other very serious and profound political issues that are at the very heart of the European project. The European project depends upon states pooling their sovereignty, giving up some of their earlier sovereign national independence in order to achieve a greater project. The question arises: How much sovereignty are European states willing or able to give up or to continue giving up? And the greatest question of all that in some sense links up with the way in which we have tried to accent how understandings of Europe and what it means to be European have changed over this period is the question of whether today a common European identity is evolving. Are French, German, Spanish, or British people inclined to view themselves first of all as Europeans downgrading an earlier national identification? And then there's a key question, which is obviously of existential importance as well—the key question of how relations between the European Union and the United States will evolve after decades of American urgings for European unity have, as it turns out, come to pass.

Let's turn now to a question of another important change in our own times, and that's the expansion of NATO. NATO was a key institutionalization of European-American cooperation during the Cold War, but there was some question whether there was any need for it after the Cold War's end. In spite of such suggestions, NATO did expand in Eastern Europe testifying to a felt need on the part of many Eastern European countries for continued security against a revival of Great Power competition in that part of the world. So, clearly earlier patterns still resonate in the anxieties of the present day. In April 1999 the Czech Republic, Poland, and Hungary were formally admitted, and then in its fifth and largest round of expansion in its history, NATO also accepted Estonia, Latvia, Lithuania, Bulgaria, Romania, Slovakia, and Slovenia in March of 2004 presenting a wider zone of stability to the satisfaction of the new member states.

There was also in this period a crucial test of whether new dynamics or older dynamics would rule the day, and that was the Yugoslav War. As the communist federal state of Yugoslavia unraveled, a series of wars broke out concerning its future from 1991 on and dragged out with a horrific record in our own times. Sometimes these wars have been called by historians who simply love to reference earlier precedents, the "Wars of Yugoslav Succession," meaning what follows after the Yugoslav Federal Republic under the leadership of the communist Tito. This is meant to echo earlier conflict like the Wars of the Spanish Succession or the Wars of the Austrian Succession—perhaps too clever a name for this bloody conflict of our own times.

After the communist leader Tito, who had to a great extent held together the Yugoslav state died in 1980, eventually the Serbian politician Slobodan Milosevic became head of the Serbian communist party in 1987. He replaced the patent and clear bankruptcy of Communism as an orthodox ideology with a new ideology that he put in its place. That was a Nationalist ideology of greater Serbia. This would imply nationalist expansion and domination in the region. When Slovenia and Croatia—that earlier had been constituent parts of Yugoslavia—declared their independence in June of 1999, Serbian forces attacked and soon captured a significant chunk of Croatia. In December of 1991, reacting to this resurgence of bloodshed to the south, Germany unilaterally recognized Slovenia and Croatia without consulting in advance all of the countries of the European Union. This was a worrisome moment for many European diplomats and policymakers who now worried that Germany might in some sense be carving out a new and more unilateral role for itself that some felt was almost inevitable after German unification.

Early in 1992, however, many European states followed the German lead as did the United States and recognized Croatia, Slovenia, and Bosnia-Herzegovina. But nonetheless, Serb forces took 70 percent of Bosnia and enacted a horrific program of what has come to be called in our own times ethnic cleansing, which describes the policy of terrorizing ethnic groups different from one's own into fleeing through a horrific record of murder, rape, and devastation.

It needs to be added that in a cycle of violence throughout the region after Serb forces had initiated this sort of a policy toward non-Serbs in the region, Serbian minorities in turn in other parts of that region would be subjected to similar ethnic cleansing as well. This was a moment when it seemed that European politics might be brought to bear through the efforts of the European Union to stamp out this sort of recurrence of the horrors of previous ages in Europe in the present day. Indeed the Foreign Minister of the European state of Luxembourg, Jacques Poos, declared ringingly that "this is the hour of Europe." But nonetheless, in spite of this promise, resolute action on the part of European states in concert lagged, and a crowning horror came in July of 1995 when Serbian paramilitary forces overran a United Nations "safe haven," as it was called, an area that was supposed to be immune from this sort of bloodshed and havoc, by the name of Srebrenica, which was guarded by Dutch peacekeepers who were taken prisoner by the Serb paramilitaries as 7,000 Bosnian Muslims were killed in an act of genocide perpetrated in Europe in our own times.

In 1995, Bosnian and Croatian forces counterattacked and NATO launched air strikes against the Serb paramilitaries in the first combat experience of the alliance in its history. The so-called Dayton Accords signed in Dayton, Ohio, were negotiated from November 1995, and a peace was signed in December 1995 in Paris bringing, so it seemed for a while, the violence to a close. Then violence returned as war broke out again in the summer of 1999 over Kosovo. This event is worth looking at in some detail. It was an instance, you might say, of the primacy of domestic policy—one of those concepts we advanced right from the start of our course—the way in which the imperatives of the internal politics can shape foreign policy actions.

Slobodan Milosevic as a dictator had pursued antagonisms with neighboring ethnic groups in order to consolidate his own power as a necessary Serb nationalist leader, but the process these conflicts, one after another, had the inadvertent effect of steadily shrinking the size of the Serbian state. Some Serbians bitterly joked at the time that if things continued in this way Milosevic would be left essentially with downtown Belgrade as his sole area of control. This new conflict, the final conflict as it turns out, centered on Kosovo, which is a history-soaked ground where the fateful defeat in 1389 of Serb armies by Ottoman's advancing upon Europe had taken place. You will recall that the World War I had been launched with the assassination in Sarajevo on the date that commemorated precisely this fateful historic defeat of 1389 in a place where historical memory is very rich.

The earlier autonomy of Kosovo, which had over time gained a large Albanian majority, was revoked and clashes took place between this ethnic group and the Serbian government. When ethnic massacres of Albanians took place, NATO responded by bombing Yugoslav positions from March to June of 1999 without United Nations approval in advance. What was fascinating in this context was the German role. In a profound sea change of earlier German reticence and a subordinate role in foreign policy, Germany now took both an active role in the promptings for dynamic action as well as the operation itself under the social democratic leadership of chancellor Gerhard Schröder and Foreign Minister Joschka Fischer, earlier student radicals of the 1960s.

In June 1999, Milosevic gave in and withdrew Serbian forces. At long last in 2000, domestic changes finally came into play as Serbian protests ousted Milosevic who was put on trial for war crimes and then died in custody in 2006. The German role, which was so new and in some sense unprecedented, was based on the calculus that it was precisely Germany's devastating record during the Nazi years that in this case meant that intervention to prevent genocide was crucially necessary and morally imperative.

Let's turn now to examine a key role of a Great Power that often has experienced ambivalence about what its role might be, and that's the role of Russia, which spans Eurasia and thus is a vast area that needs to be taken into account and retains a crucial role in Europe. Under Yeltsin, Russia had undergone a difficult transition. Yeltsin's government had sought to join Western structures and become integrated, but at the same time Russian forces had waged from 1994 a brutal war in the break-away region of Chechnya until a ceasefire in 1996.

Fatefully, as we see in hindsight, in 1999 Yeltsin appointed Vladimir Putin, a former K.G.B. officer as his Prime Minister; later he became Yeltsin's successor as president. His term in office is due to expire in 2008. Putin relaunched the Chechen War in September of 1999. He called the break up of the Soviet Union the "greatest geopolitical tragedy of the 20th century," and sought a renewed Great Power or even imperial role for Russia. Russia's aggressive foreign policy, buoyed by its massive oil wealth, worried many neighbors of this power, especially as Russia no longer seemed to be seeking a European identity but carving out a new role for itself outside of those structures.

Finally, let's examine looming issues for Europe and the world not by way of foretelling the future but of bringing into focus some key issues that are likely to be of abiding importance. From the 1970s to September 11, 2001, and on to our own present day, fears and anxieties about terrorism and terrorist attacks continue to present challenges—how best to meet precisely this challenge. It's unfortunately true that diplomats have often been targeted by terrorism and the necessity of shielding one's self against those terrorist attacks has to the regret of many diplomats foreclosed some options for more open diplomacy that would be preferable.

Also unclear is fundamentally the role of diplomacy in dealing with "rogue states," as they're called, which are fired by ideology or by dictatorship as well as non-governments, non-state actors like terrorist groups, which may not in fact have the attributes of sovereignty and a state that can be targeted in case one wanted to deter attacks. Here are fundamental questions: Can one negotiate with such political units? Can one deter such forces? Another key question of abiding significance in international politics is American-European relations. While French politicians have sometimes bitterly spoken of the necessity of resisting American "hyper-power," not even superpower but something even bigger, "hyper-power," a balancing off against the United States that realists would have predicted has not yet found a real resolute institutional expression. Indeed, after the 9/11 attacks of 2001, NATO reacted by invoking its clause, which had pled solidarity in the face of an attack on one to be considered an attack against all, and this was a historically unprecedented move on its part. What followed then was an interesting process. While generally NATO allies cooperated in the war in Afghanistan from 2001, disagreements did arise over the Iraq War launched by U.S. President George W. Bush in March of 2003. These disagreements were not monolithically American versus European. Among the disagreements were serious divides among European states themselves in how they wanted to react to this action.

More generally however, there's also the question of the strategic concepts of American policymakers and European policymakers. The political commentator Robert Kagan has written a provocative book in 2003 titled, *Of Paradise and Power: America and Europe in the New World Order*, which advances the controversial argument that in some sense America and Europe have diverged in important ways to the point where they increasingly inhabit separate universes psychologically with different values based on different strategic concepts. Kagan, in fact, renders this in sort of the language of modern relationship manuals or self-help books as follows: Americans are from Mars, and Europeans are from Venus. The book, however, also notes some important reflections of differing strategic values.

Current U.S. defense spending is roughly double that of European defense spending. The European unity project has, in fact at its very foundation, been motivated by the determination to avoid war, especially a war in Europe of the sort that devastated the continent again and again over the course of centuries. We also see subtler disagreements on a range of international topics especially as diplomacy's reach has spread. Differences in values concern initiatives such as those about how best to react to environmental crises. They involve the 2002 launching of the International Criminal Court, the idea of multilateral approaches to foreign policy versus unilateralism in general, and divergences of this sort on principles can also lead to differences on specific issues like the best response to the Middle East crisis of today. Some commentators have in our own times looked back to the schemes of earlier diplomats like Metternich and have argued for a fundamental re-founding of European-American relations in the form of a new Concert of Democracies, not a Concert of Europe but a Concert of Democracies harkening back to Metternich's guidance of Europe. But this begs the question—not all democracies always agree on what best action should be taken in any circumstances. So, abiding questions will remain.

Let's close precisely with some of these abiding issues, evidence of change, and challenges. By way of conclusion, we can see that over five centuries that span our course of lectures, Europe's state system has been marked by tremendous changes, and those changes have been part of an overall trajectory of repeated disasters and repeated reinventions. Just to recap the long-term trajectory, we might note that the earlier state system of Europe expanded to encompass the wider world, and it changed in the process. It was so successful in expansion, indeed, that Europe is no longer the center but part of a larger world.

An overview of major changes since the year 1500 with which we began is striking. From the Renaissance on, European states crafted patterns of diplomatic exchange and communication with one another that would later expand. In answer in particular to a succession of hegemonic challenges, think of the Habsburgs and their dream of universal empire, religious war and the way in which it racked Europe from within on the basis of faith and differing interpretations of doctrines of faith. Then, Europe's state system in response to that ordeal was fundamentally restructured in a dramatic new way in the Treaty of Westphalia of 1648, a true watershed in many ways as we've seen in this course.

From then on, Great Powers states, as they were called, claimed sovereignty; they dominated the international scene. Eventually, in the course of the 19th century in particular through the scramble of imperialism, they eventually dominated the globe as well. They interacted with one another in a dynamic way with shifting alliances and coalitions first against French bids for hegemony, then against German bids for hegemony in the 20th century. World War I was another watershed moment. It destroyed the Classical period of Europe's balance of power, wrecking that traditional balance of power system of Europe and European supremacy. We saw instead, non-European powers rising on the flanks of the European system, joining that system, and then eventually dominating that system in the Cold War after World War II, the role of the United States and the Soviet Union as superpowers.

With the end of that bipolar confrontation of the Cold War, from 1991 on, will the expanded state system be restructured yet again? Clearly, one of the themes of our course has been just how very much a part of human nature it is in diplomacy to pursue stability, but we have seen that stability is illusive in particular in a world of constant political change. Future questions will remain pressing. Among them is whither Europe and European identity? Where is Europe headed? Where are Europeans headed? Well, we see indications in our own times of some dramatic changes. The balance of power, which had been celebrated in earlier ages in that Classical period, as the inner constitution, the key of the European state system, now is rejected—not just marginalized but explicitly rejected.

In a speech that he gave while Foreign Minister of Germany, Joschka Fischer said that the "core of the concept of Europe after 1945 … is a rejection of the European balance-of-power principle and the hegemonic ambitions of individual states that had emerged following the Peace of Westphalia in 1648."—a rejection of the balance of power, a rejection of the sovereign system of states that emerged after 1648. Other observers suggest that in some sense maybe the European Union has come full circle back to the period before 1648. Some observers have suggested that the European Union represents in some way a late vindication of the principles that came before the Treaty of Westphalia, the decentralized and diverse feudal structures of the Holy Roman Empire in a period before Nationalism.

We can say with certainty that European identity is still under construction. It remains an open question how European identity will evolve from here on in. We've also seen in this course, as one of the themes we've tried to pursue, the expansion of diplomacy as a vital issue. Diplomacy has opened out to broader participation beyond narrow, aristocratic elites or circles, exclusive circles of crowned heads and emperors. Besides states, other players are now playing important roles on the scene. These include corporations; businesses; as well as so-called NGOs, or non-governmental organizations like the Red Cross, Amnesty International, or Greenpeace. They have important roles in contemporary diplomacy. Fundamentally, however, public involvement goes further still. Public involvement in and knowledge of foreign affairs, whether by ordinary citizens taking out a passport to travel or seeking understanding of the past as well as the present in its diplomatic dimension, all of this is perhaps also a diplomatic act of participation and promise for the future.

I would like to close on this note: This is an undertaking open to all of us to seek to understand diplomatic history in its past and present as we seek to understand the scourge of war even when it seems necessary, the profound gift of true peace when it's achieved, and the potentialities as well as the perils of the use of power. After our survey of 500 dynamic years of European diplomacy, let me conclude on this note by thanking you so much for your interest in these lectures.

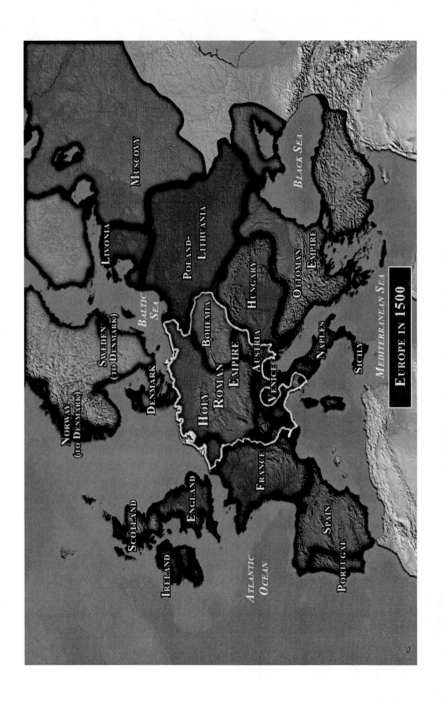

EUROPE IN 1500

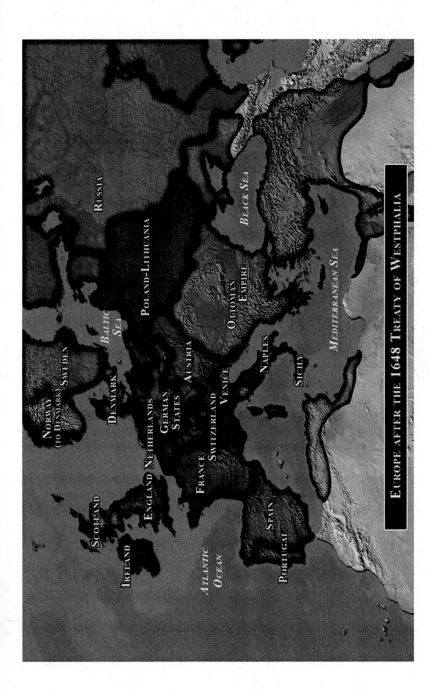

EUROPE AFTER THE 1648 TREATY OF WESTPHALIA

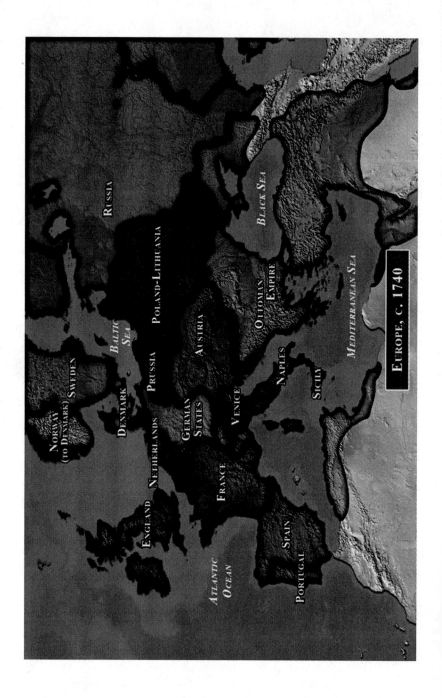

Europe, c. 1740

©2007 The Teaching Company.

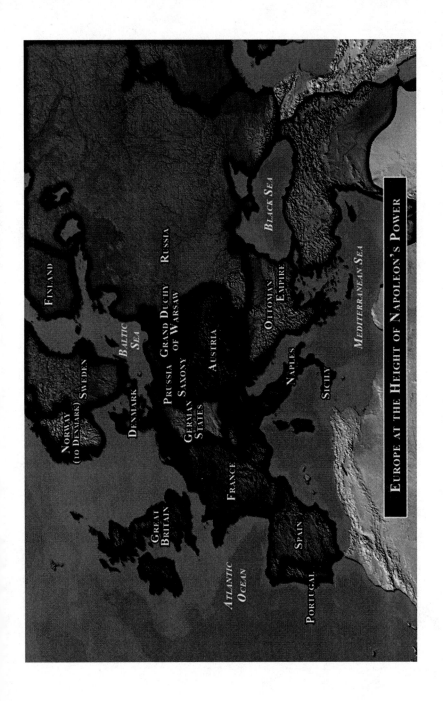

Europe at the Height of Napoleon's Power

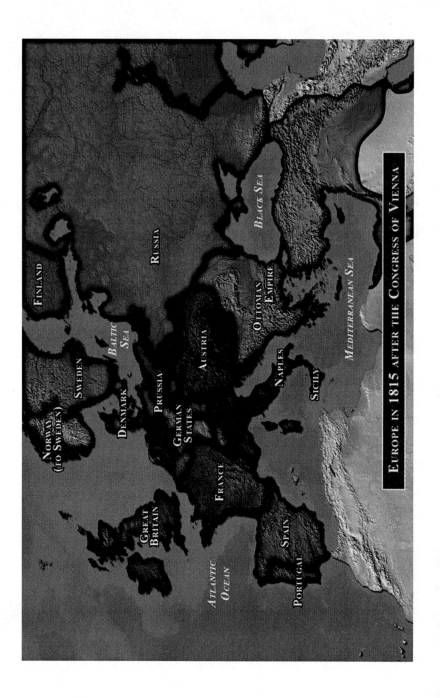

Europe in 1815 after the Congress of Vienna

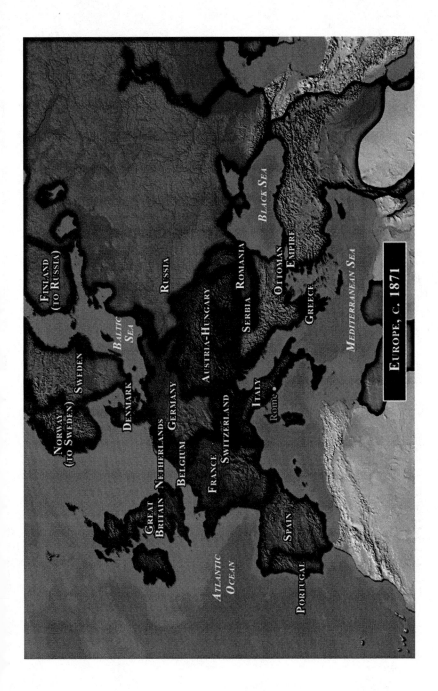

EUROPE, c. 1871

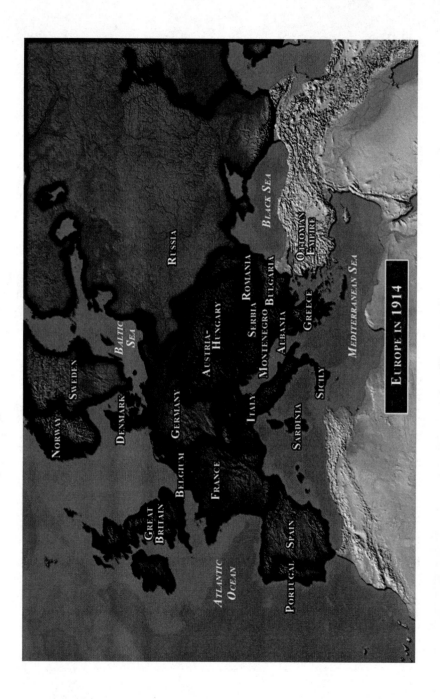

EUROPE IN 1914

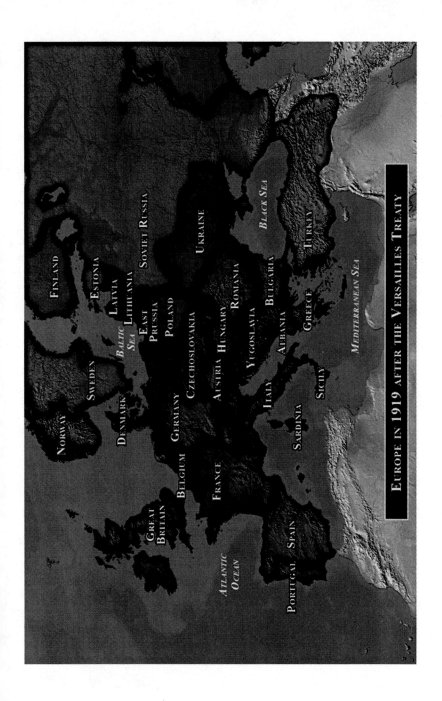

EUROPE IN 1919 AFTER THE VERSAILLES TREATY

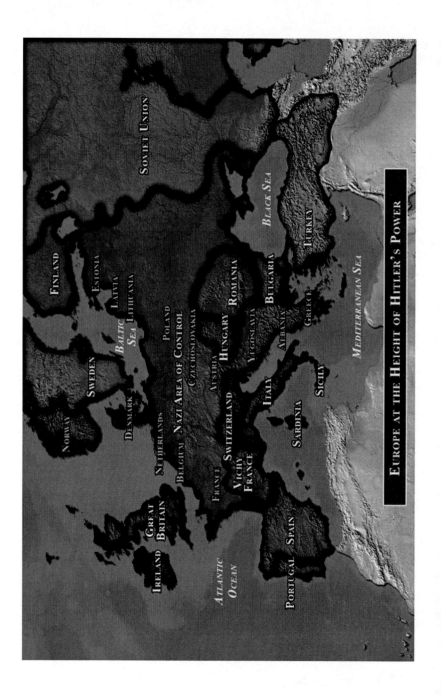

Europe at the Height of Hitler's Power

©2007 The Teaching Company.

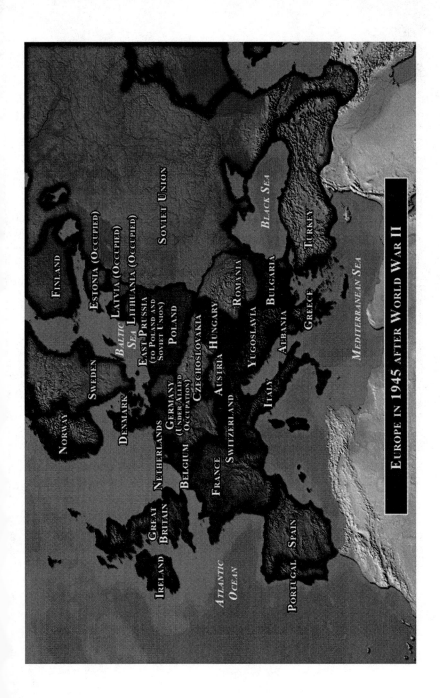

EUROPE IN 1945 AFTER WORLD WAR II

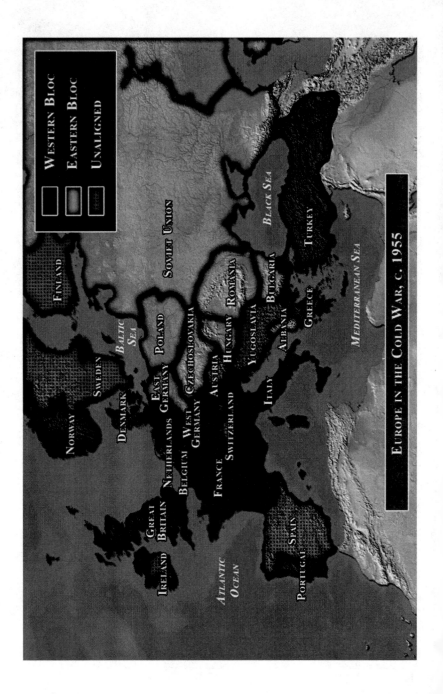

Europe in the Cold War, c. 1955

©2007 The Teaching Company.

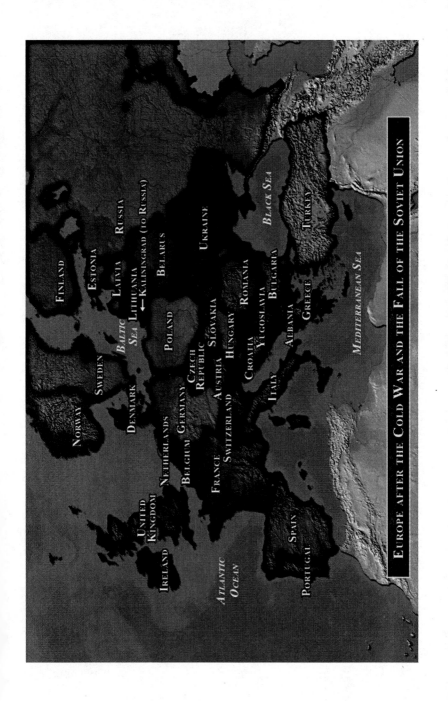

Europe after the Cold War and the Fall of the Soviet Union

Timeline

1494	French invasion of Italy.
1515	Machiavelli completes *The Prince*.
1519	Charles V of Habsburg becomes Holy Roman Emperor.
1555	Peace of Augsburg in Holy Roman Empire.
1618–1648	Thirty Years' War.
1620s	Richelieu rises to power as chief minister to Louis XIII.
1648	Treaty of Westphalia ends Thirty Years' War.
1659	Peace of the Pyrenees between France and Spain.
1661–1715	Personal reign of Louis XIV of France.
1683	Ottoman siege of Vienna defeated.
1700–1721	Great Northern War, ending in victory of Peter the Great of Russia.
1701–1713	War of the Spanish Succession pits France against coalition.
1713	Treaty of Utrecht.
1740–1748	War of the Austrian Succession.
1756	Diplomatic Revolution of Empress Maria Theresa of Habsburg.
1756–1763	Seven Years' War (known as the French and Indian War in the U.S.).
1772–1795	Poland partitioned by Russia, Prussia, and Austria.
1775–1783	American War of Independence.
1789	French Revolution.

1792–1802	French Revolutionary Wars across Europe.
1804	Napoleon crowns himself emperor.
1806	Holy Roman Empire abolished.
1807	Treaty of Tilsit between France and Russia; British parliament abolishes slave trade.
1812	Napoleon launches failed invasion of Russia.
1815	Congress of Vienna, hosted by Prince von Metternich; Napoleon's final defeat at Waterloo; Holy Alliance organized by Russia, Austria, and Prussia.
1815–1822	Functioning Concert of Europe system.
1821–1830	Greek War of Independence.
1823	U.S. Monroe Doctrine announced.
1830	Revolutions in France, Belgium, Italy, and Poland.
1839	British First Opium War in China.
1840	Middle East crisis.
1848	Revolutions across Europe, "Springtime of Nations."
1852	Napoleon III crowned French emperor.
1853–1856	Crimean War, concluded by Congress of Paris.
1858–1861	Italian unification.
1861–1865	American Civil War.
1862	Otto von Bismarck becomes chancellor of Prussia.

1864	Founding of Red Cross.
1866	Austrian-Prussian War.
1869	Suez Canal opened, wave of "High Imperialism" begins.
1870–1871	Franco-Prussian War; defeat of Napoleon III.
1871	German Empire founded after Franco-Prussian War.
1873	First Three Emperors' League founded, including Germany, Austria-Hungary, and Russia.
1875–1878	Great Eastern Crisis.
1878	Congress of Berlin hosted by Bismarck: Serbia, Montenegro, Rumania independent; Bulgaria autonomous.
1879	Dual Alliance of Germany and Austria-Hungary.
1882	Britain occupies Egypt; Triple Alliance of Germany, Austria-Hungary, and Italy established.
1884–1885	Berlin Africa Conference hosted by Bismarck.
1885–1887	Bulgarian Crisis.
1887	Germany and Russia sign Reinsurance Treaty.
1890	Bismarck resigns; Reinsurance Treaty allowed to lapse.
1894	Russian-French military alliance.
1896	First Nobel Peace Prize awarded to founder of Red Cross; Revived Olympic Games held in Athens.
1897	German *Weltpolitik* launched.

1898	Fashoda Incident between Britain and France; Spanish-American War.
1899–1901	Boxer Rebellion in China.
1899–1902	South African War pits Britain against Boers.
1902	British-Japanese Alliance.
April 1904	Britain and France establish Entente Cordiale.
1904–1905	Russo-Japanese War.
1905	Revolution of 1905 in Russia; Norway peacefully splits off from Sweden.
July 1905	Björkö meeting of Russian Tsar and German Kaiser.
1905–1906	First Moroccan Crisis.
1906	Algeciras Conference; British dreadnought class of battleships launched.
1907	Triple Entente of France, Russia, and Great Britain.
1908	Bosnian Crisis.
1911	Second Morocco Crisis (Agadir Crisis).
1912	First Balkan War.
1913	Second Balkan War and London Conference.
June 28, 1914	Archduke Franz Ferdinand assassinated in Sarajevo.
July 23, 1914	Austrian ultimatum to Serbia.
July 28, 1914	Austrian declaration of war on Serbia.
August 4, 1914	Europe's Great Powers at war.

1915	Italy enters the war on the Allied side.
Febuary 1916	Sykes-Picot Agreement on Middle East.
February 1, 1917	Germany declares unrestricted submarine warfare.
March 15, 1917	Revolution in Russia: Tsar Nicholas II abdicates; provisional government takes power.
April 6, 1917	The U.S. enters the war.
November 1917	Balfour Declaration.
November 6–7, 1917	Bolsheviks overthrow provisional government in Russia and take power.
January 1918	President Wilson's Fourteen Points speech.
March 3, 1918	Treaty of Brest-Litovsk between Central Powers and Bolsheviks.
November 11, 1918	Armistice.
January 18, 1919	Paris Peace Conference opens.
June 28, 1919	Signing of Versailles Treaty by German representatives.
March 1920	U.S. Senate refuses to ratify Versailles Treaty.
November 1920	First meeting of League of Nations General Assembly.
1920–1921	Soviet-Polish War.
1922	Mussolini comes to power in Italy; Genoa Conference; Treaty of Rapallo signed by Soviets and Germans.
1923	Ruhr Crisis as French invade Germany.

1923–1929.................................Gustav Stresemann German Foreign Minister.

1925 ....Treaties of Locarno.

1928 ....Kellogg-Briand Pact outlaws war.

1929 ....Stalin secures personal power in Soviet Union; Geneva Convention; Wall Street crash and Great Depression.

1931 ....Japanese invasion of Manchuria.

1932–1934.................................Geneva World Disarmament Conference, ending in failure.

January 30, 1933 ....Hitler becomes chancellor of Germany.

1935 ....Italy invades Ethiopia; Hitler announces German rearmament; Anglo-German Naval Treaty.

1936 ....Hitler marches into Rhineland.

1936–1939.................................Spanish Civil War.

September 29, 1938 ....Munich Conference and appeasement of Hitler.

August 23, 1939.........................Nazi-Soviet Pact.

September 1, 1939 ....World War II begins with German attack on Poland.

1940 ....Fall of France; Winston Churchill becomes British Prime Minister.

June 22, 1941 ....Hitler attacks Soviet Union.

August 1941...............................Roosevelt and Churchill sign Atlantic Charter.

December 1941 ....Japan attacks U.S.; Hitler declares war on U.S.

1943 ....Teheran Conference of Stalin, Roosevelt, and Churchill.

June 1944	Normandy invasion.
February 1945	Yalta Conference.
May 1945	German surrender after Hitler's suicide in April.
June 1945	United Nations founded.
July–August 1945	Potsdam Conference.
August 1945	U.S. drops two atomic bombs on Japan.
1946	Tensions build to Cold War; Churchill's "Iron Curtain" speech.
1947	Paris Peace Treaties with Germany's allies; Truman Doctrine announced; Marshall Plan for European reconstruction.
1948	Communist coup in Czechoslovakia.
1948–1949	Berlin Crisis (Stalin's blockade and British-American airlift).
1949	NATO founded; founding of western and eastern German states; Soviets explode atomic bomb.
1950	Korean War outbreak with implications for European international politics.
1951	European Coal and Steel Community founded.
1955	Federal Republic of Germany joins NATO; Warsaw Pact founded; Austrian State Treaty.
1956	Suez Crisis; Hungarian Revolt crushed by Soviets.
1957	Treaty of Rome establishes European Common Market.

1961	Vienna Convention on Diplomatic Relations signed; Berlin Wall built.
1963	Franco-German Elysée Treaty.
1966	De Gaulle removes French forces from NATO command.
1968	Warsaw Pact intervenes in Czechoslovakia.
1969–1974	*Ostpolitik* ("Eastern Policy") of German chancellor Willy Brandt.
1973	"Oil shock" follows Yom Kippur War.
1975	Signing of Helsinki Final Act.
1979	Soviets invade Afghanistan; "Second Cold War" era begins.
1980	Solidarity movement in Poland.
1985	Mikhail Gorbachev becomes Party Secretary in Soviet Union.
1987	Single European Act signed.
1989	Fall of communist regimes in eastern Europe.
1990	First Gulf War.
October 3, 1990	German Reunification.
November 1990	Paris Accord signifies conclusion to World War II issues.
1991	Fall of Soviet Union.
1991–1995	Yugoslavian War.
1992	Maastricht Treaty creates European Union.
1999	Kosovo War; Vladimir Putin becomes Russian Prime Minister, later president.
September 11, 2001	Al Qaeda attacks the U.S.

Glossary

alliance: A formal association of states in pursuit of a common cause.

ambassador: Highest rank of representative in residence in a foreign state.

annexation: The formal incorporation of disputed territory by a state.

autonomy: Rights of self-governance within a territory, short of independence.

balance of power: Dynamic interrelation of powers where no one power is capable of dominating the others.

Balfour Declaration: British declaration of 1917 offering support for the creation of a national Jewish homeland in Palestine.

Balkan Wars: Two wars in 1912 and 1913 that saw the expulsion of Ottoman Turkey from most of the Balkans and further fighting among Balkan states, showing the region's instability.

Brest-Litovsk, Treaty of: Signed March 3, 1918, a harsh peace settlement imposed by Germany on defeated Russia in World War I.

Brezhnev Doctrine: Soviet maxim from the 1960s that attempts to reverse communist control that will provoke intervention.

Central Powers: In World War I, Germany, Austria-Hungary, and Turkey, later joined by Bulgaria.

coalition: An alliance of a temporary character directed against a common adversary.

Cold War: In general, political and military confrontation short of warfare; bipolar confrontation between the United States and the Soviet Union and their respective alliance systems from 1946–1991.

collective security: The premise that all participating states will treat aggression as directed against all and collectively resist.

Concert of Europe: After the 1815 Congress of Vienna, the sentiment that European Great Powers should consult and work together to ensure stability.

Congress System: After the 1815 Congress of Vienna, a series of congresses and conferences in pursuit of common stability. It broke down in the 1820s.

containment: A policy of blocking the advance or expansion of another state; United States policy toward the Soviet Union during the Cold War is an example.

cordon sanitaire: A belt of states to hem in an adversary. French policy between the World Wars tried to use this policy to contain both Soviet Russia and Germany.

Dardanelles: See **Turkish Straits.**

démarche: A diplomatic statement or protest; a significant change in policy.

détente: Process of lessening of tensions between states.

diplomacy: Relations between sovereign states through negotiations.

diplomatic immunity: The practice of exempting diplomatic representatives from ordinary legal processes in the country hosting them.

dispatch: A speedy official communication.

Dual Alliance: Bismarck's key 1879 alliance of Germany with Austria.

Eastern Question: An abiding issue in European diplomacy, concerning the fate of the Ottoman Empire in the Middle East and especially its European territories.

entente: An understanding or relationship, short of an alliance commitment.

Entente Cordiale: 1904 French and British settlement of colonial conflicts.

European Union: An evolving project for European unification, starting in 1957 and formalized in the 1992 Maastricht Treaty.

Fascism: Aggressive political movement founded in Italy in 1919, celebrating the state, strong leadership, and militarism.

Fourteen Points: United States President Woodrow Wilson's announcement of American war aims on January 8, 1918.

Great Power: A power of the first rank whose interests must be consulted by other powers.

hegemony: A position of overwhelming power or influence among states.

High Imperialism: Intense "scramble for empire," especially in Africa and Asia, from 1869 to 1914.

Idealism: In diplomatic history, the theoretical concept that states are driven by ideologies and the nature of their political systems.

irredenta: "Unredeemed territories" craved by nationalists (originally Italian, but the term later applies elsewhere).

July Crisis: The escalating political and military crisis in 1914 following the assassination in Sarajevo that led to the outbreak of World War I.

London, Treaty of: Secret agreement between the Allies and Italy signed on April 26, 1915, bringing Italy into the war with promises of territory.

Monroe Doctrine: American declaration in 1823 that the western hemisphere was closed to European ambitions.

Nazism: A radical movement espousing "national Socialism." It was founded immediately after World War I in defeated Germany and led to power in 1933 by Adolf Hitler.

Nazi-Soviet Pact: Agreement of Nazi Germany and the Soviet Union dated August 23, 1939, dividing eastern Europe between the dictators Hitler and Stalin; instrumental to the outbreak of World War II.

Ostpolitik: German "Eastern Policy" aimed at détente with eastern European states; pursued by Chancellor Willy Brandt from 1969.

Paris Settlement: The comprehensive set of treaties negotiated with the defeated powers of World War I (including with Germany at Versailles) in 1919–1920.

precedence: Ceremonial order of rank and respect on formal occasions.

primacy of domestic policy: A disputed theoretical postulate that imperatives of domestic politics shape policy more than international factors.

primacy of foreign policy: A disputed theoretical postulate that imperatives of international politics shape policy more than domestic factors.

propaganda: The systematic shaping of political opinions.

protocol: The ritual and manners of diplomatic interaction, such as issues of precedence, freighted with symbolic significance and bearing on the prestige of states.

raison d'état: Meaning "reason of state"; the doctrine (most often associated with Cardinal Richelieu) that a state is impelled above all to protect its interests and survival, justifying the means needed.

Realism: In diplomatic history, the theoretical concept that states are driven by the search for security and realities of relative power.

Realpolitik: Meaning "politics of Realism"; the doctrine (most often associated with German Chancellor von Bismarck) that a state must be guided by calculations of power and national interest.

Reinsurance Treaty: German-Russian Treaty of 1887 negotiated by Bismarck to forestall conflict between the conservative powers.

reparations: Payments made by a defeated power.

revisionism: In diplomatic history, the role of a state demanding changes to the status quo.

revolutionizing: The policy of seeking to subvert enemy populations and disaffected minorities.

Schlieffen Plan: German secret plan for victory on two fronts drafted before World War I, calling for an attack on France through neutral territory.

self-determination: The nationalist demand for sovereign independence by ethnic groups.

Socialism: Based on the ideas of Karl Marx, socialists (or social democrats) envisioned a world reshaped by the international supremacy of the working class.

sovereignty: Independence of action of a state.

Soviet Union: New communist state (also U.S.S.R. for "Union of Soviet Socialist Republics") formed in 1922 and ending in collapse in 1991.

special relationship: Concept of a unique tie between the United States and Great Britain based on cultural and political affinities.

Straits: See **Turkish Straits**.

Sublime Porte: Traditional name of the seat of Ottoman diplomacy.

summit meeting: A conference attended by the very highest officials of participating states.

Sykes-Picot Agreement: British and French secret agreement of February 1916, dividing the Middle East into respective spheres of influence.

total war: A concept developed during World War I to express the all-encompassing nature of the conflict, drawing in entire populations, economies, and societies.

Triple Alliance: From 1882, an alliance of Germany, Austria-Hungary, and Italy (when Italy dropped out, Germany and Austria-Hungary formed the core of the Central Powers).

Triple Entente: From 1907, the bloc of France, Russia, and Britain who become the Allies in 1914.

Turkish Straits: Narrow straits separating the Black Sea from the Mediterranean in Turkey; a coveted strategic point where Europe and Asia meet (also called Dardanelles, Bosporus, or simply "The Straits").

ultimatum: A demand communicated to another state with the implication of harsh consequences for a negative reply.

Versailles, Treaty of: Treaty signed by the victors of World War I with Germany on June 28, 1919 (part of the overall Paris Settlement), with restrictions on German armaments, loss of territory, reparations, and admission of war guilt.

War Guilt Clause: Article 231 of the Versailles Treaty, by which Germany officially accepted responsibility for unleashing the war.

Weltpolitik: From 1897, aggressive German foreign policy claiming superpower status.

Westphalia, Treaty of: The general peace settlement of 1648 ending the Thirty Years' War; the first of the great modern peace conferences, often seen as the establishment of the modern state system.

Biographical Notes

Bismarck-Schönhausen, Otto von (1815–1898): Descendant of Prussian nobility, Bismarck possessed a volatile character. In 1862 he was appointed chancellor of Prussia after serving in diplomatic posts in France and Russia. In a series of wars, Bismarck brought about a united German state under Prussian leadership in 1871 and became known as Germany's "Iron Chancellor." Once unification was achieved, Bismarck's great challenge was to embed Germany in the European state system, which he managed to do through webs of alliances until he was forced from office in 1890. He is credited with a gift for restraint and a sense of limits in his pursuit of *Realpolitik* (power politics), but his real beliefs remain enigmatic.

Catherine the Great of Russia (1729–1796; r. 1762–1796): Born a German princess of the House of Anhalt-Zerbst, Catherine came to power in Russia in 1762 after the murder of her husband, Peter III. She combined a Russian imperial ideology with new Enlightenment ideas. Her foreign policy built on the gains of Peter the Great, with dramatic expansion to the south (against the Ottoman Turks) and west (including the partitions of neighboring Poland). As a result, the Russian Empire became a key player in the European state system as one of the Great Powers.

Cavour, Count Camillo di (1810–1861): Prime minister of the Italian state of Piedmont (Kingdom of Sardinia) who engineered Italian unification by 1861. His sentiments were Realist and royalist, and he admired Liberal Britain as a model of modernity. Reacting to the failures of 1848, Cavour constructed a Realist political solution to the Italian Question. He won Western sympathies for Piedmont by participating in the Crimean War and then crafted a secret agreement with France's Emperor Napoleon III in 1858, leading to war against Austria in 1859. In the aftermath, Cavour skillfully responded to nationalist demands by joining other territories (without Venetia) to form a united Italy under King Victor Emanuel II in 1861. Cavour died soon after; whether Italy truly had Great Power status was a question that haunted his successors.

Charles V (House of Habsburg) (1500–1558; r. 1519–1556): Elected Holy Roman Emperor after a perfect storm of inheritances from the Habsburg legacy (at his election he was already Duke of Burgundy and King of Spain). He presided over a vast empire, including colonies in the Americas. He sought an ideal of universal empire that led to conflicts with France, German princes, and the Ottoman Turks. Ultimately exhausted by the challenge, Charles abdicated his titles in 1556 and retired to a Spanish estate. His ideals passed to his son, King Philip of Spain, but whether anyone could effectively rule this vast realm remained an open question.

Churchill, Winston (1874–1965): Descendant of a famous British political family (and with an American mother), Churchill's career was badly battered in World War I. During years in the political wilderness, Churchill increasingly warned of Hitler's aggressive intentions. Churchill became Prime Minister of Britain as Nazi Germany launched its attack on France in May 1940. He rallied Britain against the Axis Powers and won the Soviet Union and the United States as Allies in the struggle. Churchill was voted out of power in 1945 while at the Potsdam Conference (he returned as Prime Minister later in 1951–1955). In his 1946 "Iron Curtain" speech in Fulton, Missouri, Churchill called attention to the emerging Cold War and urged a "special relationship" between Britain and the United States. He won the 1953 Nobel Prize in Literature.

De Gaulle, Charles (1890–1970): A French military and political leader always motivated by what he called "a certain idea of France": glorious, eternal, and respected. During World War II, he led the Free French movement and after the liberation of his country headed the government, before retiring. With the Fourth Republic's fall sparked by the Algerian crisis of 1958, De Gaulle returned to power and created the Fifth Republic, ruling as its president until 1969. In foreign policy he sought French independence between the Cold War blocs, cooperating with the Federal Republic of Germany and removing France from NATO command.

Disraeli, Benjamin (1804–1881): Famous author, dandy, and British conservative political leader. He was the son of a Jewish convert to Anglicanism. Elected to Parliament in 1837, Disraeli forged a remarkable career for himself. Upon the death of Sir Robert Peel, Disraeli became leader of the Tories and built the Conservative Party. In 1868, he became Prime Minister for the first time. From 1872, Disraeli worked for the creation of a mass party espousing the ideals of "Tory democracy" and a reinvigorated Imperialism. Disraeli and Gladstone clashed often in a famous rivalry. Returning as Prime Minister in 1874–1880, Disraeli gained control of Suez Canal shares in 1875 and made Queen Victoria Empress of India in 1876.

Gladstone, William (1809–1898): Leader of the Liberal Party in Britain and Prime Minister four times, in a close rivalry with the conservative Disraeli. Son of a Liverpool merchant, his political affiliation shifted from Tory to Whig. Deeply religious and infused with liberal ideology, Gladstone opposed Imperialism, advocated a principled foreign policy, and advanced liberal ideas of establishing peaceful international relations later taken up by Woodrow Wilson. He became Prime Minister for the first time in 1868. In opposition, Gladstone launched powerful criticisms of Disraeli's foreign policy in the Midlothian campaign of 1879–1880. As Prime Minister again, Gladstone reluctantly oversaw the British occupation of Egypt in 1882.

Gorbachev, Mikhail Sergeyevich (b. 1931): Last leader of the Soviet Union, from 1985 until 1991. Rising through the ranks of the Communist Party after studying law, Gorbachev was chosen in 1985 as general secretary after a series of old and ill leaders. As a committed believer in Leninism, Gorbachev launched a series of reform programs to revive the Soviet system, summed up in the slogans of *Perestroika* ("restructuring") and *Glasnost* ("openness"). He also initiated a withdrawal from the Cold War, given the vast expense of the confrontation. Eastern European satellite states now went their own way, and (to his surprise) demands for democracy and national self-determination also spread to the Soviet Union itself. Gorbachev shifted toward a reactionary stance, and Soviet forces cracked down with violence in the Baltic countries. In August 1991, hardliners around Gorbachev attempted a coup that soon collapsed into farce, and the Soviet Union dissolved by the end of the year.

Hitler, Adolf (1889–1945): Dictator of Nazi Germany. Of Austrian origin, Hitler was an aimless youth until the formative experience of World War I, where he served in the trenches as a volunteer in the German army. At first shattered by German defeat in 1918, Hitler launched a political career around the National Socialist (Nazi) party, preaching anti-Semitism, revisionism, and renewed German greatness while denouncing democracy. After a failed coup attempt in 1923, Hitler was briefly imprisoned and set forth his creed in *Mein Kampf*. Economic and political crises in Germany led Hitler to become chancellor in January 1933. Promptly "nazifying" German society and state, Hitler provoked a diplomatic revolution in Europe by smashing the Versailles Treaty and rearming, at first encountering appeasement rather than counterforce. After the Nazi-Soviet Pact of 1939, Hitler launched World War II with the attack on Poland, then defeated France and attacked his Soviet ally in 1941. He enacted his genocidal plans against the Jewish populations of occupied Europe in the "Final Solution." As the war turned against Germany, Hitler committed suicide in a bunker in Berlin in 1945, his toll a continent in ruins and mountains of countless dead.

Lenin, Vladimir Ilyich (1870–1924): Russian revolutionary leader of the radical Bolshevik wing of the Social Democrats. Lenin championed the concept of a "vanguard party" of professional revolutionaries catalyzing upheaval. He spent the first part of World War I in exile, until German officials intending to "revolutionize" Russia arranged to ship him back to Petrograd in April 1917. Once there, Lenin preached revolutionary defeatism and led the Bolshevik seizure of power in November 1917, overthrowing the fragile liberal provisional government. Expecting the imminent outbreak of worldwide revolution, Lenin negotiated peace with the Germans. Disappointed by the delay in global revolution, Lenin built up the Soviet dictatorship. After his death in 1924, his associate Stalin achieved control.

Louis XIV (House of Bourbon) (1638–1715; r. 1643–1715): The "Sun King" of France. On the death of his father, Louis XIII, in 1643, Louis became king with his mother as regent; he was advised by Cardinal Mazarin, who directed his education. Revolts known as the Fronde shook the young monarch. He assumed personal rule in 1661 upon the death of Mazarin and set out to gain a record of glory in the form of almost unceasing wars: against Spain, the Netherlands, the League of Augsburg, and finally a Grand Alliance of European powers reacting to his bid for hegemony. The resplendent Palace of Versailles remains the perfect embodiment of his claims to Absolutism. His reign of 72 years is one of the longest on record and left French grandeur, crippling debts, and systemic problems in its wake.

Machiavelli, Niccolò (1469–1527): Florentine diplomat and political philosopher. Soon after the breakdown of the Italian diplomatic system of the 15th century, Machiavelli served the republic of

Florence on diplomatic missions in Europe. When the Medici family restored its rule in the city in 1512, Machiavelli was imprisoned and tortured. In retirement, he wrote provocative new works of political philosophy, among them *The Prince* (completed by 1515). In this work he described politics not in terms of ideals but in terms of the realities of human nature and behavior and urged leaders to establish strong and effective states, setting personal ethics aside. Machiavelli's own deepest convictions are debated to this day, but his comprehensive rethinking of politics had an explosive impact on later leaders: Many denounced "Machiavellian" politics even as they practiced them.

Maria Theresa (House of Habsburg) (1717–1780; r. 1740–1780): Monarch of Austria. Her succession to the Austrian Habsburg throne in 1740 was disputed by other European powers in spite of earlier agreements to respect her claims. Prussia's King Frederick II attacked and seized the province of Silesia. In response, Maria Theresa dramatically rallied her subjects and diverse realms, showing a deep strength of character. With her chancellor Count von Kaunitz, she engineered the "Diplomatic Revolution" of 1756 to oppose Prussia in the Seven Years' War (1756–1763) but was unable to regain Silesia. Her record of overcoming crisis brought her considerable popular devotion as the "mother of the country."

Metternich, Klemens von (1773–1859): Masterful and subtle Austrian diplomat. A descendent of a noble family from the German Rhineland, Metternich became Austrian Foreign Minister in 1809 at an hour of humiliation for the empire, which had been defeated by Napoleon. Metternich strove to regain maneuvering room for Austria. After Napoleon's defeat, Metternich organized the Congress of Vienna of 1815, which established a remarkably durable order for the European state system. Through the Concert of Europe and its values, Metternich sought to suppress radical, liberal, and nationalist ideas while also fending off Russian predominance on the continent. His very subtlety, however, provoked many expressions of distrust from contemporaries. Metternich fell from power in the Revolution of 1848 and fled into exile.

Mussolini, Benito (1883–1945): Dictator of Italy and leader (*Duce*) of the Fascist movement. Of humble family origins and originally a Socialist, Mussolini's pivotal experience during World War I set him on a new course. His Fascist creed emphasized an all-powerful militarized state with a strong leader, primed for war and expansion. Mussolini came to power in Italy with the 1922 "March on Rome," but this street theater disguised the fact that elites had agreed to his accession. In 1935, Mussolini's aggressive foreign policy (promising a revival of the glories of the ancient Roman Empire) culminated in the unprovoked invasion of Ethiopia, and was only wanly resisted by the League of Nations, whose weakness was then clear. Allying himself with Hitler, Mussolini intervened in the Spanish Civil War and invaded Albania, France, and Greece. With military failures, Italy became increasingly dependent on its Nazi patron. As the Allies invaded Italy, Mussolini was deposed by his own associates. He was briefly reinstated as a puppet ruler in the north by Hitler, and then captured and executed by partisans in 1945.

Napoleon I (Napoleon Bonaparte) (1769–1821): Self-made emperor of the French and prototype for later dictators. Born on Corsica to lower nobility, Napoleon was sent to France for military education and began a meteoric career along avenues opened up by the French Revolution of 1789. He became a hero to many with the campaigns in Italy and Egypt and swooped back to France to take power in a coup in 1799. In 1804 he crowned himself emperor and was driven by ambition to establish continental dominion. Napoleon's growing power provoked repeated and ineffective coalitions of European powers to resist him, until he overreached in his disastrous invasion of Russia in 1812. Upon his defeat by allied European powers, he abdicated and was sent into exile on the island of Elba but grew bored and returned for a rampage of 100 days, which ended with his final defeat at Waterloo and his exile to St. Helena in the Atlantic. Decades later, his remains were brought back to Paris and are enshrined in a splendid mausoleum, reflecting a durable hero cult surrounding his complex person and legacy.

Philip II of Spain (House of Habsburg) (1527–1598; r. 1556–1598): Son of Emperor Charles V and successor to the throne of Spain upon his resignation in 1556. Viewing himself as a new Habsburg champion of Catholicism and Universalism, he presided over a period of Spanish greatness. His forces won dominance in Italy, defeated the Ottoman navy at Lepanto, and took Portugal. Indicating the sweep of empire in his possession, the Philippines are named after him. Overextension, however, ultimately led to crisis, as revolt broke out in the Netherlands, the Spanish Armada met disaster, and financial crises wracked the realm.

Richelieu, Cardinal Armand Jean du Plessis (1585–1642): French cardinal and chief minister to King Louis XIII. Richelieu's energetic foreign policy often set aside religious affiliation to pursue state interests, especially opposition to Habsburg power in Europe. Through permanent negotiations, Richelieu fostered resistance to the Habsburgs by Protestant allies, and later intervened directly in the Thirty Years' War. His signature concept was *raison d'état* ("reason of state"); Henry Kissinger calls him "the father of the modern state system." Under Richelieu's leadership, France rose to a new prominence in Europe.

Roosevelt, Franklin Delano (1882–1945): American Democratic statesman and president of the United States from 1933–1945. After he came to office in the wake of the Great Depression, Roosevelt's New Deal sought to restore public confidence. In spite of strong isolationist sentiment at home, Roosevelt sought to aid embattled Great Britain in the first stages of World War II. After Japan's attack on Pearl Harbor in 1941, Roosevelt took the U.S. into the war as one of the "Big Three," along with Britain and the Soviet Union. During the war, Roosevelt sought to craft a postwar order in summit meetings (including Yalta) with the Allies, with the United Nations as a centerpiece, replacing the failed League of Nations. He died shortly before the end of World War II.

Stalin, Joseph (1879–1953): Dictator of the Soviet Union. Of Georgian origins, Stalin rose through the Bolshevik ranks through ruthless realism and bureaucratic skill. After Lenin's revolutionary party came to power in Russia in 1917, the shadowy Stalin became general secretary of the party in 1922 and edged out rivals to succeed Lenin in the years after his death in 1924. He pursued intense purges, mass arrests, executions, and forced industrialization of the country. In a near-fatal miscalculation, Stalin allied with Hitler in the 1939 Nazi-Soviet Pact, only to be attacked by his erstwhile associate in 1941. Stalin then allied with Great Britain and the United States. After the end of World War II, Stalin reconsolidated his personal rule and died in 1953 while apparently planning another campaign of internal terror. Stalin is one of the greatest mass murderers in history, with his toll estimated at 20 million dead.

Stresemann, Gustav (1878–1929): German Foreign Minister (1923–1929) and briefly chancellor during Germany's democratic Weimar Republic. Stresemann was an ardent nationalist and imperialist during World War I but turned to policies of reconciliation in western Europe (while still holding out hopes for revision in eastern Europe). Stresemann cooperated in the crafting of the Locarno Treaties of 1925, which stirred a spirit of great hope in international cooperation, and gained Germany's admission into the League of Nations. He won the Nobel Peace Prize in 1926. After his untimely death in 1929, he was hailed as a "great European," but some questioned his ultimate sincerity.

Talleyrand, Charles-Maurice de (1754–1838): French statesman, diplomat, and former bishop. He is sometimes called "the greatest of diplomats," but his ultimate devotion was to his own interests, as he survived repeated regime changes in France with amazing suppleness and flexibility of conviction. A revolutionary in the upheavals of the French Revolution from 1789, he escaped the Reign of Terror by exile in the United States, returning to France to become Foreign Minister and helping Napoleon seize power. Later, as he saw Napoleon overreaching, he distanced himself from the emperor and after his defeat, negotiated on behalf of fallen France at the 1815 Congress of Vienna. In a masterstroke, Talleyrand parleyed a weak position into remarkable influence and restored France to the ranks of the Great Powers.

Wilson, Woodrow (1856–1924): American academic, university president, and president of the United States from 1913 to 1921. At first pursuing neutrality for the United States during World War I, Wilson later sought to mediate the crisis. Public outrage against German submarine warfare and the Zimmermann Telegram led Wilson to ask Congress to declare war against Germany in April 1917. The United States joined the Allies as an "Associate Power." In his Fourteen Points speech on January 8, 1918, Wilson announced the American war aims of expanding democracy and replacing the balance of power with a new international politics. Wilson traveled to Paris to share in the negotiations for the peace treaty and the League of Nations, but domestic opposition in the United States and his own intransigence led to the failure of his plans. Nonetheless, his message of self-determination and lasting peace had real appeal to millions of Europeans.

Bibliography

Albrecht-Carrié, René. *A Diplomatic History of Europe since the Congress of Vienna*. Revised edition. New York: Harper and Row, 1973. A classic survey of modern diplomatic history, readily available at better libraries.

Anderson, M. S. *The Rise of Modern Diplomacy 1450–1919*. New York: Longman, 1993. A work of exemplary clarity, it is really three books in one, discussing in turn the evolution of diplomatic method, balance of power theorizing, and projects for peace.

Berman, Paul. *Power and the Idealists: Or, The Passion of Joschka Fischer, and Its Aftermath*. New York: W. W. Norton & Company, 2005. This very readable extended essay examines how legacies of the 1960s counterculture now crucially affect the use of power in international politics.

Bobbitt, Philip. *The Shield of Achilles: War, Peace, and the Course of History*. New York: Anchor Books, 2002. A provocative and erudite argument positing the evolution of states, with our own age experiencing an emerging new form of state.

Carr, Edward Hallett. *The Twenty Years' Crisis, 1919–1939: An Introduction to the Study of International Relations*. New York: Harper and Row, 1964. Despite its main title, a thoughtful consideration of crucial theoretical concepts in diplomatic history.

Dehio, Ludwig. *The Precarious Balance: Four Centuries of the European Power Struggle*. New York: Alfred A. Knopf, 1962. Classic and elegant meditations on the larger picture of state contests of the last four centuries by a German historian.

Fink, Carole. *Defending the Rights of Others: The Great Powers, the Jews, and International Minority Protection, 1878–1938*. Cambridge: Cambridge University Press, 2004. Examines the mixed record of the first efforts to intervene to protect minority groups; clearly a topic that remains no less relevant today.

Gaddis, John Lewis. *The Cold War: A New History*. New York: Penguin Press, 2005. An overview of "a necessary contest that settled fundamental issues once and for all," in the author's view.

Gallagher, John and Ronald Robinson. "The Imperialism of Free Trade." *The Economic History Review* (Second Series) 6, no. 1 (1953): 1–15. A much-cited and debated argument concerning

British "informal empire"; that is, empire beyond areas of direct control.

Garton Ash, Timothy. *In Europe's Name: Germany and the Divided Continent*. New York: Vintage Books, 1994. Germany's division and approaches to eastern Europe shed light on larger European issues.

Hinsley, F. H. "The Concert of Europe," *in Diplomacy in Modern European History*. Edited by Laurence W. Martin. New York: Macmillan, 1966: 43–57. Examines the evolution of the system established at the Congress of Vienna in 1815.

Hochedlinger, Michael. "Who's Afraid of the French Revolution?: Austrian Foreign Policy and the European Crisis 1787–1797." *German History*, 21, no. 3 (2003): 293–318. An in-depth look at traditional decision making in reaction to revolutionary diplomacy.

Hurewitz, J. C. "Ottoman Diplomacy and the European State System." *Middle East Journal* 15 (1961): 141–152. A lucid and useful overview of the evolution of Ottoman diplomatic ties with European diplomacy.

Johnson, Paul. *Napoleon*. New York: Penguin, 2002. In Johnson's critical vision of Napoleon, he was both an opportunist and a precursor to later ideological dictators.

Joll, James. *The Origins of the First World War*, 2nd ed. New York: Longman, 1992. A sophisticated discussion and evaluation of the many contexts of the outbreak of the first total war.

Kagan, Robert. *Of Paradise and Power: America and Europe in the New World Order*. New York: Alfred A. Knopf, 2003. A provocative essay that sees a crucial divergence between the strategic cultures of America and Europe in our time.

Keegan, John. *Winston Churchill*. New York: Penguin, 2002. A compact and eloquent biography of a leader the author admiringly calls "a strange man."

Kennedy, Paul. *The Rise and Fall of the Great Powers: Economic Change and Military Conflict from 1500 to 2000*. New York: Random House, 1987. A best-selling narrative of how states grow, overextend, and decline in the modern era.

Kissinger, Henry. *Diplomacy*. New York: Simon and Schuster, 1994. A scholar and controversial practicing diplomat surveys the sweep of diplomatic history.

Lee, Stephen J. *The Thirty Years War*. New York: Routledge, 1991. Paradoxically, a brief and elegant treatment of a long and crude conflict.

Macfie, A. L. *The Eastern Question 1774–1923*, 2nd ed. New York: Longman, 1996. A very useful narrative of a crucial dimension in European diplomatic history with a long trajectory.

Machiavelli, Niccolò. *The Prince*. Translated by William J. Connell. Boston: Bedford St. Martins, 2005. Includes a useful introduction, notes, and related documents.

Mack Smith, Denis. *Cavour: A Biography*. New York: Alfred A. Knopf, 1985. A master biographer's vision of a master politician.

MacMillan, Margaret. *Paris 1919: Six Months That Changed the World*. New York: Random House, 2002. A dramatic and detailed story of the "peacemakers" who gathered in Paris after World War I and the clashes of personalities that ensued.

Mattingly, Garrett. *Renaissance Diplomacy*. New York: Dover, 1988. A reprint of the enduring classic originally published in 1955.

Mazower, Mark. *The Balkans: A Short History*. New York: Modern Library, 2000. A brief treatment, including good maps, of the political, social, and ideological history of the troubled region.

Nicolson, Harold. *The Congress of Vienna: A Study in Allied Unity, 1812–1822*. New York: Harcourt, Brace and Company, 1946. A fascinating case study and dissection of the dynamics of alliance during attempts at comprehensive peacemaking.

Reynolds, David. "The Origins of the Cold War: The European Dimension, 1944–1951." *The Historical Journal*. 28, no. 2 (June 1985): 497–515. A lucid discussion of the early stages of the Cold War.

———. "A 'Special Relationship'? America, Britain and the International Order since the Second World War." *International Affairs*, 62, no. 1 (Winter 1985–1986): 1–20. This article contextualizes the storied special tie between America and Britain, showing its limits and potentials.

Rich, Norman. *Hitler's War Aims: Ideology, the Nazi State, and the Course of German Expansion*. New York: W.W. Norton, 1973. An incisive analysis of the ideology and institutions behind Hitler's expansive foreign policy.

Ritter, Gerhard. *Frederick the Great: A Historical Profile*. Translated by Peter Paret. Berkeley: University of California Press, 1968. A notable German historian's meditations on different facets of this ruler's complex and contradictory record.

Roshwald, Aviel. *Ethnic Nationalism and the Fall of Empires: Central Europe, Russia, and the Middle East, 1914–1923*. London: Routledge, 2001. A valuable examination of the explosion of demands for national self-determination that intersected with World War I and destroyed multinational states.

Schroeder, Paul. "Did the Vienna Settlement Rest on a Balance of Power?" *American Historical Review*. 97 (June 1992): 683–706. An important article that sparked debate among diplomatic historians.

———. *The Transformation of European Politics, 1763–1848*. Oxford: Oxford University Press, 1994. Powerful thesis of a shift in "rules, norms, and practices of international politics" in the early 19th century, with crucial implications.

Schulz, Matthias. "A Balancing Act: Domestic Pressures and International Systemic Constraints in the Foreign Policies of the Great Powers, 1848–1851." *German History*. 21, no. 3 (2003): 319–346. A clear and subtle analysis of states' reactions in a time of revolutionary crisis.

Scott, H. M. *The Emergence of the Eastern Powers, 1756–1775*. Cambridge: Cambridge University Press, 2007. Explores and explains the dramatic shift and expansion of the European state system eastward.

Seaman, L. C. B. *From Vienna to Versailles*. New York: Harper and Row, 1963. Lively and contrarian essays challenging orthodox opinions on a range of important issues.

Smith, Simon C. *British Imperialism 1750–1970*. Cambridge: Cambridge University Press, 1998. This brief treatment explores particular issues (missionary activity, antislavery efforts, India, free trade) in the much larger history of British Imperialism.

Strachan, Hew. *The First World War*. New York: Viking, 2003. The best one-volume treatment of the devastating conflict.

Taylor, A. J. P. *Bismarck: The Man and the Statesman*. New York: Vintage Books, 1955. A characteristically witty and irreverent treatment.

————. *The Struggle for the Mastery of Europe, 1848–1918.* Oxford: Oxford University Press, 1954. A classic, witty account of the paradoxes at the core of the period of Europe's classical balance of power.

Trachtenberg, Marc, ed. *Between Empire and Alliance: America and Europe during the Cold War.* Lanham, Maryland: Rowman and Littlefield, 2003. Focused on the era 1950–1974, this collection of articles illuminates the complex dynamic between America and its western European allies.

Troubetzkoy, Alexis. *A Brief History of the Crimean War.* New York: Carroll & Graf, 2006. A well-written and lively summary of an obscure but important conflict.

Viroli, Maurizio. *Niccolò's Smile: A Biography of Machiavelli.* Translated by Antony Shugaar. New York: Hill and Wang, 2000. This admiring biography claims for Machiavelli the status of "great moral philosopher."

Wesseling, H. L. *The European Colonial Empires 1815–1919.* This study examines European imperialism over a longer period than other works, balancing treatment of the British Empire with the records of continental European countries.

Wright, Jonathan. *The Ambassadors: From Ancient Greece to Renaissance Europe, The Men Who Introduced the World to Itself.* New York: Harcourt, Inc.: 2006. This sweeping survey of pre-modern diplomatic traditions argues that while there is "no obvious sense of progress" in diplomatic practice, there are durable parallels.

————. *Gustav Stresemann: Weimar's Greatest Statesman.* Oxford: Oxford University Press, 2000. An admirably balanced and searching examination of this crucial German statesman's political evolution from annexationist to democratic peacemaker.

Internet Resources:

"The Avalon Project at Yale Law School," Yale University. A digital collection of documents relating to diplomatic, legal, economic, and political history. www.yale.edu/lawweb/avalon/avalon.htm.

"Documents of Diplomatic History," Mount Holyoke College. A large collection of documents relating to diplomacy (for example, treaties, contemporary accounts, and letters). www.mtholyoke.edu/acad/intrel/irhistry.htm.

"H-Diplo," H-Net. This website is a member of the network named H-Net (Humanities and Social Sciences Online) and features reviews, roundtable discussions, essays, and useful links on international and diplomatic history. www.h-net.org/~diplo.

"League of Nations Photo Archive," Indiana University. A fascinating collection of photographs from the League of Nations that evoke the hopes and spirit of a vanished era. www.indiana.edu/~league.

Notes

Notes